THE UNIQUE CREATION OF ALBERT CAMUS

The
Unique
Creation
of
Albert
Camus

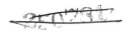

DONALD LAZERE

New Haven and London
Yale University Press
1973

Published with assistance from the Louis Stern
Memorial Fund.

Designed by Sally Sullivan
and set in Linotype Granjon type.
Printed in the United States of America by
Vail-Ballou Press, Inc., Binghamton, N.Y.

Published in Great Britain, Europe, and Africa by
Yale University Press, Ltd., London.
Distributed in Latin America by Kaiman & Polon,
Inc., New York City; in Australasia and Southeast
Asia by John Wiley & Sons Australasia Pty. Ltd.,
Sydney; in India by UBS Publishers' Distributors Pvt.,
Ltd., Delhi; in Japan by John Weatherhill, Inc., Tokyo.

Grateful acknowledgment is made to:
Alfred A. Knopf, Inc., for use of selections from the copyrighted works of Albert Camus.
George Braziller, Inc., for use of selections from *The Words* by Jean-Paul Sartre, translated
from the French by Bernard Frechtman; reprinted with the permission of the publisher.
English translation copyright © 1964 by George Braziller, Inc.
George Braziller, Inc., for use of selections from *Situations* by Jean-Paul Sartre, translated
from the French by Benita Eisler; reprinted with the permission of the publisher. English
translation copyright © 1965 by George Braziller, Inc.

In Memory of Justin O'Brien

(1906–1968)

Contents

Preface

The main purpose of this book is to present a systematic interpretation and evaluation of Camus as a literary artist and aesthetician. I see as the most distinctive quality of his art the dialectical interrelations between all his individual novels, stories, plays, and philosophical, lyrical, and journalistic essays that unite them thematically and stylistically into what is in effect a single, dynamic creation. Because the development between these works is not chronologically or even thematically linear, but circular—and multileveled, due to his habitual use of parallel structure—his entire creation demands intensive rereading and reference forward and back. One consequence is a kaleidoscopic effect whereby different readers' overall interpretation of Camus will vary according to the sequence in which they read his works. This circularity makes it difficult to organize a systematic critical exposition and particularly to figure out where to break into the circle. Rather than beginning with complete analyses of separate works by chronology or genre, I have chosen to approach his oeuvre as a whole in my first four chapters by tracing several central themes and stylistic patterns as they run throughout the fiction, drama, and essays. After these overall patterns are established in Part One, the autonomous literary qualities of the major individual works are analyzed and evaluated in more detail in Part Two. This approach necessitates an unusual number of cross-references within my own text and a certain amount of jumping back and forth by my readers—though less, one can hope, than is necessary in reading Camus himself.

A secondary purpose of the book evolved as a result of its being written by a critic of contemporary American culture and being addressed primarily to American general readers, college students, and teachers of English and world literature rather than to specialized scholars in French (although I hope the latter will also find it of interest). In the United States Camus is more than just one major foreign author among others. After World War II he became a surrogate great American author during the period of literary decline here following the rich creative era between the 1920s and the war. I have tried, peripherally throughout the book and centrally in the concluding chapter, to define his special significance for American readers, his affinities to the Anglo-American literary tradition, what he had to say to us that contemporary domestic writers were not saying, and the way American critics have interpreted him. It may be that the picture of Camus that emerges is somewhat different from that familiar to French readers, but then he is simply not the same author to Americans that he is to the French. By the same token the French are entitled to *their* Poe, Faulkner, James M. Cain, or Howard Hawks, unrecognizable though they may be to us.

I use an eclectic variety of critical approaches, the natural consequence of attempting to encompass an author whose hallmark is an exceptional versatility, and multidimensionality. American academic literary criticism in this century, especially since World War II, has tended to be regrettably proscriptive, with the advocate of each theory—New Critical or neo-Aristotelian formalist, Marxist, Freudian, Christian traditionalist, archetypist, or stylistician—obsessed with finding fallacies in and excommunicating all other sects but his own. The comprehensiveness of a writer like Camus demolishes the notion that one aesthetic necessarily negates the value of any other or can provide the sole legitimate criterion for interpreting a literary artist. For Camus and his sympathetic critic the challenge of literature is not to restrict or fragment our vision but continually to make it more inclusive and integrative through creations whose myriad facets reflect the human condition in its full range of existential and social components. This perspective should not be confused with the debased form of liberal "pluralistic" tolerance that suspends all judgments and evades commitment. Rather, while striving toward commitment to a unified ideological and aesthetic vision, it recognizes that for any such vision to be legitimate it must give full credit to competing views and assimilate rather than ignore or revile them. There has been, for example, an excessive degree of closed-mindedness in our time between intellectual advocates and opponents of Marxism, which Camus himself fell victim to increasingly during the 1950s, in a lapse from his own ideal tolerance. While there are very substantial differences between Camus and Marxist literary critics, I find over the course of this study that they have more in common than either was willing to concede. Similarly, I find that Camus subsumes much of what is valid in the New Critical aesthetic, which appears on the surface to be diametrically opposed to his beliefs.

Camus advocated and practiced the militant engagement of the artist's sensibility in the spiritual and social problems of his historical moment. In his view, partisan commitment and autonomous, complex literary creation reinforce one another rather than being mutually exclusive, as American writers and readers, whether political or apolitical, left-wing or right-wing, have been prone to regard them in recent years. Similarly for the critic, ideological commitment need not preclude careful, just analysis of a text, literary or political, on its own terms; he must constantly try to coordinate the two. Thus, while Camus's writing lends itself to close critical attention to the internal dynamics of individual works and dialectical tensions between different ones, a method I use through a large part of the book, it would be a gross distortion to treat his moral and political concerns merely as incidental aesthetic raw material. These concerns, then, are not subordinated here, but they are dealt with for the most part as he dramatizes and structures them through literary means.

This approach necessitates restricting my treatment of his political thought mainly to those areas where it intersects with his literary practice and theory regarding such issues as the political responsibility and vantage point of the man of letters. Those areas are extensive, to be sure, increasingly so in his later works. Furthermore, the changing political attitudes wrought by world events and New Left ideology in the 1960s have significantly altered our viewpoint on Camus's literary meaning and merits, as I have indicated where warranted in the chapters on individual works in Part Two. (By "New Left" I refer throughout this book to the general movement of social activism, disillusionment with Cold War liberalism, and reevaluation of radical ideology in the sixties, rather than to any particular factions.) The ups and downs of his political relevance and reputation in the United States have been so prominent as to demand extended discussion in themselves in the concluding chapter, within the framework of a sketch of American cultural history from the 1940s to 1970s.

Analysis in depth of Camus's positions on certain highly controversial political issues, however, such as the Algerian War, French internal politics, or Hegelian and Marxian formal philosophy, would be impractical within the scope of the present study. Fortunately, several books dealing more extensively with these topics have appeared in America since about 1965, correcting somewhat the inadequate scrutiny of Camus's politics in previous American criticism. Among these works Emmett Parker's *Albert Camus: The Artist in the Arena* and Fred Willhoite's *Beyond Nihilism: Albert Camus' Contribution to Political Thought* do little to challenge the facile assumptions of Cold War liberalism accepted by most influential earlier critics of Camus in this country. Only Conor Cruise O'Brien's *Albert Camus of Europe and Africa* has broken out of this mold, raising the necessary, hard questions demanded by a post-Cold War perspective, regarding issues like Camus's racial attitudes toward Arabs. Cruise O'Brien's book has provoked a heated response by Germaine Brée in her recent *Camus and Sartre: Crisis and Commitment,* and the biographical references in these two books provide an ample guide toward further study on the points of disagreement between them.

I have found that a psychoanalytic perspective reveals a significant additional dimension on which Camus's works coalesce into an aesthetic whole. But, being aware of the danger of its overshadowing all other critical approaches, I have chosen to restrict it mainly to one chapter, the fourth. To those with a bias against Freud or against critics whom J. D. Salinger disdainfully calls "aesthetic pathologists" in "our busy neo-Freudian Arts and Letters clinics," I can only testify that my purpose is not to expose Camus's neuroses— I find, in fact, that he provides a model of relatively healthy adjustment to potentially incapacitating emotional stresses—or to simplistically reduce his ideas to sublimations of his repressed impulses. While I do see certain correspondences between his psychological formation and his philosophical and political attitudes, I do not mean to suggest that their congruities or contradictions per se either confirm or refute the inherent ideological validity of those attitudes.

I can anticipate one possible criticism of my interpretation: that I excessively schematize Camus's themes and techniques, especially in my first three chapters. Certainly I am applying a more explicitly systematic framework than Camus himself did, and I have the warning of his own wariness of oversystematizing. My justification is the necessity to clarify easily confused distinctions and correlations that he made calculatedly though tacitly and that are vital components in the intricate clockwork of his literary art. I can only hope that I have succeeded in reducing confusions rather than compounding them and that I am not schematizing all life out of his writing. There is really little danger of doing the latter to a work so multifaceted and mercurial that any attempt to encompass it is bound at best not only to be sketchy but to provoke many valid alternate interpretations and discoveries of new dimensions at the same time that it is reducing the number of invalid readings. Furthermore, I can foresee that the appearance of some previously inaccessible work by Camus or new interpretation by another critic may knock my analysis askew and require still another rereading of his complete works from that altered perspective. (His previously unpublished first novel, *A Happy Death,* appeared in French and American editions shortly before this book went to press. There still remain to be published volumes of his notebooks after 1952 and his travel journals plus, possibly, fragments of the works in progress at the time of his death, mainly a novel and a play.)

The book's American orientation dictates citing in my text the English translations of Camus published in this country for the most part by Alfred A. Knopf, Inc. The translations, however, frequently deviate from or miss an important shade of meaning in the French text, and in such instances I have suggested an alternate translation, along with the original French where useful, in brackets. Single quotation marks are used to distinguish these interpolations from other authorial comments.

It should be acknowledged from the start that translation is a thankless task; its critic tends to take perfect accuracy and grace for granted while perforce singling out any passage that falls short. Space does not allow extensive remarks on the many artful touches in the American versions. Suffice it to say that my suggested alternate readings are not meant to deny the generally competent quality of most of the translations. The most prominent exceptions are *The Stranger* and *The Rebel,* in both of which cases a strong argument can be made for a completely new translation. Anthony Bower's version of *L'Homme révolté* is stylistically ponderous, often obscures meaning through imprecise or garbled syntax, and takes gratuitous liberties with Camus's text; several whole chapters were cut in the Knopf edition but restored in the Vintage text. Stuart Gilbert's version of *L'Etranger,* Camus's most widely read book here, has never been updated to include the author's 1953 revisions, and although it has its own charms, too many of them, alas, are Gilbert's invention rather than Camus's. (For further support of this point, see Helen Sebba, "Stuart Gilbert's Meursault: A Strange 'Stranger,'" *Contemporary Literature* 13, no. 3 [Summer 1972]: 334-40.)

The one glaring flaw in Ellen Conroy Kennedy's otherwise satisfactory rendition of the *Lyrical and Critical Essays* is the overly literal translation of *L'Envers et l'endroit* as *The Wrong Side and the Right Side,* which is disastrously misleading in its implied value judgment—exactly the kind of proscriptive distinction Camus constantly rejected. The "front and back" of a fabric or "heads and tails" of a coin comes closer to the noncommittal sense of the French phrase. References in my text will retain the French title in this one case.

My being a devoted former student of Justin O'Brien may raise some question of bias when I assert that he consistently served Camus more faithfully than any other translator. Anyone, however, who closely compares the French and English texts will find it obvious that O'Brien, with relatively few lapses, is most scrupulous in striving for the closest English equivalents while at the same time conveying a sense of Camus's style in clear and graceful English.

I owe thanks for suggestions on parts or the whole of the present manuscript to Frederick Crews and his graduate students in the psychoanalytic study group in the English Department of the University of California at Berkeley, to Albert J. Guerard, Richard Bridgman, Richard Hutson, Peter Dale Scott, Kenta Duffey, Alan Hausman, Sara Lazere, and to Merle Spiegel at Yale University Press. None of the above, however, is responsible for the opinions expressed herein, which have in fact occasioned some spirited disagreements. I would also like to thank the following teachers who earlier stimulated my interest in Camus: William Fick, Armand Renaud, Louis Rossi, Leon Roudiez, and, above all, Justin O'Brien, who for ten years advised and encouraged my studies but who, in one of those cruel Camusian ironies, died before their culmination here. In completing this book I have continued to draw sustenance from the memory of Professor O'Brien's expositions of twentieth-century French literature—enlivened by anecdotes about his personal encounters with its luminaries—and his exceptional personal kindness, qualities that endeared him to Columbia students for over a third of a century.

French Texts and English Translations

It is useful throughout this study to keep in mind the following chronology of Camus's major works in their first French editions, which differs widely from the sequence of their translations in the United States. Where page numbering differs between the American hard-cover and paperback or Modern Library editions, the less expensive edition will be cited in quotations. Where more than one translation is available I have chosen whichever is preferable for each particular passage quoted. I have translated all quotations from French texts that have not been published in English versions.

L'Envers et l'endroit. Algiers: Charlot, 1937. Reprinted by Gallimard, Paris, in 1958 with a new preface.

The Wrong Side and the Right Side, in *Lyrical and Critical Essays.* Translated by Ellen Conroy Kennedy. New York: Alfred A. Knopf, 1968; Vintage, 1970. Contents: "Preface," "Irony," "Between Yes and No," "Death in the Soul," "Love of Life," "The Wrong Side and the Right Side."

Noces. Algiers: Charlot, 1939.

Nuptials, in *Lyrical and Critical Essays.* Contents: "Nuptials at Tipasa," "The Wind at Djémila," "Summer in Algiers" (also in *The Myth of Sisyphus and Other Essays*), "The Desert."

L'Etranger. Paris: Gallimard, 1942; revised 1953. 1955 foreword written for American textbook edition (New York: Appleton-Century-Crofts, 1955) and translated in *Lyrical and Critical Essays.*

The Stranger. Translated by Stuart Gilbert. New York: Alfred A. Knopf, 1946; Vintage, 1954. Based on 1942 text.

Le Mythe de Sisyphe. Paris: Gallimard, 1942; revised 1948, 1957.

The Myth of Sisyphus and Other Essays. 1955 preface written for American edition. Translated by Justin O'Brien. New York: Alfred A. Knopf, 1955; Vintage, 1960. Based on 1948 text.

Le Malentendu. Paris: Gallimard, 1944; revised 1947. First staged in 1944.

The Misunderstanding in *Caligula and Three Other Plays*. Translated by Stuart Gilbert. 1957 preface by Camus written for American edition and translated by Justin O'Brien. New York: Alfred A. Knopf, 1958: Vintage, 1962. Based on 1947 text. Camus's extensive revisions of this play, as well as *Caligula* and *The Just Assassins,* for various productions are transcribed in *Théâtre, récits, nouvelles* (see below).

Caligula. Paris: Gallimard, 1944; revised 1947, 1958. Written in 1938 but not staged until 1945.

In *Caligula and Three Other Plays*. Based on 1947 text.

Lettres à un ami allemand. Paris: Gallimard, 1945.

"Letters to a German Friend," in *Resistance, Rebellion, and Death*. Translated by Justin O'Brien. New York: Alfred A. Knopf, 1961; Modern Library, 1963.

La Peste. Paris: Gallimard, 1947.

The Plague. Translated by Stuart Gilbert. New York: Alfred A. Knopf, 1948; Modern Library, 1961; Vintage, 1972.

L'Etat de siège. Paris: Gallimard, 1948. First staged in 1948.

State of Siege, in *Caligula and Three Other Plays*.

Actuelles I (Chroniques 1944–1948). Paris: Gallimard, 1950. Thirty-eight journalistic articles, of which the following are translated in *Resistance, Rebellion, and Death:* "The Blood of Freedom," "The Night of Truth," "The Flesh," "Pessimism and Courage," "Defense of Intelligence," "The Unbeliever and Christians," "Why Spain?" *Neither Victims nor Executioners* was translated by Dwight Macdonald in the July-August 1947 issue of *Politics* and has been reprinted in pamphlet form by *Liberation,* New York, and World without War Council, Berkeley; the 1968 edition of the pamphlet is the source for page references here. "The Artist as Witness of Freedom" ["Le témoin de la liberté"] appeared in *Commentary* in December 1949.

Les Justes. Paris: Gallimard, 1950. First staged in 1949.

The Just Assassins, in *Caligula and Three Other Plays*.

L'Homme révolté. Paris: Gallimard, 1951.

The Rebel. Translated by Anthony Bower. New York: Alfred A. Knopf, 1954 (abridged); Vintage, 1956 (unabridged). Foreword by Herbert Read.

Actuelles II (*Chroniques 1948–1953*). Paris: Gallimard, 1953. Seventeen
journalistic articles, of which the following are translated in *Resistance,
Rebellion, and Death:* "Bread and Freedom," "Homage to an Exile."
"The Artist and His Time" is translated in *The Myth.*

L'Eté. Paris: Gallimard, 1954.
Summer, in *Lyrical and Critical Essays.* Contents: "The Minotaur, or
Stopping in Oran" (also in *The Myth*), "The Almond Trees,"
"Prometheus in the Underworld," "A Short Guide to Towns without a
Past," "Helen's Exile" (also in *The Myth*), "The Enigma," "Return to
Tipasa" (also in *The Myth*), "The Sea Close By."

La Chute. Paris: Gallimard, 1956.
The Fall. Translated by Justin O'Brien. New York: Alfred A. Knopf,
1957; Vintage, 1963; Modern Library, n.d.

L'Exil et le royaume. Paris: Gallimard, 1957.
Exile and the Kingdom. Translated by Justin O'Brien. New York:
Alfred A. Knopf, 1958; Vintage, n.d.; Modern Library, n.d. Contents:
"The Adulterous Woman," "The Renegade" ("Le Renegat ou Un esprit
confus"), "The Silent Men" ("Les Muets"), "The Guest" ("L'Hôte"),
"The Artist at Work" ("Jonas, ou L'Artist au travail"), "The Growing
Stone."

"Réflexions sur la guillotine," in *Réflexions sur la peine capitale.* Paris:
Calmann-Lévy, 1957.
"Reflections on the Guillotine," in *Resistance, Rebellion, and Death.*

Requiem pour une nonne. Paris: Gallimard, 1957. First staged in 1956.
Dramatic adaptation of the novel *Requiem for a Nun* by William
Faulkner. Camus's foreword translated in *Lyrical and Critical Essays.*

Actuelles III (*Chroniques algériennes, 1939–1958*). Paris: Gallimard, 1958.
Nine journalistic articles, of which the following are translated in
Resistance, Rebellion, and Death: "Preface to Algerian Reports,"
"Letter to an Algerian Militant," "Appeal for a Civilian Truce,"
"Algeria 1958."

Discours de Suède. Paris: Gallimard, 1958. Two addresses. "Speech of
Acceptance upon the Award of the Nobel Prize for Literature." Translated by Justin O'Brien. *Atlantic Monthly* (May 1958), pp. 33–34;

Alfred A. Knopf, 1958 (the more widely accessible *Atlantic* text is the source for page references here). "Create Dangerously" ("L'Artiste et son temps"), in *Resistance, Rebellion, and Death*.

Les Possédés. Paris: Gallimard, 1959. First staged in 1959.

The Possessed. Translated by Justin O'Brien. New York: Alfred A. Knopf, 1960; Vintage, 1964. Stage adaptation of the novel by Fyodor Dostoevsky.

Carnets 1935–1942. Paris: Gallimard, 1962.

Notebooks 1935–1942. Translated by Philip Thody. New York: Alfred A. Knopf, 1963; Modern Library, 1965.

Carnets 1942–1951. Paris: Gallimard, 1964.

Notebooks 1942–1951. Translated by Justin O'Brien. New York: Alfred A. Knopf, 1965; Modern Library, 1970.

Théâtre, récits, nouvelles. Paris: Gallimard, 1962. Edited and annotated by Roger Quilliot.

Essais. Paris: Gallimard, 1965. Edited and annotated by Roger Quilliot and Louis Faucon.

These last two volumes, posthumous collections in the *Bibliothèque de la Pléiade* series, are indispensable for their definitive texts of virtually all of Camus's works except the notebooks and *A Happy Death*—they are the source for my references to the French texts—as well as annotations and variant readings between different manuscript versions. They contain many pieces otherwise uncollected in French book form, including the following, all in *Essais*, translated as "Kadar Had His Day of Fear," "Socialism of the Gallows," and "The Wager of Our Generation" (all first published in 1957) in *Resistance, Rebellion, and Death*, "The Rains of New York" (1947) and all the critical essays and interviews in *Lyrical and Critical Essays*, written between 1939 and 1959.

La Mort heureuse. Edited and annotated by Jean Sarocchi. Paris: Gallimard, 1971. Camus's first novel, written between 1936 and 1938 but unpublished in his lifetime.

A Happy Death. Translated by Richard Howard. New York: Alfred A. Knopf, 1972; Vintage, 1973.

Abbreviations of Camus's Works
Cited in Text

CTOP *Caligula and Three Other Plays*
EK *Exile and the Kingdom*
HD *A Happy Death*
LCE *Lyrical and Critical Essays*
Myth *The Myth of Sisyphus*
N1 *Notebooks 1935–1942*
N2 *Notebooks 1942–1951*
NP *Speech of Acceptance upon the Award of the Nobel Prize for Literature*
NVNE *Neither Victims nor Executioners*
RRD *Resistance, Rebellion, and Death*
TRN *Théâtre, récits, nouvelles*

PART ONE

I

Camus's Artistic System

Λ

I

Albert Camus is a much more complicated and elusive literary artist than has generally been recognized, especially in the United States, where his books have been translated in a desultory sequence that has obscured their full scope and plan. Many American readers, exposed in college courses only to *The Stranger* or *The Plague* as samples of "the existentialist novel," regard him exclusively as a thesis novelist. Others read on into a few of the plays or essays and, finding ostensibly the same themes, may criticize him for being monolithic and sententious—especially if they are followers of the New Criticism, with its emphasis on poetic ambiguities, ironic tensions, and organic dynamics. At the opposite critical pole, some Marxists and other leftists, again usually reading *The Stranger* or *The Myth of Sisyphus* alone, have downgraded him for having an undialectical mind or for neglecting historical and social reality in his self-centered preoccupation with metaphysical speculation. Georg Lukács similarly dismisses *The Plague:* "The lives of his characters are without direction, without motivation, without development. Camus's plague—the choice of subject-matter is characteristic—is not shown as an accidental disaster, as a horrific interlude in the continuity of human life. The plague is the reality of human existence itself, the terror of which has no beginning and no end."[1] Even critics sympathetic to Camus have sometimes misread particular works by interpreting them either in isolation or in an over-simplified, one-to-one correlation to his other writings.

Perhaps these are justifiable reactions to a partial exposure to Camus. Certainly he is repetitious, even monotonous—though not necessarily in

1. *Realism in Our Time* (New York: Harper Torchbook, 1971), p. 59 (original German edition, 1956).

3

an undesirable sense. In his notebooks and *The Myth* he speaks admiringly of the monotony of certain great artists, most eminently "the terrible [or 'terrific,' in the sense of 'awesome'] monotony of Proust" (*N 1*, pp. 202–3), referring both to Proust's art and to his theory that the artist creates a unified world view by infusing a diversity of subjects with his own distinct personality. But beyond his Proustian singleness of vision, or the artist's unique "resonance," as Camus terms it, he creates a sequence of theme-and-variation between virtually all his works that simultaneously unifies them into a complex, dynamic whole and multiplies the ironies and tensions in each individually.

As for his works that leftists have alleged to be unpolitical or undialectical, he sets them, and sometimes different levels within them, against others as theses or antitheses toward a dialectical synthesis combining metaphysical and historical or sociopolitical, egocentric and communal themes. His method is fundamentally akin to Marxian dialectics, although he strongly disagreed with Marxism on several crucial points. (His more enlightened Marxist critics have in turn pointed out serious shortcomings in his thought and art traceable to his specific political perspective, that of an independent, democratic socialist with tendencies toward nonviolent anarchosyndicalism. These disagreements among leftists of differing tendencies will be duly considered in later chapters.)

To appreciate Camus fully, then, it is necessary to encounter as an ensemble his novels, stories, plays, philosophical and lyrical essays, journalistic political criticism, speeches, interviews, and notebooks, as though they formed a single, multivolumed creation like Proust's *Remembrance of Things Past* or Durrell's *Alexandria Quartet*.

Camus makes it clear that this is how he conceived his own art in *The Myth*:

> Too often the work of a creator is looked upon as a series of isolated testimonies. Thus, artist and man of letters are confused. A profound thought is in a constant state of becoming; it adopts the experience of a life and assumes its shape. Likewise a man's sole creation is strengthened in its successive and multiple aspects: his works. ['De même, la création unique d'un homme se fortifie dans ses visages successifs et multiples que sont ses oeuvres' (*Essais*, p. 190). A closer translation would be, 'Likewise, a man's unique (or "single")

creation fortifies itself in its successive and multiple faces that are his works.'] One after another, they complement one another, correct or overtake one another, contradict one another too. . . . To be sure, a succession of works can be but a series of approximations of the same thought. But it is possible to conceive of another type of creator proceeding by juxtaposition. Their works may seem to be devoid of inter-relations. To a certain degree, they are contradictory. But viewed altogether, they resume their natural grouping. [Pp. 84–85]

"Another type of creator" is obviously Camus, the wording being typical of his somewhat coy reluctance to talk about himself directly. He does speak more personally in his reply to an interviewer's question as to which technique—fiction, the theater, or the essay—gave him the most satisfaction: "The alliance of all these techniques in the service of a single work" (*LCE*, p. 362). And in a 1948 notebook entry he speaks about the "necessity of a style for each subject, not altogether different because the author's special language belongs to him. But it so happens that it will bring out, not the *unity* of this or that book, but the unity of the entire work" (*N2*, p. 185).

II

The reader is likely to get his first concrete indication of Camus's dialectical method from his unorthodox custom of making explicit cross-references between his fictitious works. Meursault in *The Stranger* reads a newspaper account of the murder of a son by his mother and sister—the story of *The Misunderstanding*. Cottard in *The Plague* speaks sympathetically of the trial of a man who shot an Arab in Algiers—Meursault. Jean-Baptiste Clamence in *The Fall* provides a gloss on the character of Salamano in *The Stranger:* "I am well aware that one can't get along without domineering or being served. Every man needs slaves as he needs fresh air. . . . The lowest man in the social scale still has his wife or his child. If he's unmarried, a dog" (p. 45).

A second unifying technique is certain key images that Camus uses repeatedly, from his first to last writings, as titles and motifs: the stranger, the plague, the fall, the judge, the condemned man, the sun and sea, the two sides of the coin, exile and kingdom, lucidity and indifference, speech and silence, solitude and solidarity. His thematic associations with these images are usually fairly constant, so that they become a kind of shorthand for his continuing preoccupations. Sometimes, however, he works ironic variations on them or gives them multiple meanings, thereby creating tension between their appearances in different contexts. For example, the theme of exile and kingdom, which provides the title for his last published book of fiction in 1957, already appears in his first book, *L'Envers et l'endroit,* in 1937, in the essay "Between Yes and No," where he uses it to introduce a nostalgic reminiscence on his mother and childhood: "An emigrant returns to his country" (*LCE,* p. 30). But he also considered using *The Exile* as an alternate title for *The Misunderstanding,* the story of a son who returns home from abroad and is murdered by his mother. After Camus has moved to France during World War II he uses the phrase most frequently to refer to his exile from his Algerian homeland, but for several of the French Algerians in *Exile and the Kingdom,* which was published at the height of the Algerian War, Algeria too has become a place of exile. In *The Myth* he begins by evoking the phrase's religious associations in speaking about the absurd man's alienation from belief in God (among other lost illusions): "His exile is without remedy since he is deprived of the memory of a lost home or the hope of a promised land" (p. 5); but later, in extolling the absurd man's agnostic acceptance of a life without illusions, he reverses the biblical images: "This hell of the present is his Kingdom at last" (p. 39). (Similar variations that Camus works on the image of the stranger will be discussed in chapter 8 below.)

Certain pairings of whole books have also been widely recognized: *The Stranger* and *The Myth, The Plague* and *State of Siege* are clearly companion pieces; *The Rebel* is a sequel to *The Myth,* and the themes of *The Plague* modify those of *The Stranger.* But the exact relation between these pairs is not so simple as generally supposed, most notably in the case of *The Stranger* and *The Myth. The Stranger* has frequently been interpreted as a point-by-point dramatization of the themes of *The Myth,* or *The Myth* as a gloss on *The Stranger* (as Jean-Paul Sartre saw it in his 1943 explication of *The Stranger*). Some critics have considered it a weakness in Camus that his books should need this kind of extrinsic commentary. The correspondences, however, are not simply one to one; while there are some congruencies between the two books, in several vital respects they supplement and even contradict, or at least counterbalance, each other, as will be detailed throughout this study. Their interdependency, then, rather than diminishing the intrinsic literary value of each, enriches it with an additional dimension of ambiguity. In a 1936 note he reveals his plan to set up a tension between philosophical and literary works and to "show no emotion about this tension—despise comparisons" (*N1*, p. 27). ['Scorn comparisons' would be closer to the tone of *mépriser*.]

The notebooks reveal that beyond these pairings he also envisioned his works falling into larger groups to form "series" or "cycles":

FEBRUARY 21, 1941

Finished *Sisyphus*. The three absurds are now complete. Beginnings of liberty. [*N1*, p. 189]

JUNE 17, 1947

Without sequel

First series. Absurd: *The Stranger—The Myth of Sisyphus—Caligula* and *The Misunderstanding*.

Second series. Revolt: *The Plague* (and annexes)—*The Rebel*—Kaliayev [*The Just Assassins*].

Third series. Judgment—The First Man.[2]

Fourth series. Love sundered ['déchiré']: The Stake ['Le Bûcher']—On love—The Charmer ['Le Séduisant'].

Fifth series. Creation corrected or The System: Big novel + great meditation + unplayable play. [*N2*, p. 158]

MAY 27, 1950

I. The Myth of Sisyphus (absurd)—II. The Myth of Prometheus (revolt)—III. The Myth of Nemesis [in "Helen's Exile" (1948) he had referred to 'Nemesis, goddess of moderation, not of vengeance']. [*N2*, p. 257]

MARCH 7, 1951

Finished the first writing of *The Rebel*. With this book the first two cycles come to an end. Thirty-seven years old. And now, can creation be free? [*N2*, p. 270]

---

2. In its chronology and concern with judgment, this series would seem to include *The Fall, Exile and the Kingdom,* and the novel on which Camus was working at the time of his death entitled "The First Man." There are, however, few specific anticipations of these works in the notebooks of this period, and since they were inspired in large part by events of the 1950s (the unfinished novel culminates with the Hungarian uprising in 1956), it must be surmised that his plans for them were only vaguely formulated.

To a remarkable degree, Camus seems to have outlined his entire writing career from the beginning. The more one reads and rereads him, the more it appears that the spacing of his published works over nearly twenty-five years does not represent a progression of separately conceived projects so much as simply the time span he needed to fill in the details of a largely preordained pattern. Consequently, trying to discern chronological development in his writing can be very tricky. I have often thought I had seen a radical change in attitude or new line of thought between one work and a later one, only to go back to the first or an even earlier one and discover the "later" attitude already hiding there; the philosophy of limits, for instance, that is central to *The Rebel,* already appears in *The Myth* and some of the early lyrical essays, though not as conspicuously. Or else I had concluded that one group of his works in a certain period expresses his prevailing personal outlook at that time, only to realize that contemporaneous works in other genres or his personal activities express quite a different outlook—the way, for example, the egocentricity of all his early creative writing through *The Myth* is offset by his social commitments in journalism and political activism during the same period.

One also learns to guard against the temptation to conclude that when Camus has contradicted himself from one work to another—as he does, say, on the subject of whether art embodies disunity or unity, which will be discussed in chapter 3—he has committed himself exclusively to the later position and renounced the earlier one. It is closer to Camus's own way of thinking to consider his reversals, no matter how clear-cut, not as mutually exclusive but only as two possible alternatives, the two sides of the coin. His method was to fragment in each work one facet of his personality, one line of argument, one of several possible responses to a common condition such as the absurd, in such a way that only assembled in their totality would they reveal his full intention. This method enabled him to temper the intense emotionality that most readers associate with his writing with an equal measure of ironic detachment that he is not usually credited with. The following is a 1949 notebook entry:

> First cycle. From my first books (*Noces*) to *La Corde* [later *Les Justes—The Just Assassins*] and *The Rebel,* my whole effort has been in reality to depersonalize myself (each time, in a different tone). Later on, I shall be able to speak in my own name. [*N2*, p. 210]

Readers frequently make the mistake of identifying Camus completely with Meursault or Caligula or Clamence, but as he observes in *The Rebel,* "A character is never the author who created him. It is likely, however, that an author may be all his characters simultaneously" (p. 37). Even his essayistic positions sometimes constitute a persona; he begins *The Myth* by dramatically setting a tone of despair and knocking down all conventional values, only to end up reaffirming life's worth and reconstituting a value system within the terms of the absurd, and this final position in *The Myth* in turn becomes only a preamble or point of departure to *The Rebel.*

III

Bearing in mind all of the foregoing reservations about the difficulties of linear exposition in interpreting Camus, we can at least hazard a brief preliminary summary of his themes. *L'Envers et l'endroit* and *Nuptials* are concerned primarily with the necessity to detach oneself periodically from both legitimate social commitments and the flux of habitual social routine, with its illusions of immortality, stability, and self-importance, in order to establish an identity in solitary relation to the indifferent natural world and thereby to confront one's own mortality as a part of nature and to heighten appreciation of being alive. The sense of solitude and personal insignificance resulting from this dislocation of everyday routine in face of death, which is regarded as valuable in his first two books, regresses at the beginning of *The Myth* into a source of anxiety as one aspect of "the absurd," along with other aspects including the apparent non-existence of God, the lack of unity, purpose, or rationale in the natural universe, and the frustrating restrictions of human understanding. Camus ends up accepting absurd alienation in *The Myth,* concluding that the insignificance and ephemerality of the individual's existence actually constitute its unique, irreplaceable value. He introduces the theme of metaphysical revolt in calling for the man of absurd awareness to rise above his overwhelming, lonely fate by bearing it defiantly rather than killing himself, to stave off death through prolonging and savoring every moment of life, and to combat the limitations of reason by maintaining constant lucidity.

The Stranger and *The Misunderstanding* dramatize more fully than

The Myth that aspect of the absurd concerning the capricious twists of fate, while *The Stranger* and *Caligula* add to metaphysical absurdity and revolt the parallel dimension of revolt against the social absurdity of conventional morality and arbitrary legal authority, especially in the extreme form of capital punishment. *The Stranger,* like *The Myth,* asserts the primacy of individual, flesh-and-blood reality against any abstract notion that claims to supersede it. This assertion becomes the basis for Camus's opposition to political abstractions like nationalism, capitalist commodity fetishism, and communist collectivism; he does believe, though, that decentralized, worker-controlled socialism contains the most potential for maximizing each individual's personal fulfillment and freedom, and thus moves from individual revolt to the solidary struggle for working-class liberation.

In both *The Stranger* and *Caligula* social revolt leads in the negative direction of unbridled egocentric license and nihilistic murder. This direction is counterbalanced in the characters of Cherea and Scipio in *Caligula,* Rieux and Tarrou in *The Plague,* and Kaliayev in *The Just Assassins* and is systematically repudiated in *The Rebel* in favor of metaphysical and social revolt that limits itself from killing, thereby asserting the absolute value of every life and the solidarity of all men in revolt against death.

The absurd takes a political form in *The Rebel* and other writings after World War II about the capricious course of modern history, particularly in revolutions that have miscarried and ended up reinstitutionalizing murder as a political policy in both bourgeois and communist states. A total commitment to nonviolent resistance expressed in *Neither Victims nor Executioners* and by Tarrou in *The Plague* is modified in *The Rebel* and *The Just Assassins* to a doctrine of "limited guilt" whereby the rebel recognizes that he may have to kill in a just revolution or war, but only as a last resort and on the condition that he be willing to sacrifice his life in return so as to avert a cycle of revenge-killings or the political legitimization of murder. The works following *The Rebel* add no radically new themes; the significance of subsequent major works like *The Fall, Exile and the Kingdom,* and essays on politics and art lies in variants on previous motifs and in Camus's efforts to sustain his position in face of the increasingly tortuous dilemmas of the Cold War and Algerian crisis.

This thematic line is elaborated through Camus's underlying vision of life's ambiguity and its reflection in his literary style through his frequent use of parallelism, antithesis, paradox, and ironic reversal. (Detailed analysis of parallelism will be deferred to chapters 2 and 3, which deal with two of his most important systems of parallels, metaphysical and human judgment and the metaphysical and epistemological dimensions of the absurd.) In his world view the natural universe and man's fate are enigmatic, capriciously fluctuating forces, and our experiences are charged with many levels of possible meanings and implications that are sometimes complementary or parallel to one another, sometimes antithetical. His fascination with ambiguity shows in his titles—*L'Envers et l'endroit,* "Between Yes and No," "Irony," "The Enigma," "The Minotaur" (in its association with labyrinthine puzzles), *Exile and the Kingdom*—and in his frequent use of dualistic phrases like "solitary/solidary," "judge-penitent," "ambivalence," "equilibrium," "duplicity," and "equivocation." In *The Fall* Clamence describes his "shop sign": "A double face, a charming Janus, and above it the motto of the house: 'Don't rely on it' " (p. 47), and later observes, "The world's order likewise is ambiguous" (p. 113).

For Camus this pluralism pervading every area of life is sometimes a cause for anxiety—as in the early chapters of *The Myth* and in *The Rebel,* his two surveys of man's perpetual quest for unity—but it is also the source of a benign, Montaignian skepticism and tolerance, a distaste for absolutism, whether in politics, philosophy, morality, or aesthetics; Montaigne's "Que sais-je?" echoes through Camus's writing, even down to Meursault's offhand expressions in *The Stranger* like "You never know" ['On ne peut jamais savoir,' 'On ne sait jamais ce qui peut arriver']. This pluralism provides, above all, an ennobling challenge to encompass and hold in dynamic balance the whole range of complex, self-contradictory possibilities that life offers. Camus evokes the seventeenth-century French neoclassical ideal of *le balancement* in quoting Pascal in the epigraph to "Letters to a German Friend": " 'A man does not show his greatness by being at one extremity, but rather by touching both at once' " (*RRD,* p. 1). Camus apparently never read F. Scott Fitzgerald, but the two have many affinities, and on this theme Camus distinctly echoes Fitzgerald's *The Crack-Up:*

> The test of a first-rate intelligence is the ability to hold two opposed ideas in the mind at the same time, and still retain the ability to

function. One should, for example, be able to see that things are
hopeless and yet be determined to make them otherwise. . . . I must
hold in balance the sense of the futility of effort and the sense of the
necessity to struggle; the conviction of the inevitability of failure and
still the determination to "succeed." [3]

IV

Among Camus's array of balanced antitheses, the less complicated include unity and diversity (discussed more fully in chapter 3), pessimism
and optimism, sensuality and intellectuality, and the life-giving and destructive sides of nature. Disillusioned recognition of life's limitations is
offset by its intensification of the values remaining within those limitations: "The loftiest work will always be, as in the Greek tragedians,
Melville, Tolstoy, or Molière, the work that maintains an equilibrium
between reality and man's rejection of that reality. . . . The world is
nothing and the world is everything—this is the contradictory and tireless
cry of every true artist" (*RRD*, p. 203). Skepticism about an afterlife and
about the stability of earthly happiness or social progress—and even about
society's survival in the nuclear age—is countered by faith in the individual's capacity to withstand the worst twists of fate, to shape his own
destiny in part, and to reduce in some measure the amount of suffering
in the world: "If Christianity is pessimistic as to man, it is optimistic as to
human destiny. Well, I can say that, pessimistic as to human destiny, I am
optimistic as to man" (*RRD*, p. 55).

He values both sensuality and intellect without ever indicating any
sense of conflict between the two. In an essay called "Defense of Intelligence" he rejects "the spurious romanticism that prefers feeling to understanding as if the two could be separated" (*RRD*, p. 48). In essays
like "Summer in Algiers" he identifies with the spontaneous pleasure
seeking of uneducated workers, but his own intellect obviously distinguishes him from them at least partially, and he augments their uncere-
bral sensualism with the articulateness and mental intensity that only the
intellectual can know. And if he gives an intellectual dimension to passion, he is also impassioned in celebrating the intellect: "To a man devoid
of blinders, there is no finer sight than that of the intelligence at grips
with a reality that transcends it" (*Myth*, p. 41).

3. *The Crack-Up* (New York: New Directions, 1956), pp. 69–70.

Nature is two-faced in Camus's literary world, giving life and taking it away equally gratuitously. It provides man's joys and his tragedies: flowers, the warm Algerian seashore—and the plague. Nature's ambiguity is epitomized in the "inexhaustible sun" of Algeria, which in its life-giving aspect shines "in the center of our work, dark though it may be" (*LCE*, pp. 160–61), but which can also be "insatiable, one by one devouring victims lying crucified upon the beach at the funereal hour of noon" (*LCE*, p. 166). He compresses this duality into the oxymoron of "black sunlight" (*LCE*, p. 65) or "dark flame" (*LCE*, p. 105) and in "The Enigma" uses it as a symbol of the tragic vision: "Aeschylus is often heartbreaking; yet he radiates light and warmth. At the center of his universe, we find not fleshless nonsense but an enigma, that is to say, a meaning which is difficult to decipher because it dazzles us" (*LCE*, p. 160). While Camus's themes are so universal that trying to trace them to sources in his personal life is often a somewhat academic exercise, it is tempting to see a great deal of significance in his statement, during an informal written interview, attributing his first attack of tuberculosis at seventeen to "Excess of sport. Fatigue. Excess of exposure to the sun. Hemoptysis."[4]

A more complex series of antitheses stems from possible alternative attitudes toward death. First there is terror in facing it, balanced by the pride of acknowledging it honestly: "I want to keep my lucidity to the last, and gaze upon my death with all the fullness of my jealousy and horror" (*LCE*, p. 78). He also finds this lucidity toward death to be a means of intensifying life's joys, in the *carpe diem* tradition: "There is no joy of life without despair of life" (*LCE*, p. 56). For Camus the most privileged moments are those when danger brings us to the brink of death and simultaneously to peak awareness of being alive: "I have always felt I lived on the high seas, threatened, at the heart of a royal happiness" (*LCE*, p. 181). In *The Myth* he exalts awareness of the absurd in images of "being able to remain on that dizzying crest" (p. 37) and "the extreme limit of the condemned man's last thought, that shoelace that despite everything he sees a few yards away, on the very brink of his dizzying fall" (p. 41). The intense beauties of nature provide a further imperative to seize each moment away from death. Amid the Roman ruins and primitive countryside of Djémila, "I think of flowers, smiles, the desire for women, and realize that my whole horror of death lies in

4. Carl Viggiani, "Notes pour le futur biographe d'Albert Camus," *Revue des lettres modernes*, nos. 170–71 (1968), p. 209.

my anxiety to live. I am jealous of those who will live and for whom flowers and the desire for women will have their full flesh and blood meaning. I am envious because I love life too much not to be selfish. What does eternity matter to me" (*LCE*, p. 78).

A frequent theme in the early works is that we are all indifferent to the death of others. It is often ambiguous, though, whether this indifference entails a greater appreciation that *we* are still alive or an impassivity toward the prospect of our own death. In passages that suggest the latter, the lesson of nature lies, not in its beauty that inspires us to seize the day, but in its impersonality, its superhuman scale that negates social life and reduces man to the level of every other creature that is born only to die in an indifferent universe. This ambiguity pervades *The Stranger* and will be discussed therein at greater length in subsequent chapters. In the last paragraph, for one instance, when Meursault, facing execution, speaks of being liberated and opening his heart to the benign indifference of the universe ['la tendre indifférence du monde'], it is unclear whether he is feeling liberated from social concerns, the attitude described in *The Myth* as "the divine availability of the condemned man before whom the prison doors open in a certain early dawn, that unbelievable disinterestedness with regard to everything except for the pure flame of life" (p. 45), or whether it is life itself to which he has become indifferent. Meursault's earlier preoccupation with the natural setting at his mother's funeral presents the same ambiguity, as does a scene that prefigures it in "Irony," the earliest essay in *L'Envers et l'endroit*. There Camus as a child is distracted from his grandmother's burial by the magnificent seaside setting of the cemetery in Algiers, a setting that recalls Valéry's poem *Le Cimetière marin*, in which ambivalence between life and death is similarly symbolized in the juxtaposition of a cemetery with the Mediterranean. This cemetery reappears in two later lyrical essays, "Death in the Soul" and "Summer in Algiers," in both of which he ironically disparages the sentimental epitaphs hypocritically expressing grief for the departed by those still enjoying life: " 'Eternal regrets' on an abandoned grave" (*LCE*, p. 51). The theme of "Irony" is summed up in its closing lines: "Death for us all, but his own death to each. After all, the sun still warms our bones for us" (*LCE*, p. 29) ['La mort pour tous, mais à chacun sa mort. Après tout, le soleil nous chauffe quand même les os' (*Essais*, p. 22)]. If we interpret the burial scene in light of the references to the cemetery in the other essays, these lines seem to imply that others' deaths are of no concern to those of us whose living bones are still warmed by the sun. But the lines might equally well be read with the opposite meaning, that we foresee our own death in that of others and learn from their diverse deaths that it is a matter of indifference how we live and die, since after death the sun warms everyone's bones impartially.

Camus's fascination with the inhuman face of nature sometimes not only signals indifference toward life rather than determination to appreciate it fully but verges on a suicidal attraction toward death as a Lucretian merging with the inanimate world, a consummation devoutly to be wished. At the dead city of Djémila, "All through this country I followed something that belonged not to me but to it, something like a taste for death we both had in common" (*LCE,* p. 76). His strongest leanings toward suicide appear in the earlier writing, when the suffering of his first attacks of tuberculosis may have caused him, like Keats, to be "half in love with easeful death." In *The Myth* he clearly repudiates the death wish and in *The Rebel* delimits the temptation to merge with nature when he criticizes the extreme manifestations of it, the drive toward necrophilia, irrationalistic self-annihilation, or mystic transcendence of the ego that he sees in the literature of the romantic movement, Lautréamont, and the surrealists. After a tubercular relapse in 1949, however, he returns poignantly to Keats's dying letters, which he quotes in the notebooks: " 'I am glad there is such a thing as the grave' " (*N2,* pp. 223–24). The later notebooks continue to refer to his resisting a temptation toward suicide, and as late as the 1958 preface to *L'Envers et l'endroit* he speaks of returning to "that tranquil land where death itself is a happy silence" (*LCE,* p. 16). Moreover, throughout his later writings, as will be seen in chapter 4, there persists on a subliminal level an association of death with sexuality, keyed to his ambivalent feelings of love and hostility toward his mother and women in general and closely paralleling the theme of nature's duality.

It can be argued that, at least on a conscious level, the passages welcoming death do not represent a romantic death wish so much as an ultimate stoic resignation to death as an inevitable part of the natural process: when you have lived to the utmost, in full harmony with nature, you can face death with equanimity. As he puts it in "The Wind at Djémila":

It is to the extent I cut myself off from the [natural] world that I fear death most, to the degree I attach myself to the fate of living men instead of contemplating the unchanging sky. Creating conscious deaths is to diminish the distance that separates us from the world and to accept a consummation without joy, alert to rapturous images of a world forever lost. [*LCE*, p. 78]

This is clearly the theme of "Death in the Soul," where he encounters death in both Prague and the Italian countryside near Vicenza but is repulsed more by the former because it takes place in the artificial atmosphere of the somber, chilly city, alienated from nature. Similarly, in his writing during and after World War II, it is the *unnaturalness* of death contrived by war and capital punishment that by contrast gives natural death a nostalgic appeal.

This whole set of attitudes toward death becomes subsumed in the first half of a larger antithesis in which the solitary egocentricity of Camus contemplating nature and natural death is balanced against his social conscience: "I hold onto the world with every gesture, to men with all my gratitude and pity. I do not want to choose between the right and wrong sides ['cet endroit et cet envers'] of the world" (*LCE*, p. 61). And, "To correct a natural indifference, I was placed halfway between poverty and the sun. Poverty kept me from thinking all was well under the sun and in history; the sun taught me that history was not everything" (*LCE*, pp. 6–7). The difficulties of maintaining a balance between solitude and solidarity are summed up in the short story "The Artist at Work" in *Exile and the Kingdom,* at the end of which the painter Jonas, exhausted by public demands on his time, can only scribble in a corner of his last canvas a partially illegible word that may be either "solidaire" or "solitaire."

Even in the earliest lyrical essays Camus emphasizes that his contemplative retreats into nature are only a brief respite from political commitments. The extraordinary authenticity of this balance in his life is confirmed by our knowledge that the Rousseauan solitary wanderer meditating on mortality in the Roman ruins of Tipasa and Djémila or celebrating the noble savages of Algerian beaches was in the same early period of his adulthood, from about 1934 to 1939, starting a radical theater troupe (Le Théâtre du travail, later Le Théâtre de l'équipe), joining the

Communist party and quitting it a year or so later because of its manipulative tactics among the Moslems, and getting in trouble with French colonial authority as a left-wing newspaper reporter for exposing conditions of Arab poverty. His later liberal-reformist position on Algerian politics has occasioned much criticism from the revolutionary left, but the fact of his continuing journalistic and personal efforts over the years trying to avert civil war there is sufficient in itself at least to offset any inference that might be drawn from the lyrical essays that egocentricity led him to blindly romanticize his homeland.

Camus comes to relate the solitary/solidary antithesis to the geographical contrast between Mediterranean sunshine and northern Europe's gray climate. Occasional interludes of self-gratifying solitude were possible during his youth in Algeria, but from the time he moved to Paris just before the Nazi occupation in 1940, he associated Europe with all-consuming obligations to maintain solidarity with the victims of history, first in the French Resistance (whose leading newspaper, *Combat,* Camus edited), then, immediately thereafter, in the Cold War with its unrelenting threat of nuclear holocaust and in postwar society where plaguelike political injustices infested both bourgeois and communist countries. In 1958 he writes, "Though born poor in a working-class neighborhood, I never knew what real misfortune was until I saw our chilling suburbs. Even extreme Arab poverty cannot be compared to it, because of the differences in climate. But anyone who has known these industrial slums feels forever soiled, it seems to me, and responsible for their existence" (*LCE,* p. 8).

A corollary here is that the interminable struggle for social justice can only be sustained if it is undertaken toward the goal of winning the freedom, for both the victims of injustice and Camus himself, to be an egocentric hedonist. Returning to Tipasa in the early 1950s for another brief respite, he writes:

Europe hates the daylight and can do nothing but confront one injustice with another. In order to prevent justice from shriveling up, from becoming nothing but a magnificent orange with a dry, bitter pulp, I discovered one must keep a freshness and a source of joy intact within, loving the daylight that injustice leaves unscathed, and returning to the fray with this light as a trophy. [*LCE,* p. 168]

Camus's theoretical writings about the literary artist's vocation incorporate the same balance between egocentricity and social responsibility. His conception of artistic creation as a means of intensifying existence, developed in the sections "Absurd Creation" in *The Myth* and "Art and Rebellion" in *The Rebel,* follows the nineteenth-century aestheticist tradition whose quintessential expression is the conclusion to Walter Pater's *The Renaissance:*

> Well! we are all *condamnés,* as Victor Hugo says: we are all under sentence of death but with a sort of indefinite reprieve—*les hommes sont tous condamnés à mort avec des sursis indéfinis:* we have an interval, and then our place knows us no more. . . . Our one chance lies in expanding that interval, in getting as many pulsations as possible into the given time. . . . Of such wisdom, the poetic passion, the desire of beauty, the love of art for its own sake, has most.[5]

He absorbed the Paterian influence through Proust and Gide, who had themselves absorbed it by way of Oscar Wilde. He significantly modified the theory of art for art's sake, however, along much the same lines as André Malraux—to begin with, infusing it with a heterosexual sensibility in contrast to its previous frequent association with homosexuality. Furthermore, *The Rebel* and later expressions of literary theory develop his conviction that no artist, no matter how egocentric, can work in isolation: "To me art is not a solitary delight. It is a means of stirring the greatest number of men by providing them with a privileged image of our common joys and woes. . . . The artist fashions himself in that ceaseless oscillation from himself to others, midway between the beauty he cannot do without and the community from which he cannot tear himself" (*NP,* p. 33).

The artist's love of beauty and his working conditions are self-centered, but they become communal through his urge to articulate and share them. During his solitary revery in "Nuptials at Tipasa" Camus is already sensing his compatriotism with his fellow Mediterraneans and planning to write about it. Conversely, one's art is nourished by the social involvements we all have as men, not artists. As he explains in "The Artist and His Time" of 1953, if "we speak in our works of deserts and of selfish love, the mere fact that our lives are militant causes a special tone of voice to people with men that desert and that love" (*Myth,* p. 150).

5. *The Renaissance* (New York: Meridian Books, 1961), pp. 223–24.

Finally, the writer must always draw from his time for material, and only the most effete author can remain uncommitted when faced with the urgency of our present crises. The challenge is to assimilate the present temper into works that are both significant socially and substantial aesthetically.

> The artist of today becomes unreal if he remains in his ivory tower or sterilized if he spends his time galloping around the political arena. Yet between the two lies the arduous way of true art. . . . Every work presupposes a content of reality and a creator who shapes the container. Consequently, the artist, if he must share the misfortune of his time, must also tear himself away in order to consider that misfortune and give it form. [*RRD,* p. 182]

Sartre, who derived his notion of *la littérature engagée* from the experience of French underground resistance during World War II, at which time he and Camus became associates, came to link it with socialist ideology and, increasingly in subsequent years, with intellectual subordination to revolutionary party discipline. This is one of the issues that pulled Camus and Sartre steadily farther apart after the war. In the 1950s, when Sartre was devoting his writing career more and more to supporting Third World revolutionary causes allied in varying degrees with the Communist party, Camus continued to insist that "beauty, even today, especially today, cannot serve any party" (*RRD,* pp. 204–5). The writer cannot faithfully serve art by becoming a party propagandist but should remain a political "free lance." "We must simultaneously serve suffering and beauty" (*Myth,* p. 151) by bearing independent witness to both with creative imagination, compassion, honesty, and eloquence.

His most widely inclusive antithesis is that between romantic and classical values and stylistic traits, the reconciliation of which is a rare, admirable achievement in the twentieth century, especially from the perspective of American intellectual life, which tends to lurch between unbridled romanticism and pedantic stultifications of the classical spirit. Some authors like Goethe and Chateaubriand have developed from youthful romanticism to mature classicism, but Camus—partly under the early influence of Nietzsche, Gide, and the philosopher Jean Grenier, his teacher at the University of Algiers—set out from his first works to synthesize the two. In his view, in fact, they are not entirely antithetical; classicism, rather, encompasses romanticism, since the balancing of opposites itself is a central classical and neoclassical doctrine, as he indicates in the epigraph from Pascal in "Letters to a German Friend." Furthermore, he asserts that "genuine classicism is only romanticism subdued" (*Rebel,* p. 270) and, about Gide, "His concept of classicism as a romanticism brought under control is something I share" (*LCE,* p. 353).

His instinctive sympathies are typically romantic: the love of solitary, melancholy contemplation in nature evokes Rousseau, Chateaubriand, Lamartine, Keats, Wordsworth and Thoreau; his social or metaphysical rebels like Sisyphus, Meursault, Caligula, Rieux, and Kaliayev, or Clamence in his dandyish despair, recall Byron, Shelley, Melville, Balzac, Hugo, and Stendhal. But his simultaneous concern for social commitment is in the line of the seventeenth- and eighteenth-century neoclassicists' concern with normative values for man within society, and throughout *The Rebel* and related shorter works he applies classical strictures to the excesses of the romantic spirit. He views twentieth-century political absolutism as the outgrowth of nineteenth-century German romantic philosophy from Hegel to Marx and Nietzsche. He attributes Europe's—and America's—political excesses in general to their concept of justice as an absolute, in contrast to its Greek association with *la mesure*—measure or moderation, the delineation of appropriate proportions and sensible limits. The French adjective *juste,* as used in *le juste milieu,* has this denotation of exactitude (*la justesse*) rather than moral rectitude (*la justice*), a sense in which the word is rarely used in English except for "just right." Hellenic allusions become increasingly more frequent in his postwar works such as "Prometheus in the Underworld," "Helen's Exile," and *The Rebel*—the last section of which, "Thought at the Meridian" ("La Pensée de midi"), evokes Le Midi, Mediterranean France. He had already taken a classical stance, however, in a 1937 speech, "The New Mediterranean Culture" (*LCE,* pp. 189–98), in which he identified the authentic Mediterranean tradition with the sensual love for beauty of Athens's Periclean Age, in contrast to Spartan militancy and Roman imperialism from Caesar to Mussolini. Similarly, in "Summer in Algiers" in 1939, he associated the young Algerians on the beaches with the athletes of Delos, concluding, "And still, yes, one can find a certain moderation ['une mesure'] in the strained and violent faces of these people" (*LCE,* p. 89).

But the classical spirit is subject to abuses too. Camus's exhortations to emotional and intellectual intensity are in the tradition of the romantic movement's reaction against the rigidified neoclassicism of the late eighteenth century, a reaction that has been repeated in the twentieth century by French surrealism and existentialism, and later the American beat and hippie movements, against the atrophy of the classical virtue of decorum into academic stuffiness or bourgeois insipidity and priggishness. Thus, if classicism can be seen as a controlled romanticism, controlled romanticism can also be seen, in an author like Camus, as a regenerated classicism.

A final way he combines the two traditions is to enclose his romantic subjects or heroes in a classical style and structure. Classical stylistic convention as well as ideology can be seen in his constant use of antithetical devices like parallelism, balanced sentences, chiasmus, and oxymoron. In contrast to romantic verbal effusion, involution, and rejection of set forms, his prose is typically concise and clear (aside from some lapses in *The Myth* and lyrical essays), his literary forms tightly, symmetrically structured. He indicates in "Helen's Exile" that Greek tragedy was his model for this kind of formal restraint on passionate subject matter, contrasting modern disequilibrium to "that higher equilibrium . . . which applied the music of numbers [i.e., poetic meter] even to blood-tragedy" (*Myth,* p. 135). (He fails to acknowledge that this notion of tragedy derives from Hegel and Nietzsche, allegedly the ideologists of romantic excess.) Camus has been called the classicist of French existentialism; Sartre, Simone de Beauvoir, Maurice Merleau-Ponty, or Francis Jeanson may sometimes be more advanced ideologically, but Camus certainly is the most polished stylist and master of literary forms and technique.

v

Camus blends still more antithetical attitudes into the paradoxes that mark almost every page of his writing. The paradoxes inherent in the absurd condition provide the dramatic reversals of *The Myth:* The absence of a God or transcendent meaning in life, which he begins by postulating as a justification for suicide, ends up making life *more* worth living; reason is incapable of making sense out of life, yet it is valuable insofar as it gives us a concept of what sense is and a rational articulation of its own limitations. The crucial shift in emphasis in his writing after *The*

Myth from the phase of the absurd to that of rebellion pivots on a paradox
that he expresses in the introduction to *The Rebel:* If I conclude that the
value of my freedom and egocentric pleasure make my own life worth
living, I must through simple empathy say the same about everyone else's
life. Therefore, murder as well as suicide is proscribed, my freedom must
be limited where it interferes with others', and in order to defend the
principle of the value of life, freedom, and pleasure, I may have to sacrifice my own when others' are threatened. Thus Camus in his personal
dialectical development recapitulates the ambivalence from total irre-
sponsibility to total responsibility that is central to existentialist thought
from Dostoevsky to Sartre.

He continually works further variations on the paradoxes of solitude
and solidarity. Chapter 1 of *The Rebel* concludes:

> The first progressive step for a mind overwhelmed by the strangeness
> of things is to realize that this feeling of strangeness is shared with all
> men. . . . The malady experienced by a single man becomes a mass
> plague. In our daily trials rebellion plays the same role as does the
> "cogito" in the realm of thought: it is the first piece of evidence.
> But this evidence lures the individual from his solitude. It founds its
> first value on the whole human race. I rebel—therefore we exist.
> [Literally, 'I rebel, therefore we are,' which more closely maintains
> the play on Descartes's 'I think, therefore I am.'] [P. 22]

In other words, we are all together in being alone—the references to
strangeness and a mass plague suggesting the progression on this theme
between Camus's first two novels. Or, in the 1958 preface to *L'Envers
et l'endroit:*

> Sometimes on those opening nights at the theater, which are the
> only times I ever meet what is insolently referred to as "all Paris," it
> seems to me that the audience is about to vanish, that this fashionable
> world does not exist. It is the others who seem real to me, the tall
> figures sounding forth upon the stage. Resisting the impulse to flee,
> I make myself remember that every one in the audience also has a
> rendezvous with himself: that he knows it and will doubtless be
> keeping it soon. Immediately he seems like a brother once more;
> solitudes unite those society separates. [Camus nicely reinforces the

paradox grammatically by reversing the expected 'solitude unites.']
[*LCE*, p. 12]

Similarly, in his literary theory he transmutes the narcissism and political escapism or elitism usually identified with art for art's sake into
a politically committed, democratic aesthetic. He argues that even when
artistic gratification is individualistic and self-centered it cannot in good
conscience be restricted to socially privileged individuals. To help make
art accessible to all men, the artist and art lover must actively support
universal freedom and the elimination of poverty and exploited labor.
Oscar Wilde, the popular stereotype of the dandyish aesthete but, like
Camus, a master of paradox, adumbrated this dialectical synthesis in his
little-publicized essay *The Soul of Man under Socialism,* where he conceded that the egocentric aesthete ought to support socialism because it
will allow everyone the leisure, cultivation, and opportunities for selfish-
ness necessary to become an aesthete. Wilde's personal awakening to
tragic compassion after his imprisonment inspired Camus to write a
preface to a French edition of *De Profundis* and *The Ballad of Reading
Gaol,* predictably entitled "The Artist in Prison," [6] in which he suggests
that these works ennoble Wilde's earlier life and writings by turning
their frivolity into half of the two-sided coin of joy and sorrow, egocentricity and communality, that marks the highest art.

Another form of paradox is the ironic reversal by which a line of
action carried too far merges with its opposite or the condition against
which it was intended to rebel. An excess in one's assertion of freedom
destroys others' freedom and eventually his own, as in the case of Caligula. Rebellion against a murderous universe (Caligula) or society
(Meursault) can make the rebel a competitor in murder. The romantic
quest for apocalyptic transcendence of bourgeois banality can end in intellectual or physical self-annihilation that is equally banal. And if one
fixates on the absurdist attitude without seeing it as a point of departure,
then "the absurd, which claims to express man in his solitude, really
makes him live in front of a mirror. And then the initial anguish runs
the risk of turning to comfort" (*Rebel,* pp. 8–9). These reversals reinforce
his classicist's credo that ethical values are not to be found in absolutes
but in keeping everything in proper proportion.

6. Reprinted in *Encounter,* Mar. 1954, pp. 26–29, trans. Antonia White.

VI

A full recognition of the protean, unpredictable side of Camus's writing that emerges from these patterns of ambiguity, antithesis, ambivalence, paradox, and ironic reversal shows how far off the mark are those readers and critics who regard him as somber, monolithic, or unremittingly tendentious. One of his key words is *jouer*, in its multiple senses of acting, gambling, and playing sports or games; his motto, like Clamence's, could be: "Don't rely on it." In fact, his flair for playing riddle games and for shifting roles was so strong that he must have come to feel misgivings about its tendency to undercut his more serious, straightforward intentions. Such misgivings are suggested by his criticisms of the romantic dandy in *The Rebel*, who "plays [or 'acts'] at life because he is unable to live it" (p. 52), and of Clamence in *The Fall*, who confesses, "I have never been really able to believe that human affairs were serious matters. I had no idea where the serious might lie, except that it was not in all this I saw around me—which seemed to me merely an amusing game, or tiresome" (pp. 87–88). Although he does not say so outright, it can be surmised that similar apprehensions effect a change in his literary technique from the ambiguities of *The Stranger* and *The Myth* to the more straightforward exposition of *The Plague* and *The Rebel*, in the latter of which he states, "Every ambiguity, every misunderstanding, leads to death; clear language and simple words are the only salvation from this death" (p. 282). (The return to the technique of ambiguity in *The Fall*, of course, can be seen as part of his critical portrait of Clamence.) In a 1949 notebook entry he appears to be approving of ambiguity in artistic creativity but not in intellectual discourse:

> Monnerot. "The fecundity of a producer of ideas (he is speaking of Hegel) is proven by the multiplicity of possible *translations* (interpretations)." [Camus's parentheses.]
> Of course not. That is true of an artist, absolutely false of a thinker. [*N2*, p. 222]

The monumental artistic plan and ideological comprehensiveness of Camus's total work approach a complete world system, a synthesis of metaphysics, ethics, history, political theory, social psychology, aesthetics, and semantics into a single, consistent viewpoint. Part of his fascination is the same as that of other philosophical or literary system builders like Plato and Plotinus (Camus wrote his thesis for the Diplôme d'études supérieures on neoplatonism and Christian metaphysics), Saint Thomas Aquinas, Dante, Spenser, Milton, Spinoza, the Encyclopedists, Hegel, Marx, Freud, Proust, and Sartre. And he is open to the same criticism, on philosophical if not on artistic grounds, that he sometimes oversimplifies or bends reality in trying to make everything fit his system. He shows his attraction toward systematizing in the notebook entries planning a 1500-page series of works that he called "The System" and his recognition of its drawbacks in a 1951 entry: "After *The Rebel*. Aggressive, obstinate rejection of the system. The aphorism henceforth" (*N2*, p. 269).

All of the foregoing indicates why he is a difficult author. It is not that he is prone toward obscure, scholarly allusions in the manner of T. S. Eliot, or toward the occultism and private fantasies of symbolist and surrealist poets, or even the rigorous formal philosophy of Sartre. It is, rather, that assimilating the magnitude, complexity, and kaleidoscopic dynamics of all his major works combined presents the reader with an aesthetic challenge on the scale of *The Divine Comedy, Remembrance of Things Past,* or *A Portrait of the Artist as a Young Man, Ulysses,* and *Finnegans Wake.* Camus remarks in *Nuptials* that "it takes ten years to have an idea that is really one's own" (*LCE*, p. 76). Likewise, a comprehensive interpretation of Camus can be ten years in formation—as this book attests. The aesthetic challenge is further compounded by his rare power to engage the reader in an emotional confrontation. Like a small number of other artists and thinkers such as Marx, Dostoevsky, Freud, Proust, and Sartre, he can get into the bloodstream, haunt the mind, radically alter one's perception of the world and the course of his life—a quality which has inspired one American author, Hayden Carruth, to write a book called *After the Stranger: Imaginary Dialogues with Camus.*[7]

In the end, it is ironic that Camus, who has generally been underestimated by both Marxist and formalist critics—two schools that he considered to be at equally excessive poles in their exclusivity—actually provides an exemplary subject of study for the combination of aesthetic and

7. *After the Stranger* (New York: Macmillan, 1965).

political concerns valued by the former and for the literary complexity valued by the latter. His artistic theory and practice in fact subsume and transcend the aesthetic of formalists such as the New Critics in England and America. T. E. Hulme, T. S. Eliot, and I. A. Richards early in the twentieth century, and William Empson, John Crowe Ransom, Allen Tate, Cleanth Brooks, Robert Penn Warren, W. K. Wimsatt, R. P. Blackmur, Northrop Frye, René Wellek, and Austin Warren, among others more contemporaneously with Camus, performed a valuable service in seeking to delineate precisely what distinguishes literature from ordinary expository discourse and to analyze in close detail the formal techniques through which literature embodies ideas. The unfortunate aftermath of their efforts, however, was that they and, more often, their pedestrian academic followers tended to turn this analytic method into the ultimate criterion of literary value, as though the ideological content of a work was irrelevant and only the complexities of its technical dynamics were of any interest or worth for students of literature.

Camus's aesthetic is closer to that of Coleridge, who is often cited as a forerunner of the New Critics; in contrast to the latter, though, for Coleridge as for Camus the internal dynamics of the literary work are not constrictingly divorced from the external world but are enriched all the more by being viewed as a microcosm of the artist's organically unified world view. Part of Camus's unique accomplishment in our time is that his stylistic and formal elaborateness is not an aesthete's affectation or attempt to flee reality into an artificial paradise but an integral extension of and key to his total vision of reality. Proust had similarly asserted that "style is for the writer, as for the painter, a question, not of technique but of vision." [8] Camus's distinctive vision, moreover, includes a leftist political ideology and an imperative for militant involvement by the artist in the struggles of his historical moment. In this he was opposed to the conservative Coleridge and the politically retiring Proust, as well as to most twentieth-century formalist critics (Empson in England being one exception) and other prominent literary artists like Yeats, Eliot, Pound, Stevens, Valéry, Lawrence, Joyce, Fitzgerald, and Faulkner, who either leaned toward the right or advocated the insulation of art from political partisanship. Thus Camus could synthesize Coleridge and Marx in proposing art as a paradigm for postindustrial, classless society: "The

8. *Remembrance of Things Past* (New York: Random House, 1932), 2 : 1013.

type of civilization that is inevitable will not be able to separate, among classes as well as among individuals, the worker from the creator; any more than artistic creation dreams of separating form and substance, history and the mind" (*Rebel,* pp. 273–74).

2.

Metaphysical and Social Courtrooms

I

The most prominent motif unifying Camus's writing is the problem of judgment, to whose multiple forms he attributes the crucial spiritual and social ills of the twentieth century. He develops some aspects of this theme in expository order in the essays, while in the fiction and drama he reveals other aspects through a variety of literary techniques: images of the judge, jury, prosecuting and defense attorneys, witness, guilty verdict, prison, and death sentence run all through these works on the level of literal action and as metaphor, symbol, and allegory. His system here involves four parallel elements: metaphysical and human judgment and the rational and irrational forms they both take. Camus does not set up these categories so explicitly; I base them, however, on his distinctions in *The Rebel* between metaphysical and historical rebellion and rational and irrational terrorism, and on the following notebook entry from 1942: "*The Plague* has a social meaning *and* a metaphysical meaning. It's exactly the same. Such ambiguity is in *The Stranger* too" (*N2*, p. 36).

The imagery of rational metaphysical judgment derives from the Christian conception of God as the final judge, who omnisciently dictates standards of innocence and guilt and accordingly rewards or punishes men after death. Camus sees rational human judgment as society's appropriation of God's judicial powers. In *The Rebel* he traces the bloody history of Europe's attempt to transfer the kingdom of God to earth, first in the prerevolutionary Church-State, which used "divine right of kings" to rationalize dictatorship, then in modern, secular states including those established in rebellion against religious authority from the French to the Russian revolutions, which have self-righteously established themselves as substitutes for God as absolute judge, producing an ever more murderous spiral of warfare and authoritarianism in the cause of implementing earthly justice. In the ultimate ideological struggle of the Cold War, "the atom too bursts into flame, and history ends in the triumph of reason and the death agony of the species" (*LCE,* p. 152). ("La raison" denotes not only reason but rectitude, as in *avoir raison,* "to be right.")

Governmental absolutism reveals itself not only in war but in capital punishment, which Camus repeatedly attacks as legalized, rationalized murder. In "Reflections on the Guillotine" he remarks on the distorted reasoning of the Church-State in its sanction of the death penalty: "The executioner is invested with a sacred function. He is the man who destroys the body in order to deliver the soul to the divine sentence, which no one can judge beforehand" (*RRD,* p. 171). The justifications of secular governments are even more self-contradictory:

> When an atheistic or skeptical or agnostic judge inflicts the death penalty on an unbelieving criminal, he is pronouncing a definitive punishment that cannot be reconsidered. He takes his place on the throne of God, without having the same powers and even without believing in God. He kills, in short, because his ancestors believed in eternal life. . . . In other words, after being a priest, the executioner became a government official. [Pp. 172–74]

In opposition to "rational" religious and social judgment, Camus expresses his themes of metaphysical absurdity and social nihilism in images of irrational judgment. Neither Camus nor any of his fictional heroes believes in God, an afterlife, or any rationale in the workings of the universe. In *The Myth* and other works dealing with the absurd, Camus describes natural death, the ultimate absurdity, in two metaphors: the "absurd walls" of the prison of mortality, and the guilty verdict and death sentence that nature inevitably pronounces on every man without any reason and without any possibility of grace through a Last Judgment: "The absurd is sin without God" (p. 30). Under the universal death sentence the "sinner" by Christian standards is no more or less guilty than the pious believer; therefore, recognizing the absurdity of life has the positive value of freeing one from concern about eternal salvation or damnation. Similarly, Camus and his protagonists consider society's rationalized standards of right and wrong and its power to enforce them to be groundless. Paraphrasing Nietzsche in *The Rebel,* he writes: "Judg-

ments are based on what is, with reference to what should be—the king-•
dom of heaven, eternal concepts, or moral imperatives. But what should
be does not exist; and this world cannot be judged in the name of nothing" (p. 67). Death obliterates all of society's distinctions between innocence and guilt, and a premonition of his death exposes to a man the
artificiality of society's rules, freeing him to rise above them and live any
way he pleases.

If freedom from religious and social judgment is pushed to its extremes, however, it in turn becomes another form of judgment; unlimited
freedom legitimizes nihilistic murder, by which man becomes the accomplice of the universe as capricious killer: "Nihilism . . . ends with the
conclusion that it is a matter of indifference to kill when the victim is already condemned to death" (*Rebel*, pp. 282–83). The nihilist, then, adds
irrational human judgment to the irrational metaphysical judgment of
natural death. Once again the death sentence has been transferred from
the metaphysical to the human, and while Camus asserts in *The Rebel*
that irrational murder has a more realistic metaphysical basis than rational murder—"A mind imbued with the idea of the absurd will undoubtedly accept fatalistic murder; but it would never accept calculated
murder" (p. 6)—he concludes that the two are equally pernicious. He
traces the historical line of nihilistic judgment from the theories of Sade
and Nietzsche to their grisly application by Hitler and parallels this line
of "irrational State terrorism" to the "rational State terrorism" that began
with the French revolutionary apologists and ran through Hegel and
Marx to culminate in Stalin's Russia.

All of the foregoing murderous forms of metaphysical and human
judgment figure centrally in Camus's fiction and drama as well as in the
philosophical and journalistic essays. The novels, stories, plays, and earlier
lyric essays also extend the theme of social judgment dramatically into
more mundane areas—such as the everyday, arbitrary rituals of conventional morality, the officiousness of clergymen, judges, and bureaucrats, the
petty vanity of individuals who need to give an air of importance to their
banal daily routines or to consider themselves morally superior to their
neighbors. This theme of day-to-day judgment is implicit in the self-
righteous minor characters of *The Stranger, Caligula, The Plague,* and
State of Siege and breaks out as the central subject of *The Fall,* in which
Clamence observes, "The feeling of the law, the satisfaction of being right,

'the joy of self-esteem, *cher monsieur,* are powerful incentives" (p. 18), and, "Don't wait for the Last Judgment. It takes place every day" (p. 111).

The complexity of the judgment theme can be confusing, and failure to distinguish between its multiple aspects has caused many readers and critics to miss the ironies and structural dynamics that Camus gets out of paralleling metaphysical and human, rational and irrational judgment. In *The Fall* preeminently, all four forms of judgment are closely intertwined in Clamence's fevered, devious discourse on guilt; here, and to nearly an equal degree in each of the other works, it is necessary to distinguish carefully which forms of judgment Camus is dealing with and on what literary levels they are functioning at different stages of the story. This will be my procedure in following the main lines of the theme through five major works—*The Stranger, Caligula, The Plague, The Fall,* and "The Guest." (The theme is also prominent in several other works not discussed here—as, for instance, in the characters of Judge Casado in *State of Siege* and the judge in "The Growing Stone," Kaliayev's imprisonment and execution in *The Just Assassins,* and the courtroom and prison setting of Camus's stage adaptation of Faulkner's *Requiem for a Nun.*)

II

The first half of *The Stranger* is populated by a number of minor characters each of whom has his own little way of asserting his self-importance: the officious director of the home for the aged, who makes death an impersonal business matter with his efficient, antiseptic manner; the concierge at the home, who is himself an inmate but insists on regarding himself as an official and sets himself above his fellow pensioners by referring to them as "the old folks"; Meursault's neighbors, Raymond the pimp, who describes himself as a "warehouseman," and Salamano, who gets a sense of power from beating his mangy dog—his unloved wife, who evidently served the same function as the dog, having died; and the members of a soccer team who pass Meursault's window euphoriously singing after a Sunday victory that "their club would never perish" (my translation—Gilbert's, on p. 28, departs entirely from the French text). (The little "robot woman," who organizes her daily schedule with machinelike precision, might be included in this category, but she is an ambiguous character; she might also be an alter ego to Meursault in being aware of life's brevity and amorphousness but reacting to it, in contrast to Meursault's impassivity, by organizing every minute. Her identification with Meursault is suggested by her being one of the few people who sympathize with him at his trial.)

In contrast to these self-aggrandizing characters, Meursault lives with an instinctive, unarticulated premonition of death, with its equalization of all ways of life, that relieves him of the need to justify his way of life above any other. The colloquialism "It's all the same to me" ['Cela m'est égal'] literally expresses his sense of the moral equivalence of all endeavors. When his employer offers to transfer Meursault from Algiers to Paris and suggests that the change of life should please him, he replies, "I was quite prepared to go; but really I didn't care much one way or the other [literal translation: 'Yes, but in the end it was all the same to me']. He then asked if a 'change of life,' as he called it, didn't appeal to me, and I answered that one never changed his life; one life was as good as another, and my present life suited me quite well" (p. 52).

Society, like the individuals within it, sets up arbitrary standards of importance—such as family and conjugal ties, bourgeois respectability and financial success, and patriotism—and tries to dignify them by demanding lip service to sentimental rituals like marriage, funeral services and the trappings of mourning, occupational advancement, and public honors (the director of the home for the aged wears a Legion of Honor ribbon). Meursault, however, is a simple, sensuous soul who, lacking the the aptitude and desire to play the game, is oblivious to society's artificial scale of values. His attitudes are determined solely by his physical state; he is blissful when the sun is pleasantly warm, distraught when it is too hot. His intense sensitivity to physical details often excludes more "important" matters—his main preoccupation at his mother's burial is with the red geraniums on the graves and the color of the earth and bits of roots covering her coffin. After remaining dry-eyed at the funeral, he takes a mistress, Marie, the next day and befriends Raymond the procurer. In reply to Marie's suggestion that they get married, "I explained that it had no importance really, but, if it would give her pleasure, we could get married right away. . . . Then she remarked that marriage was a serious matter. To which I answered: 'No' " (p. 53). Social and occupational advancement are also beyond his scope. When his employer accuses him of lacking ambition, he reflects, "As a student I'd had plenty of ambition of the kind he meant. But, when I had to drop my studies, I very soon realized all that was pretty futile" [literally, '. . . all that had no real importance'] (p. 52).

Meursault's innate rapport with "the benign indifference of the universe" estranges him from any need to pass judgment on people or events; his strongest opinion is that something is "very interesting." Nor can he understand why anyone should want to judge him, and he gets vaguely annoyed when people criticize him for his lack of emotion over his mother's death. But after he shoots an Arab in a moment of sun-blinded confusion, an event that could legitimately be interpreted as an accident or self-defense, he learns the full extent of society's compulsion to judge. Ordinarily, a Frenchman killing an Arab in such extenuating circumstances would be quickly exonerated of any guilt, but when he is arrested, Meursault consternates the officials by refusing to express any remorse or to try to justify his crime.[1] The very concept of "crime" is foreign to Meursault. To kill a man, when both the killer and killed must eventually die anyway, is no more right or wrong than any other act; just before he shoots the Arab, the thought crosses Meursault's mind that "one might fire, or not fire—and it would come to absolutely the same thing" (p. 72). Although he is by nature a harmless person, once circumstances have caused him to murder, he is prepared to accept the consequences of his act—as he has shown by firing four deliberate shots into the Arab's body after the first accidental one—but not to admit that it was wrong.

After his arrest Meursault is questioned by a pious examining magistrate who believes that in his profession he is executing God's judgment. When Meursault explains that he does not believe in God, the magistrate is appalled: "That was unthinkable, he said; all men believe in God, even those who reject Him. Of this he was absolutely sure; if ever he came to doubt it, his life would lose all meaning" (p. 86)—his life, and especially

---

1. In *Albert Camus of Europe and Africa* (New York: Viking, 1970), Conor Cruise O'Brien argues that the defense's failure to play on the jury's colonialist prejudices indicates that Camus was ingenuously ignoring the realities of the racial situation in Algeria. Cruise O'Brien makes a persuasive case that much in the novel reveals Camus's own unconscious racism, but it seems to me on this particular point that Camus consciously set up the circumstances of the killing so the court would have been predisposed to side with Meursault if he had cooperated and that the racism involved is so obvious that no one engaged in the trial needs to make it explicit.

his occupation. To Meursault, of course, the occupation of judge *is* meaningless; his grilling by the magistrate strikes him as a kind of game, for
ignorance of his "guilt" prevents him from playing the role of criminal.
Nor can he understand why he should be inflicted with the privations of
prison during the long months before his trial, for he can see no connection between the abstract authority of the law and the concrete restrictions it imposes on him. And when he is first brought to trial he
cannot get used to being the center of attraction; he feels, rather, like a
spectator at a play, *de trop* in the room full of men bent on judgment.
However, when the everyday acquaintances of his past life are brought
to witness against him for not crying at his mother's funeral, for beginning an affair the next day, for his lack of ambition and general social indifference, he realizes that his fellow men have been condemning
him every day of his life. The trial sequence becomes a Kafkaesque
parable in which Meursault is finally sentenced to death, not because he
has murdered a man, but because he has failed to "play the game" of
conforming to society's arbitrary rituals.

In *The Myth* Camus uses the metaphor of a prison's "absurd walls" to
describe man's frustrating constriction in an incomprehensible and cruel
universe. In *The Stranger* Meursault's imprisonment before and after his
condemnation represents society's calculated counterpart to nature's un-
calculated restrictions—a counterpart that surpasses nature's incomprehen-
sibility and cruelty precisely because it *is* calculated. Meursault's conviction and death sentence are even more outlandishly contrived and codi-
fied substitutes by society for the metaphorical guilty verdict of natural
death as a form of metaphysical absurdity in *The Myth*. As Camus puts
it in "Reflections on the Guillotine," "She [society] assumes the right to
select as if she were nature herself and to add great sufferings to the elimination as if she were a redeeming god" (*RRD*, p. 173). In "Reflections"
he also points out the appalling disparity between society's imperfect,
often arbitrary moral standards and its power to enforce them with the
absolute punishment of death. Similarly in *The Stranger*, all through
Meursault's trial and even after his sentence has been passed, he remains
incredulous that society really has the power to take a life in retribution
for breaking its taboos. Yet, although he never affirms the rectitude of
the standards of guilt that have condemned him or of society's entire
practice of putting men to premature death, he is forced to concede that

the death sentence is as inexorable as natural death. In one of Camus's most powerful expressions of society's absurdity, Meursault reflects:

> Try as I might, I couldn't stomach this brutal certitude. For really, when one came to think about it, there was a disproportion between the judgment on which it was based and the unalterable sequence of events starting from the moment when that judgment was delivered. The fact that the verdict was read out at eight p.m. rather than at five, the fact that it might have been quite different, that it was given by men who change their underclothes, and was credited to so vague an entity as the "French people"—for that matter, why not to the Chinese or the German people?—all these facts seemed to deprive the court's decision of much of its gravity. Yet I could but recognize that, from the moment the verdict was given, its effects became as cogent, as tangible, as, for example, this wall against which I was lying, pressing my back to it [cf. the "absurd walls" of natural death in *The Myth*]. [Pp. 137-38]

In the last chapter, as Meursault awaits execution, he is visited by the prison chaplain, who pleads with him in vain to take confession. In contrast to the examining magistrate who earlier equated the court's judgment with that of God, the chaplain distinguishes between the two, while Meursault remains equally skeptical toward both: "In his view man's justice was a vain thing; only God's justice mattered. I pointed out that the former had condemned me. Yes, he agreed, but it hadn't absolved me from my sin. I told him that I wasn't conscious of any 'sin'; all I knew was that I'd been guilty of a criminal offense" (p. 148).

Meursault is finally able to reconcile himself to execution through a sequence of thoughts that has begun with his imprisonment before the trial. When first imprisoned he desperately misses the pleasures of which he has been deprived: freedom of movement, women, cigarettes, and so on. But eventually he becomes acclimated: "I've often thought that had I been compelled to live in the trunk of a dead tree, with nothing to do but gaze up at the patch of sky just overhead, I'd have got used to it by degrees. . . . I remember it had been one of Mother's pet ideas—she was always voicing it—that in the long run one gets used to anything" (pp. 95-96). After he has been tried and convicted, Meursault is placed in a death cell where the only light comes from a small skylight whose narrow vista recalls the hollow tree trunk referred to earlier. Here, just as prison at first has made him intensely miss the freedom of the outside world, his impending death at first makes him passionately appreciate the life he must give up. But the idea—one that echoes throughout the book—that one gets used to anything, which has enabled him to become acclimated to prison, also ultimately enables him to become resigned to the thought of his death.

Up until the chaplain's visit Meursault has clung to a slim hope of escaping the guillotine, but in a final burst of rage against the paternalistic priest, his intuition of death's all-leveling inevitability becomes explicit, and he recognizes that it is ultimately unimportant whether he dies now or twenty years from now, whether naturally or at the hands of the executioner: "All alike would be condemned to die one day; his turn, too, would come like the others'. And what difference could it make if, after being charged with murder, he were executed because he didn't weep at his mother's funeral, since it all came to the same thing in the end?" (p. 152). (Again, it should be emphasized that Meursault's resignation does not mean that he—or Camus—is condoning the death penalty. Natural death is unpreventable and unwilled, but society can and should prevent the willful institutionalization of killing.) So Meursault goes to the guillotine impassively, content that death will provide an escape from the spurious world of society's judgment.

III

By living free from society's arbitrary values in his everyday life and by refusing to condemn others himself or to recognize the validity of the guilty verdict the court has pronounced on him, Meursault has rebelled against social judgment; but by failing to affirm any value in life that would make it worthwhile to continue living and by killing a man and then facing his own death equally impassively, he has acquiesced to the metaphysical judgment of natural death. Although Meursault murders involuntarily, when he fires the four extra shots into his victim and subsequently denies any regret, by implication he condones voluntary, nihilistic murder—the gratuitous act by which man affirms and abets the gratuitous death sentence of the natural universe.

Camus explores the extreme consequences of Meursault's course of action in *Caligula*, written in the same period as *The Stranger* and *The Myth of Sisyphus*. The Roman emperor Caligula, originally a humane and just ruler, becomes obsessed with the awareness that in the face of death all happiness is destined to perish and society's laws and conventions are ludicrously tenuous. He renounces happiness to seek godlike transcendence in becoming the equal of nature as a capricious judge. With his royal power he turns Roman justice upside down, forces his pompous courtiers into obsequious travesties, and institutes an orgy of whimsical death sentences, executing together the innocent and guilty, patricians and plebeians, friends and enemies: "Judges, witnesses, accused—all sentenced to death without a hearing" (*CTOP,* p. 17).

Caligula's nihilistic assertion of freedom from social convention is of course doomed to end, not in transcendence, but—like every other human activity—only in death. As he overhears a band of assassins arming to attack him, he admits the futility of his grisly experiment: "But killing is not the solution. Caligula! You, too, are guilty. Then what of it—a little more, a little less? Yet who can condemn me in this world where there is no judge, where nobody is innocent? . . . I have chosen a wrong path, a path that leads to nothing. My freedom isn't the right one . . . we shall be forever guilty" (*CTOP,* p. 72).

Caligula has pushed the nihilistic implications of Meursault's absurd freedom to their logical conclusions and has found no satisfaction. But while he can discover no alternative between illusory social conventions and nihilistic self-indulgence, one *is* found by two characters in the play: Cherea the humanitarian and Scipio the young artist. Cherea, in simple passion for life, and Scipio, in beauty, find values beyond those of conventional society that are worth affirming and sustaining as long as possible, in spite of their ephemerality and lack of metaphysical justification. After acknowledging the logic of Caligula's nihilism, Cherea explains: "My plan of life may not be logical, but at least it's sound. . . . What I want is to live, and to be happy. Neither, to my mind, is possible if one pushes the absurd to its logical consequences" (*CTOP,* p. 51).

In Caligula's enigmatic dying gasp—"I'm still alive!" (*CTOP,* p. 74)— perhaps he belatedly arrives at Camus's conclusion in *The Myth,* that simply being alive is a value in itself, that life's very brevity and absence of transcendent meaning make every minute all the more precious. The final implication of absurd reasoning is not that the universal death sentence dictates cutting life and happiness even shorter than nature does; on the contrary, it dictates doing everything one can to prolong his own and others' lives: "[The absurd] escapes suicide to the extent that it is simultaneously awareness and rejection of death. It is, at the extreme limit of the condemned man's last thought, that shoelace that despite everything he sees a few yards away, on the very brink of his dizzying fall. The contrary of suicide, in fact, is the man condemned to death" (*Myth,* p. 40). Cherea's plan of life is in the end more logical than that of Caligula, the "superior suicide," as Camus later described him (*CTOP,* p. vi). Rebellion against religious or social orthodoxy, while desirable within humane limits, must be restricted at the point where it too destroys life. Cherea and Scipio lead the rebellion to curb Caligula's destructive freedom, and in doing so they foreshadow a new kind of hero—one who rebels not only against rationalized religious and social judgment like Meursault and Caligula but also against the irrational forces of the universal death penalty and human nihilism. In the overall pattern of Camus's works *Caligula* marks a transition between *The Stranger* and *The Plague,* in whose heroes Rieux and Tarrou Camus combines rebellion against all four forms of judgment.

IV

In *The Plague* the epidemic that strikes the city of Oran replaces judgment as the central image of the absurdity of death, but the novel's characters repeatedly picture the plague as a judgment on them; Camus at one time considered calling the book "The Prisoners," and in one passage plague and prison merge literally:

> For though some prisoners are kept solitary, a prison forms a sort of community, as is proved by the fact that in our town jail the guards died of plague in the same proportion as the prisoners. The plague was no respecter of persons and under its despotic rule everyone, from the warden down to the humblest delinquent, was under sentence and, perhaps for the first time, impartial justice reigned in the prison. [P. 153]

The citizens' reactions to the plague allegorize various traditional answers to the problem of death. The priest, Father Paneloux, for instance, follow-

ing Catholic doctrine, tells his congregation that the plague is God's judgment against them for their sins. When he himself is stricken, he refuses
to be treated by a doctor and dies. The criminal Cottard takes advantage
of the plague in every way possible, dealing with the black market and
illicitly smuggling people out of the quarantined city. After the plague
ends, his life becomes aimless, and, going mad, he sits at his window
with a revolver and fires at passers-by until he is captured by the police.
Cottard is a nihilistic ally of Meursault and Caligula in his willingness
to become the accomplice of the universe as murderer. Camus thus
equates the rational fatalism of the Christian and the irrational
fatalism of the nihilist in their acquiescence to the universal death sentence.

Among the characters who survive the plague is the old asthma victim who, having always had a premonition of death similar to Meursault's but more articulated, has retired at fifty and spent the rest of his
days merely being conscious of life every minute. He maintains this
constant awareness by throwing away clocks and marking time by shifting peas, one by one, from one saucepan to another. (His mechanical
multiplication of life's moments allies him to the robot woman of *The
Stranger* and to Camus's quantitative ethic of the most life, rather than
the best life, in *The Myth*.) The plague presents no new danger to him,
and he mocks those who have become distraught in its presence. In contrast to Meursault, who in the face of death denies that life is worth prolonging, the old man's exposure to the plague reinforces his determination to prolong his life and earns him the right to survive the epidemic in
Camus's allegory: "There's lots of life in me yet, and I'll see 'em all into
their graves. *I* know how to live" (p. 277).

Two other survivors are the journalist Rambert, to whom physical love
gives life all its meaning, yet who reluctantly exiles himself from the
woman he loves because of his sense of responsibility to the victims of
the plague, and Grand the literary artist, who divides his time between
helping the sanitary squads fight the plague and endlessly rewriting the
first sentence of a novel in his lonely room. Despite the satirical picture
that Camus paints of his artistic activities, Grand embodies Camus's ideal
of the artist whose life fluctuates between social solidarity in helping to
alleviate the human condition and solitude in expressing it through his
art.

The fate of these secondary characters indicates that Camus's sympathy has shifted from those who accept the universal death sentence unprotestingly or become its accomplices, like Meursault, Caligula, Paneloux, and Cottard, to those who rebel against it, like Cherea, Scipio, the old asthma patient, Rambert, and Grand. The leading role of Dr. Rieux confirms this indication. In *The Rebel* Camus writes, "Human insurrection, in its exalted and tragic forms, is only, and can only be, a prolonged protest against death, a violent accusation against the universal death penalty" (p. 100), and "Metaphysical rebellion is the movement by which man protests against his condition and against the whole of creation" (p. 23). Similarly, Rieux conceives his vocation as a physician in terms of "fighting against creation as he found it" (*Plague,* p. 116). Camus draws much of his imagery of judgment and rebellion against it from Dostoevsky, and Rieux is a literary descendant of Ivan Karamazov. In *The Rebel* Camus discusses the chapter "Rebellion" from *The Brothers Karamazov,* in which Ivan rejects the traditional justifications for a God who afflicts the world with suffering and death: "Ivan Karamazov sides with mankind and stresses human innocence. He affirms that the death sentence which hangs over man is unjust" (p. 55). "'If the suffering of children,' says Ivan, 'serves to complete the sum of suffering necessary for the acquisition of truth, I affirm from now onward that truth is not worth such a price'" (p. 56). And, "'I only know that suffering exists, that no one is guilty'" (p. 57). Rieux describes himself similarly, as "a man who was sick and tired of the world he lived in—though he had much liking for his fellow men" (*Plague,* pp. 11-12). He too rejects Christian justifications for the cruelties of nature; after he and Father Paneloux have witnessed the death of a child from the plague, he tells the priest, "Until my dying day I shall refuse to love a scheme of things in which children are put to torture" (pp. 196-97). But while Ivan condones murder as an act of rivalry to a murderous universe—as do Meursault, Caligula, and Cottard—Rieux chooses to sustain life as a doctor, even though he knows that every patient he heals must eventually die.

Rieux leads the fight against the plague and at the end of the novel explains his role as the story's narrator: "Dr. Rieux resolved to compile this chronicle, so that he should not be one of those who hold their peace but should bear witness in favor of those plague-stricken people; so that some memorial of the injustice and outrage done them might endure;

and to state quite simply what we learn in a time of pestilence: that there are more things to admire in men than to despise" (p. 278). And, "Summoned to give evidence regarding what was a sort of crime, he has exercised the restraint that behooves a conscientious witness. All the same, following the dictates of his heart, he has deliberately taken the victims' side and tried to share with his fellow citizens the only certitudes they had in common—love, exile, and suffering" (p. 272). Rieux's double role of militant activist against the plague and its chronicler identifies him, along with Grand, as Camus's committed artist, and his self-image as witness for the defense coincides with Camus's imagery, in "The Artist and His Time" and the speeches following his receipt of the Nobel Prize, of art as testimony and the artist as an opponent of judges: "The artist, at the end of his slow advance, absolves instead of condemning. Instead of being a judge, he is a justifier" (*RRD,* p. 204).

As a corollary to the themes of metaphysical and nihilistic judgment in *The Plague,* Camus creates another level on which the plague symbolizes a concrete contemporary incarnation of nihilism: Nazism and the German occupation of France. The occupation is evoked by the presence in the plague-quarantined city of "isolation camps," special police, collaborators (Cottard), the black market, crematoriums, and so on; and the characters like Rieux who fight the plague symbolize the members of the Resistance.

As Dr. Rieux embodies rebellion against natural death, Jean Tarrou, the other central character of *The Plague,* embodies rebellion against the rational judgment of society. Tarrou resembles Meursault in his dislike for self-righteousness and officiousness, as well as in his half-amused observation of the petty ways in which his fellow citizens assert their self-importance. He keeps a journal noting the habits of characters like the man who bolsters his ego by spitting on cats from his balcony and the magistrate Othon, who extends his officious needs to private life by militaristically domineering his wife and children. When Othon in his passion to judge states, "It's not the law that counts, it's the sentence," Tarrou observes, "That fellow is Enemy Number One" (p. 134).

Tarrou further resembles Meursault in his distaste for the State's power to inflict the death penalty. He is particularly concerned about the political murders that twentieth-century revolutions have committed in the name of justice, to which his own answer is nonviolent resistance. In his long monologue near the end of the novel, Tarrou equates the plague metaphorically with the germ of rational murder that every man has within himself. Tarrou admits that he too had plague, long before he came to Oran, for in his youth he believed in his own self-righteousness. But he was awakened to the cruelty of his society's "justice" when he went to a courtroom for the first time and watched his father, a prosecuting attorney, demand and receive the execution of a pathetic, contrite defendant. Here again, as in *The Stranger,* Camus parallels the courtroom as a symbol of social judgment (in the Tarrou plot) to the universal courtroom of natural death (in the Rieux plot). Rebelling from this brutal image of the authority of father and society, Tarrou ran away from home to become a revolutionary—presumably a communist. "I didn't want to be pestiferous, that's all. To my mind the social order around me was based on the death sentence, and by fighting the established order I'd be fighting against murder" (p. 226).

But Tarrou has found, as Camus emphasized in *The Rebel,* that there is a difference between rebellion and revolution: the rebel renounces judgment, while the revolutionary merely replaces one standard of judgment with another. Revolutionists too pass their death sentences: "Today there's a sort of competition who will kill the most" (p. 228). Tarrou's experience with revolutionists is obviously based on Camus's own break from the Communist party when he realized that the Communists, while attempting to correct the injustices of Christianity's bloody history, have shed just as much blood in the name of justice and a future secular utopia. Here Camus makes an implicit equation, one that he often makes explicitly in his political writing, between the metaphysical rationale of Christians such as Father Paneloux and the equally murderous social rationale of the Marxists. The parallels between Rieux's and Tarrou's stories also clearly correspond to Camus's critique of Nazi irrational terrorism and communist rational terrorism in *The Rebel.*

Tarrou has not been able to reconcile himself to killing, even after he has conceded that in our age politics have reached the point where every man must become a judge—if only to restrain the killers: "I know, too, that I'm not qualified to pass judgment on those others. There's something lacking in my mental make-up, and its lack prevents me from being a rational murderer" (p. 229). So he has left the revolutionists and "resolved to have no truck with anything which, directly or indirectly, for good reasons or for bad, brings death to anyone or justifies others' putting him to death." In the political essay *Neither Victims nor Executioners,* published in 1946, a year before *The Plague,* Camus calls for worldwide, nonviolent resistance to the injustices of both the communist countries and the West. In words reminiscent of this essay, Tarrou explains why he has joined Rieux in fighting the plague at Oran: "All I maintain is that on this earth there are pestilences and there are victims, and it's up to us, so far as possible, not to join forces with the pestilences" (p. 229).

v

Out of the values of *The Stranger* and *The Plague* Camus synthesized a humanitarian ethic for our time. From *The Stranger* he retained Meursault's simple, pagan sensuality free from illusions of immortality or a God to justify one's values, as well as his freedom from society's arbitrary laws and self-righteousness. However, Meursault's is "a still-negative truth," as Camus says in a 1955 foreword to *The Stranger* (*LCE,* p. 336), because Meursault ultimately denies life's value and because he kills, albeit accidentally, without contrition. In *The Plague* Rieux and Tarrou make Meursault's negative truth positive. By battling against the plague—and, allegorically, against natural death and nihilism—Rieux attests to the value in every man's life that justifies fighting to stay its inevitable execution. Tarrou makes explicit Meursault's instinctive rebellion against social judgment in its everyday forms and especially in its most severe form, rational murder committed under the authorization of capital punishment or militant "justice." In defending human happiness against any life-threatening force—metaphysical or human, irrational or rational—Rieux and Tarrou define the boundary of individual freedom at the point where it destroys one's own or another's life. Man's earthly salvation, then, lies in enjoying and sustaining as long as possible a finite, sensual life free from the self-righteous compulsion to be judged innocent oneself, by God or society, or to condemn others, whether out of self-righteousness or nihilistic fatalism.

However, the theme of Camus's last novel, *The Fall,* is that most men today are, unfortunately, incapable of gaining this humanitarian salvation because they have been conditioned by centuries of Christianity to need a belief in the transcendent authority of God and further conditioned by recent decades of totalitarianism to need absolute social authority. Jean-Baptiste Clamence, the narrator and antihero of *The Fall,* professes to a humanitarian ethic in his life as a lawyer in Paris.[2] Free from religious illusions, he dreams of "a total love of the whole heart and body, day and night, in an uninterrupted embrace, sensual enjoyment and mental excitement—all lasting five years and ending in death" (p. 135). Eager to sustain life and ease his fellow man's suffering, he helps blind people across streets, consoles widows, gives generously to charities, and so on. He tells of a man whose friend had been imprisoned and who slept on the floor of his room every night in order not to enjoy a comfort of which his friend had been deprived. Although he admits that he himself is not capable of such extreme self-sacrifice, Clamence claims, "I'd like to be and I shall be. Yes, we shall all be capable of it one day, and that will be salvation" (p. 32). He avoids judging others, either literally or figuratively; in contrast to the prosecuting attorneys of Camus's previous novels, he is a defense attorney, specializing in "noble cases," taking the victims' side (like Tarrou), and in everyday personal conflicts he is quite self-effacing and deferential. Nor does he respect those who do judge; he expresses "an instinctive scorn for judges in general. . . . I could not understand how a man could offer himself to perform such a surprising function. I accepted the fact because I saw it, but rather as I accepted locusts" (p. 18). Clamence's expression of these ideals, however, is obviously forced, and the word "judgment" creeps into his monologue too often for his self-proclaimed state of grace to ring true. Inevitably he falls from his Eden of freedom from judgment. His ideal of himself as the self-sacrificing humanitarian is the first to crumble. When he fails to save a drowning girl, simply because there is no one around to see him do it, he admits that he has helped relieve others' suffering only when it has been convenient and advantageous for him to do so. Another night he is crossing a bridge similar to the one from which the drowning girl had jumped, and he hears mysterious laughter directed at him. Breaking into a sweat, he realizes that he is not indifferent to being judged. Finally, he is browbeaten in a traffic tie-up, for a long while afterward cherishes a dream of trouncing his annoyers, and concludes that "the truth is that

2. Clamence's monologue is partly in present tense, partly past. I have put the whole sequence of narration into present tense, both to avoid syntactic complications and to establish the chronology of the events that Clamence in his deviousness and fever jumbles together.

every intelligent man, as you know, dreams of being a gangster and of ruling over society by force alone" (p. 55).

Clamence's fall from self-esteem continues as he admits that all of his professed ideals of humaneness and freedom from judgment have really been subtle, insidious means for him to judge without being judged in return. His profession of defending attorney has "set me above the judge whom I judged in turn, above the defendant whom I forced to gratitude" (p. 25). His altruistic good deeds, friendships, and even his love affairs have all been egocentric: "Modesty helped me to shine, humility to conquer, and virtue to oppress" (p. 84).

As soon as Clamence admits that he is not immune to judging or being judged, it becomes impossible for him to escape guilt. To begin with, the world today has gone mad with judgment: "Deprived of their natural curb, the judges, loosed at random, are racing through their job" (p. 117). Christ offered men innocence, but once the authority to judge passed from Christ to the human agency of the Church, grace disappeared: "They have hoisted him onto a judge's bench, in the secret of their hearts, and they smite, they judge above all, they judge in his name. He spoke softly to the adulteress: 'Neither do I condemn thee!' but that doesn't matter; they condemn without absolving anyone" (p. 115). The compulsion to judge that has been conditioned by the Church hangs on today even in nonreligious countries, through political authoritarianism: "On dead innocence the judges swarm, the judges of all species, those of Christ and those of the Antichrist" (p. 116). "Whether they are atheists or churchgoers, Muscovites or Bostonians, all Christians from father to son" (p. 134). Here Camus is commenting once again on the similarity between the murderous rationales of Christianity and Russian communism. Furthermore, today's terroristic police state, epitomized by Nazism, needs neither God's sanction nor the rationale of justice: " 'This is the truth,' we say. 'You can discuss it as much as you want; we aren't interested. But in a few years there'll be the police who will show you we are right' " (p. 45).

Once Clamence's shield of complacency has been shattered, he discovers that even the members of his own community have a compulsion to condemn:

> Today we are always ready to judge as we are to fornicate. . . . In
> my eyes my fellows ceased to be the respectful public to which I was

accustomed. The circle of which I was the center broke and they lined up in a row as on the judges' bench. In short, the moment I grasped that there was something to judge in me, I realized that there was in them an irresistible vocation for judgment. . . . People hasten to judge in order not to be judged themselves. . . . Each of us insists on being innocent at all cost, even if he has to accuse the whole human race and heaven itself. [Pp. 77–81, passim]

Now aware that the Church, contemporary politics, and his neighbors —as well as the ultimate judge, death—are all lined up to condemn him, Clamence tries to escape from this awareness through a series of mental anesthetics—wealth, ridicule, love, debauchery—even a brief, comic experiment with chastity. He succeeds in drugging himself into "a fog in which the laughter became so muffled that eventually I ceased to notice it" (p. 106), until during an ocean voyage he momentarily mistakes a piece of driftwood in the water for a drowning person. As the guilty memory of the drowning girl he was too cowardly to save overcomes him, he knows that his attempt to escape judgment has been futile. Even if he is able to slip through the judgment of other men, he is doomed to be condemned by his own conscience for rejecting freedom and temporal salvation. "Is not the great thing that stands in the way of our escaping the fact that we are the first to condemn ourselves?" (p. 131). Throughout his writing up to this point, Camus has attacked traditional standards of innocence and guilt as being arbitrary means that the self-righteous use to justify themselves while condemning others. At this point in *The Fall*, however, Camus for the first time discloses his own conception of innocence and guilt, consistent with the ethic he synthesized from *The Stranger* and *The Plague:* innocence lies in rebellion against all forms of metaphysical and human judgment; Clamence's true guilt is his failure to save the drowning girl and to be a sincere "defense attorney" against the judgment of Church, State, judges, and community.

Even after recognizing that he could purge his guilt by rebelling against judgment, Clamence is still too weak to make the necessary self-sacrifice: "We should like, at the same time, to cease being guilty and yet not to make the effort of cleansing ourselves" (p. 83). He is afraid of the freedom he could gain by living a finite life of pure sensuality without justification, afraid to sustain life by sacrificing himself for others—

Rebels against authority

when the only reward is the silence of the grave—or to deprive his ego of the gratification of judging others. Freedom, he sighs, is a solitary, exhausting chore, and "at the end of all freedom is a court sentence" (p. 133). Even being condemned by the arbitrary standards of the Church, State, or community—or, indeed, by a purely nihilistic authority—is preferable to the responsibilities of freedom. And so, accepting his own (and every man's) inescapable guilt, Clamence becomes an apostle of universal slavery:

> Ah, *mon cher,* for anyone who is alone, without God and without a master, the weight of days is dreadful. Hence one must choose a master, God being out of style. . . . So, after all, for want of betrothal or uninterrupted love, it will be marriage, brutal marriage, with power and the whip. The essential is that everything should become simple, as for the child, that every act should be ordered, that good and evil should be arbitraily, hence obviously, pointed out. . . . On the bridges of Paris I, too, learned that I was afraid of freedom. So hurray for the master, whoever he may be, to take the place of heaven's law. [Pp. 133–36, passim]

These passages again echo Dostoevsky, this time "The Grand Inquisitor," in which Christ returns to earth, only to be imprisoned by the Spanish Inquisition and chastised by the cardinal of Seville for having burdened men with the responsibility for freely choosing their own salvation. What men really crave, the Grand Inquisitor tells Christ, is not salvation but merely some authority to whom they can hand over their freedom of choice—and the Church has provided that authority in the form of brutal moral and political absolutism. Camus's addition is a commentary on the insidious appeal of secular as well as ecclesiastical authoritarianism.

Pending universal slavery, Clamence's only consolation can be to drag down everyone he meets to his own level of guilt. Furthermore, if he can convince other men that they too are guilty, he can momentarily regain his superiority by judging them once again. As Clamence has already found, however, "the judgment you are passing on others eventually snaps back in your face" (p. 137); so he must find a way to escape the return judgment: "I discovered that while waiting for the masters with their rods, we should, like Copernicus, reverse the reasoning to win out.

Inasmuch as one couldn't condemn others without immediately judging oneself, one had to overwhelm oneself to have the right to judge others" (p. 138). All Clamence needs to do is find the one crime of which all his contemporaries are guilty, the one crime which, when Clamence accuses himself of it, they will also recognize and condemn in themselves. And this one crime is, of course, judgment itself.

And so Clamence gives up his law practice and leaves Paris to establish the profession of "judge-penitent." Taking the pseudonym "Jean-Baptiste" —prophet of universal guilt—he finds the perfect setting for his new profession: postwar Amsterdam, the scene of Nazi oppression, a fogbound northern European city where men are most prone to judge and where salvation is most obscure, a city whose concentric canals resemble the circles of Dante's hell. Yet, there are the doves perpetually circling overhead, always in sight but never coming down to roost—the doves of salvation. And Clamence carefully chooses a bar with a tropical name, the Mexico City, as the headquarters for his confessions. Just enough reminders of the freedom Europeans have rejected so that when Clamence tells his story everyone who hears it will see himself mirrored in Clamence and suffer the same remorse. The minute this self-judgment sets in on his victim, Clamence rises once more, though only for one brief, fevered moment, to the superior heights of judgment. But this last, desperate attempt to judge is abortive too; Clamence can escape the guilty memory of his own rejected freedom for no more than a moment: "Oh, sun, beaches, and the islands in the path of the trade winds, youth whose memory drives one to despair!" (p. 144).

VI

Camus follows the same general theme of men's flight from rebellion and freedom in several of the stories in his final work of fiction, *Exile and the Kingdom*. The multiple levels of the theme are most effectively embodied in "The Guest," which is primarily a dramatization of the French colonial intellectual's divided sympathies in the Algerian conflict but which also has a symbolic dimension in which Camus explores the idea of a humanitarian Christ who comes to free men from religious and social judgment.

Christian critics who have claimed to see indications of an impending

submitted blindly to
dogma "the church"

conversion by Camus in *The Fall* and other late works have missed the irony in his use of Christian imagery against orthodox Christian doctrine. In his 1955 foreword to *The Stranger* he refers to Meursault, the sacrificial victim of Christian society's judgment, as "the only Christ we deserve" (*LCE*, p. 336). In *The Rebel* he again paraphrases Nietzsche: "What is the profoundly corrupt addition made by Christianity to the message of its master? The idea of judgment, completely foreign to the teachings of Christ, and the correlative notions of punishment and reward" (p. 69). In *The Fall* Clamence speaks of the true Christ, who did not condemn the adulteress, and disparages the Church's perversion of his ethic, but Clamence likewise is a false prophet to this Christ, locating himself in the last circle of Dante's hell, that of Judas the betrayer. In "Reflections on the Guillotine" Camus writes, "There could be read on the sword of the Fribourg executioner the words: 'Lord Jesus, thou art the judge.' . . . And, to be sure, whoever clings to the teaching of Jesus will look upon that handsome sword as one more outrage to the person of Christ" (*RRD*, p. 171).

"The Guest" once more evokes Dostoevsky's "The Grand Inquisitor," in which Christ comes to free men from miracle, mystery, and authority but is spurned by the Catholic church, whose officials decree that men are happier submitting blindly to dogma. Dostoevsky's theme is that each individual must choose of his own free will to believe in God and follow Christian morality without coercion by ecclesiastical or political authority. Camus's ironic variation in "The Guest" is his ideal of freedom from *freedom* all external authority, that of God as well as of Church and State. *freedom*

The Christ of freedom is reincarnated here in the kindly schoolmaster Daru. The French title "L'Hôte" carries the dual meaning of "the guest" and "the host," as well as a connotation of "l'hostie," the eucharistic host, and its Latin meaning of "the victim" or "the sacrifice." Balducci, the old guard whose paternalistic manner suggests the Old Testament God, turns an Arab prisoner over to Daru, whom Balducci repeatedly addresses as "son." Daru in turn is supposed to keep watch on the Arab overnight and take him to prison the next morning for punishment (the Arab has committed a hot-blooded murder, which Camus always regarded as less culpable than society's premeditated murders). Daru states his reluctance to deliver the criminal, but Balducci nevertheless leaves the Arab with him. That evening Daru bakes a cake and shares it with the Arab in a eucharistic dinner. As they eat together the prisoner asks, "Are you the judge?" and Daru replies, "No, I'm simply keeping you until tomorrow" (*EK*, p. 99).

In the morning Daru again feeds the Arab cake and, after leading him to a baptismal shower, sets him on the path to freedom, not jail. The irony of "The Grand Inquisitor" and *The Fall* is repeated when the Arab, too conditioned to being judged, turns and dumbly follows the road to prison. And when Daru returns to his schoolhouse he finds a message on the blackboard: "You handed over our brother. You will pay for this" (*EK*, p. 109). Christ is again misunderstood and crucified, his self-sacrifice futile, and men have again chosen condemnation over freedom.

VII

Camus was trying in his writing to work his way through the problems of contemporary Europe so that he could return in peace of mind to the spirit of the sensuous "eternal summer" of his youth in Algeria. One of the cruelest aspects of his untimely death in 1960 was that it ended his artistic development in the pessimistic period epitomized by the fog-bound European setting of *The Fall*, whereas he had envisioned *The Fall* and *Exile and the Kingdom* as transitions to the "cycle of freedom" that he had anticipated in his notebooks. He was working on a novel about the Hungarian rebellion of 1956 and on a play about Don Juan, one of his favorite early embodiments of pagan sensuality and rebellion against authority.

Even if he had lived, however, the course of history would have been working against him. The French Algeria of his youth was gone forever. With the revolt of colonial peoples in Algeria and elsewhere throughout the Third World, the roles of victims and executioners were becoming constantly more difficult to distinguish. In his critique of *The Rebel* Sartre reproved Camus's overly facile dichotomies: "This is the explanation of why the war in Indo-China plunged you into such embarrassment. If we are to apply your principles, the Vietnamese are the colonized, and thus slaves, but they are also Communists, and thus tyrants."[3]

Moreover, positive as his works-in-progress might have been, Camus

---

3. "Reply to Albert Camus," in *Situations* (New York: Fawcett World Library, 1966), p. 66; translation of *Situations IV* (Paris: Gallimard, 1964).

was too much of an ironist to have expected to achieve in them a definitive resolution of problems that he had struggled with through more than
twenty years of writing. As he recognized as early as *The Myth,* "If
something brings creation to an end, it is not the victorious and illusory
cry of the blinded artist: 'I have said everything,' but the death of the
creator which closes his experience and the book of his genius" (p. 84).

3

Meaning and Value

One of the central, and typically ambiguous, words throughout Camus's writing is "meaning." He uses the noun *le sens* and the verbs *signifier* and *vouloir dire* to refer both to a metaphysical purpose, justification, or scale of moral values in life and to epistemological "sense"—semantic signification and the rational unification and explanation of sense experience. Both meanings of "meaning" are involved in the theme of the absurd in *The Myth, The Stranger*, and his later retrospections on these works in *The Rebel* and elsewhere.

Camus divides the multiple aspects of the absurd that he enumerates in *The Myth* into what can be termed metaphysical and epistemological absurdities. The former include the brevity of life and inevitability of death, the indifference of the natural universe to human existence and of men to one another's existence, and the absence of a God and an after-life that would give this life a transcendent purpose or universal system of moral values (although Camus approaches the existence of God more as an epistemological problem than as a metaphysical one; he does not deny God's existence but our ability to ascertain it rationally). Epistemological absurdity further entails the limitations of human understanding in general—the foundering of reason in logical dilemmas, the mind's failure to explain or unify experience totally, the frustration of our "nostalgia for unity, that appetite for the absolute . . ." (*Myth*, p. 13).

Camus summarizes all of these metaphysical and epistemological aspects of the absurd in the formulation "life has no meaning"; the central question of the book then becomes whether "refusing to grant a meaning to life necessarily leads to declaring that it is not worth living" (p. 7). He assumes that it is the belief life has a meaning, in all of the above senses, that makes most men feel it is worth living. But, he asks, is the absence of metaphysical and epistemological *meaning* in fact equivalent to the absence of all *value* in life, or can values be found that make life worth living even under the conditions of absurd meaninglessness? His answer from the beginning is, "In truth, there is no necessary common measure between these judgments" (p. 7). Indeed, he later concludes, "It was previously a question of finding out whether or not life had to have a meaning to be lived. It now becomes clear, on the contrary, that it will be lived all the better if it has no meaning" (pp. 39–40).

On the metaphysical level, he explains, the absence of God—or more precisely our absence of knowledge that there is a God—dictates existential freedom, in the manner of Ivan Karamazov's "Everything is permitted"; recognizing the brevity of life and denying an afterlife provide an imperative to savor every minute of this life; the lack of any preordained purpose or moral value system is an invitation to create one's own life style and to substitute "the quantity of experiences for the quality": "Belief in the meaning of life always implies a scale of values, a choice, our preferences. Belief in the absurd, according to our definitions, teaches the contrary. . . . What counts is not the best living but the most living" (p. 45). And all the restrictions of the absurd increase the value of man's capacity to revolt against them—the pride of bearing one's fate stoically, in the manner of Sisyphus, without surrendering to suicidal despair or to deluded hope, and the challenge to his powers of defiance to push constantly to "exhaust the limits of the possible," without false hopes of transcending them.

On the epistemological level, reason is valuable within its limitations for two reasons. To begin with, its failure to explain and unify experience is not total:

> Our appetite for understanding, our nostalgia for the absolute are explicable only in so far, precisely, as we can understand and explain many things. It is useless to negate reason absolutely. It has its order in which it is efficacious. . . . Here may intervene the notion of limit and the notion of level. The laws of nature may be operative up to a certain limit, beyond which they turn against themselves to give birth to the absurd. Or else, they may justify themselves on the level of description without for that reason being true on the level of explanation. [P. 27]

And reason provides the source not only of a minimal sense of coherence but of another form of revolt, that of the human mind defying the mindlessness of the rest of the universe and grappling with its own limitations: "To a man devoid of blinkers, there is no finer sight than that of the intelligence at grips with a reality that transcends it" (p. 41). (Note that here Camus sees meaning, i.e., reason, as a source of values in itself, in contrast to the passage where, having called into question the conventional equation of meaning with value, he has asserted that life is more valuable without meaning; he might have said more accurately that life is more valuable with only limited meaning. I stress these fine points of the relation between meaning and value because they come up again in Camus's later works.) To deny the value of reason altogether, through irrationalism, mysticism, or the religious-existentialist leap to faith in God, is to commit "philosophical suicide," the intellectual equivalent to literal suicide as a response to metaphysical absurdity.

One form of absurd "lucid reason noting its limits" is literature, which, Camus claims in the chapter "Absurd Creation," can function validly within the boundaries of epistemological absurdity:

> For an absurd work of art to be possible, thought in its most lucid form must be involved in it. But at the same time thought must not be apparent except as the regulating intelligence. This paradox can be explained according to the absurd. The work of art is born of the intelligence's refusal to reason the concrete. It marks the triumph of the carnal. . . . The absurd work requires an artist conscious of these limitations and an art in which the concrete signifies nothing more than itself. [P. 72]

Camus says of the great novelists, "The preference they have shown for writing in images rather than in reasoned arguments is revelatory of a certain thought that is common to them all, convinced of the uselessness of any principle of explanation and sure of the educative message of perceptible appearance" (p. 75). Absurd literature, then, will deal in concrete images rather than abstractions, arguments, or explanations and, furthermore, will not seek to unify experience: "Any thought that abandons unity glorifies diversity. And diversity is the home of art" (p. 86). Finally, by describing life in its full metaphysical and epistemological absurdity, the writer is affirming that there are indeed values that make life under these conditions worth living—and worth celebrating through literary imitation. Thus epistemology and metaphysics merge in the occupation of creative writing, which becomes an exercise in living the most.

II

The two meanings of meaning and their relation to life's value figure in *The Stranger* as well as *The Myth*—but with some significant differences. Deferring for the moment the epistemological dimension, we can first see clear parallels with the metaphysical themes of *The Myth* in the contrast between Meursault, with his acceptance of a life without justifications or a scale of moral values, his attitude of "It's all the same to me," and the other characters discussed in the previous chapter who need to give their life meaning through illusions of self-importance, arbitrary value judgments by which they justify themselves and condemn others, and belief in God. (When Meursault says he does not believe in God, the chaplain is reduced to tears and the examining magistrate is appalled: "That was unthinkable, he said; all men believe in God, even those who reject Him. Of this he was absolutely sure; if ever he came to doubt it, his life would lose all meaning" [*Stranger*, p. 86].)

If Meursault resembles the absurd man of *The Myth* in finding value without meaning in his everyday life, he goes in quite the opposite direction when he stumbles into committing murder and then faces execution with the attitude that "nothing had the least importance" (p. 152) and that "life isn't worth living, anyhow" (p. 142). It can be argued that Meursault's willingness to die stems exclusively from his social revolt and thus does not entail any metaphysical denial of life's value. This view, which Camus himself leans toward in his 1955 preface (*LCE*, pp. 335–37), would salvage consistency between *The Stranger* and *The Myth*, since the latter purposely excludes the question of dying for social motives. I disagree with this interpretation, for reasons explained in greater detail in chapter 8 below; briefly, my reading is that beyond Meursault's social defiance, he also displays a natural indifference toward averting his death —if not a definite attraction toward dying—in clear contrast to the absurd man of *The Myth*, for whom preserving his life as long as possible is the supreme goal. The following two passages epitomize the opposition between the two books:

In the long run, I was aware that whether I died at thirty or at seventy had little importance, since, naturally, in both cases other men and other women will be living, and that will be true for thousands of years. Nothing was clearer, in fact. It was still me who would be dying, whether now or in twenty years. At that moment, what bothered me a little in my reasoning was the frightful upsurge that I felt inside me at the thought of twenty years to come. But all I had to do to stifle it was imagine what my thoughts would be in twenty years when I would still have to arrive at that point. From the moment that one dies, how and when has little importance, obviously. [*Stranger*, pp. 142–43, although I have departed entirely from Gilbert's translation, which is quite unfaithful here.]

Let us say that the sole obstacle, the sole deficiency to be made good, is constituted by premature death. Thus it is that no depth, no emotion, no passion, and no sacrifice could render equal in the eyes of the absurd man (even if he wished it so) a conscious life of forty years and a lucidity spread over sixty years. Madness and death are his irreparables. . . . There will never be any substitute for twenty years of life and experience. [*Myth*, pp. 46–47]

Although the passage from *The Stranger* comes when Meursault is still emotionally unresigned to dying, he ultimately confirms his reasoned conclusions here in abandoning his appeal and virtually welcoming death. Camus's obviously conscious parallel between these two sections supports the view that in some respects the two books counterbalance rather than support one another, as most critics assume, and that Camus intended Meursault to embody a more negative response to the absurd than the one he advocates in *The Myth*.

It is not necessary to look to *The Myth* or Camus's other, more affirmative works of the same period in order to find an alternative attitude to Meursault's; for within *The Stranger* itself there is a contradiction between Meursault the hero and Camus the author. Camus in effect refuted certain phases of Meursault's logic by the very act of writing *The Stranger*. To what extent he was conscious of doing so at the time is an interesting speculation, one to which we will return; however, it is clear that he was perfectly aware of having done so by the time he reexamined the concept of the absurd in that all-important summary of the development of his thought from *The Myth* and *The Stranger* to *The Fall,* the introduction to *The Rebel:*

> The absurd is, in itself, contradiction.
>
> It is contradictory in its content because, in wanting to uphold life, it excludes all value judgments, when to live is, in itself, a value judgment. To breathe is to judge. Perhaps it is untrue to say that life is a perpetual choice. But it is true that it is impossible to imagine a life deprived of all choice. From this simplified point of view, the absurdist position, translated into action, is inconceivable. [P. 8]

In a passage in "The Enigma," written in 1950, that almost duplicates the introduction to *The Rebel* and the chapter in the latter work on rebellion and the novel, Camus protests against having been stereotyped as an author of despairing or nihilistic literature simply because he analyzed the contemporary malaise of the absurd in *The Myth,* even though he ended up transcending it:

> Refusing the world all meaning amounts to abolishing all value judgments. But living, and eating, for example, are in themselves value judgments. You choose to remain alive the moment you do not allow yourself to die of hunger, and consequently you recognize that life has at least a relative value. What, in fact, does "literature of despair" mean? Despair is silent. Even silence, moreover, is meaningful if your eyes speak. True despair is the agony of death, the grave or the abyss. If he speaks, if he reasons, above all if he writes, immediately the brother reaches out his hand, the tree is justified, love is born. Literature of despair is a contradiction in terms. [*LCE,* p. 160]

This passage is even more pertinent to *The Stranger,* which, in the author's ostensible sympathy with its indifferent hero, is certainly a more pessimistic book than *The Myth.* Meursault chooses not to maintain life, not to go on breathing or eating, and thereby denies that life is worth living. But if a man chooses not only to go on living but to write a book, as Camus did *The Stranger,* he has undeniably demonstrated that he believes it is worth living.

III

So far, we have only examined the metaphysical side of meaning and value in *The Stranger*. There is an epistemological parallel, and it involves a similar implicit self-contradiction. Meursault's mentality reflects the incoherence, inexplicability, and nonabstractability of the absurd condition described in *The Myth*. Jean-Paul Sartre, in his incisive 1943 "Explication of *The Stranger*,"[1] and several subsequent critics, such as Armand Renaud[2] and M.-G. Barrier,[3] have analyzed how this disparity of perception is expressed in Meursault's narrative style in the short, choppy sentences, the paratactic juxtaposition of clauses without any causal conjunction, and the use (in the French version) of the *passé composé,* or present perfect tense, which gives the verb a disjointed, passive connotation and makes the narrative seem to follow events from minute to minute. Because Meursault does live only from minute to minute, he cannot sustain his emotions beyond the time when the object that stimulated them is present; he *was* fond of his mother and of Marie, but once the one has died and he is separated by imprisonment from the other, his fondness naturally wanes. His sense of the disunity of experience obviously precludes any idea of an underlying order in life, an organizing force that guides the course of events toward a logical goal. " 'Do you wish my life to have no meaning?' " (p. 86) implores the examining magistrate, for Meursault would divest his life of both heavenly authority and earthly cogency. Meursault himself perceives no unity in his personal experience. His future is amorphous—hence his lack of ambition or of any kind of complex, foreseeing motivation—and he doesn't think much about his past. What retrospection he does undertake is an attempt, not to unify past events, but merely to bring physical sensations back to memory. For Meursault, the antithesis of Proust's narrator, the past is no more susceptible to organization than the present; events retain their concreteness and discontinuity in his memory, without coalescing into meaningful patterns.

1. In *Camus: A Collecton of Critical Essays,* ed. Germaine Brée (Englewood Cliffs, N. J.: Prentice-Hall, 1962), pp. 108–21; French text in Sartre's *Situations I* (Paris: Gallimard, 1947).
2. "Quelques remarques sur le style de *L'Etranger*," *French Review* 30, no. 4 (Feb. 1957): 290–96.
3. *L'Art du récit dans "L'Etranger" d'Albert Camus* (Paris: A. G. Nizet, 1962).

It is a strain for Meursault's purely sensory consciousness, absorbed in the distinct sensations of each separate moment, to abstract sense impressions into words and syntactical order—one reason for his taciturnity. The more abstract a concept is, the farther removed from physical reality it is, and the more incomprehensible to Meursault. In the first paragraph of the book, when Meursault remarks about the complimentary closing of the director's telegram—"Deep sympathy" ['Sentiments distingués']— that "that doesn't mean anything," ['cela ne veut rien dire'] he refers not only to the phrase's emotional emptiness but to its semantic emptiness as well.[4] When he tells the chaplain, "I wasn't conscious of any 'sin'" (p. 149) [literally, 'I didn't know what a sin was'], he means quite literally that he does not know what the word "sin" means. And when Marie asks him if he loves her and he replies that "her question meant nothing" (p. 52) [literally, 'That signified nothing'], both senses of "signify" are involved: "significance"—love is not an important matter—and "signification"—the abstraction "love" signifies no physical reality. Camus says in *The Myth,* "Of love I know only that mixture of desire, affection, and intelligence that binds me to this or that creature. That compound is not the same for another person. I do not have the right to cover all these experiences with the same name" (p. 55). Or as Sartre says in his explication, "What we call a feeling is merely the abstract unity and the meaning ['signification'] of discontinuous impressions."[5] Meursault simply cannot assemble his passing impressions and feelings into universal categories like "love"; similarly, during his interrogation he cannot understand that he has become one of the linguistic class of "criminals." Ultimately the character of Meursault raises the possibility of a person for whom mankind's entire intellectual faculty for abstracting sense impressions into the symbolic realm of language is alien, a man of exclusively sensory consciousness for whom the universally accepted convention that words "mean" or "signify" objects in the physical world and that the flow of events can be organized into the syntactic order of discourse is too artificial to comprehend. *The Stranger* takes epistemological absurdity one step further than *The Myth* in implicitly calling into question the validity of any semantic meaning.

Semantic disorganization and nonsignification preclude analysis. Meur-

4. See the discussion of the translation and interpretation of the first paragraph of *The Stranger* below in chap. 8, sec. II.
5. *Camus: A Collection of Critical Essays,* ed. Brée, p. 113.

sault, like the "concrete" novelists discussed in *The Myth,* is "convinced
of the uselessness of any principle of explanation" and consequently of any
principle of justification or judgment. The man who feels obliged to
justify his motivations must explain, interpret, and evaluate his actions.
And his need to justify himself is inextricably connected with the need
to condemn those whose actions contradict his own values, to attribute
evil motivations to them. It follows naturally that Camus should throughout his works identify verbosity with those who have an obsession to
justify and judge—most prominently Clamence of *The Fall* and the "garrulous slave" of "The Renegade"—and taciturnity with those like Meursault who are indifferent to judgments of innocence and guilt. As Camus
says in a 1937 notebook entry, "The innocent is the person who explains
nothing" (*N1,* p. 71).

We are now in a position to see how the theme of semantic meaning
enters into the discrepancy between the Arab's murder in Part One and
its verbal reexaminations during Meursault's interrogation and trial in
Part Two. Camus's brilliant dramatization of this discrepancy dominates and balances the novel's central portion. When Meursault is questioned by the examining magistrate, he noncommittally recounts the
series of events on the beach. When he is asked, however, to explain why
he shot the Arab—"*Why?*" the magistrate repeats five times—Meursault
recalls the physical sensations of the moment that were the real cause but
cannot translate them into explanatory language: "I seemed to see it
hovering again before my eyes, the red glow of the beach, and to feel that
fiery breath on my cheeks—and, this time, I made no answer" (p. 84).

At the trial Meursault finally makes a feeble attempt "to explain that it
was because of the sun, but I spoke too quickly and ran my words into
each other. I was only too conscious that it sounded nonsensical, and, in
fact, I heard people tittering" (p. 130). When the prosecuting attorney
"reconstructs" the crime, we the readers, having been eyewitnesses to the
actual scene in Part One, are appalled at the breach between the two
versions. Even if his description were factual, it would not be able to
recapture Meursault's vivid, confused sensations on the beach. Sartre is
highly perceptive on this point: "The reader, [having been] brought
face to face with simple reality, [finds] it again, without being able to
recognize it in its rational transposition. This is the source of the feeling
of the absurd, that is, of our inability to *think,* with our words and con-

cepts, what happens in the world." According to Sartre, the trial represents "an absurd justice, incapable of ever understanding or even of making contact with the deeds it intends to punish," an attempt "to use words to describe a world that precedes words." [6]

As for Meursault's "motive," the simple truth that the murder was unmotivated is *too* simple before a courtroom-theater audience that demands eloquent self-exoneration or the kind of malevolent calculation that the prosecuting attorney imputes to Meursault. And the two attorneys' evaluations of Meursault's retrospective attitude toward his deeds—the prosecution's image of a stonyhearted, remorseless criminal, and the defense's image of a penitent bearing the weight of eternal remorse—are equally erroneous. "I didn't feel much regret for what I'd done. Still, to my mind he overdid it, and I'd have liked to have a chance of explaining to him, in a quite friendly, almost affectionate way, that I have never been able really to regret anything in all my life. I've always been far too much absorbed in the present moment, or in the immediate future, to think back" (p. 127). As the lawyers' progression from verbal reconstruction to motivational analysis to condemnation or exoneration leads the trial further and further away from the physical realities of the shooting and from physical reality altogether, Meursault gets the feeling that the trial has nothing to do with him and completely loses interest. Only the shrill horn of an ice-cream vendor outside the building, a brief reminder of the world of sensuous immediacy, pierces through the unintelligible, irrelevant babble of an absurd "justice."

The epistemological self-contradiction in *The Stranger* stems from the theory of total semantic nonsignification implicit in Meursault's character. It seems to have been only novelistic expediency that prevented Camus from making Meursault completely mute, as he should be as the theoretical absurd hero. But the fact that he can speak at all is a flaw in the theory. Any speech whatsoever, even on the least complex level, is an abstraction of sense experience into verbal symbols and an ordering of disparate phenomena into syntactic sequence. In the passage from *The Rebel* quoted earlier in which Camus says that the absurdist contradicts himself in precluding value judgments and yet making the value judgment of continuing to live, he continues that the absurd "is equally inconceivable when translated into expression. [Literal translation: 'Any philosophy of

6. Ibid., p. 115.

nonsignification survives on a contradiction by the very fact of expressing itself.'] Simply by being expressed, it gives a minimum of coherence to incoherence, and introduces consequence where, according to its own tenets, there is none. Speaking itself is restorative. The only coherent attitude based on non-signification would be silence—if silence, in its turn, were not significant. The absurd, in its purest form, attempts to remain dumb" (p. 8). And in the paragraph quoted earlier from "The Enigma," where he again parallels the metaphysical and semantic paradoxes in the absurd, he articulates it more succinctly: "The moment you say that everything is nonsense you express something meaningful [literally, '. . . something that makes sense']" (*LCE*, pp. 159–60). A single spoken word, a single sentence, is a Cartesian *cogito,* a first step toward possible formulation of the qualities that are beyond Meursault's capacities: abstract concepts, sustained emotions, and the continuity of thought necessary to constitute complex motivation and a scale of values—all the qualities except a need to justify and to judge, for Camus never became reconciled to the self-righteous, arbitrary values that society uses to excuse rational murder; the central problem in *The Rebel,* in fact, is how to reconstitute from the absurdist point of departure a humane scale of values while stopping short of any value that justifies killing.

This inconsistency does not negate Meursault's verisimilitude as a character. It is still credible that a certain man may lack the capacity to unify and evaluate his experience beyond a primitive level. A contradiction becomes involved only if *The Stranger* is regarded as postulating a theory of nonsignification. So regarded, it presents a further paradox. Meursault cannot put his sense experience into language; yet Camus the author must use language to convey these experiences to the reader. (Sartre recognizes this difficulty but approaches it only as a challenge to novelistic technique, without pursuing the contradiction that it implies.) The disparity between the actual events surrounding the murder and their verbal reconstruction by the attorneys at the trial is somewhat diminished by the fact that what is being verbally reconstructed is not really Meursault's firsthand experiences but Camus's own verbal reconstruction of them in turn; we have been twice removed from reality. In this one respect, *The Stranger* might be more effective as a play or film than as a novel. On the stage or screen we could see and *feel* the scene on the beach, without the numbing intermediary of verbal description; then the irrelevance of the trial would strike us in its full absurdity. (Visconti's generally faithful but un-inspired 1966 film cut the verbal reconstruction—a regrettable failure to take advantage of the cinematic medium.) Camus must have sensed, at least half-consciously, this particular paradox when he was writing the book, because he uses considerable literary sleight-of-hand to surmount—or mask—it. W. M. Frohock has analyzed Camus's heightened use of metaphoric images in the murder scene in an attempt to jump the gap of descriptive language and make the climactic passage as vivid as possible.[7] Camus achieves his effect but does not resolve the paradox; semantically, metaphor is one step *farther* away from direct experience than straight descriptive language. (John Cruickshank makes the interesting suggestion that Camus intended Meursault's lapse into metaphor to indicate his temporary hallucinatory state—an interpretation that would support my point.) [8]

The murder scene is only the most prominent example of the sleight-of-hand that Camus uses throughout the book toward the same general purpose, that of creating the illusion that *The Stranger,* consonant with Meursault's fragmented consciousness, is an unstructured, nonliterary work, an antinovel—while in reality it is a conventionally structured, highly literary novel. The supremely paradoxical fact is that the structure of *The Stranger* presents the exact antithesis of Meursault's structureless world view. Meursault sees life as disunified, nonsequential, and nonsignificative; but *The Stranger* is a work of meticulous organization, logical sequence, and signification—rigorously constructed on a symmetrical framework of analogy, metaphor, and symbolism. As Camus was to state positively in his chapter on rebellion and the novel in *The Rebel,* literary form is standing evidence against the apparent amorphousness of life: "What, in fact, is a novel but a universe in which action is endowed with form, where final words are pronounced, where people possess one another completely, and where life assumes the aspect of destiny?" A footnote adds: "Even if the novel describes only nostalgia, despair, frustration, it still creates a form of salvation [literally, '. . . creates form and salvation']. To talk of despair is to conquer it. Despairing literature is a contradiction in terms" (pp. 262–63). (Camus seems unclear here on whether

---

7. *Style and Temper: Studies in French Fiction, 1925–1960* (Cambridge: Harvard University Press, 1967), pp. 107–11.
8. *Albert Camus and the Literature of Revolt* (London: Oxford University Press, 1959), pp. 156–58.

he is speaking about despair over life's formlessness or its valuelessness. Having carefully distinguished meaning, in both senses, from value in *The Myth,* he may be falling inconsistently into equating value with epistemological meaning. On the other hand, his consistency might be salvaged by reading this passage as an extension of his acknowledgment in *The Myth* that reason is capable of unifying experience to a limited degree and that this minimal sense of unity is one of the values that makes the absurd life worth living.) In countering Meursault's antiformalism with the form of *The Stranger* itself, Camus has provided both poison and antidote, just as he has done on the metaphysical level by countering Meursault's denial of life's value with the affirmation of remaining alive himself and writing the novel.

The failure of many of Camus's critics to pick up his hints for understanding the counterpoise between the explicit theme and the form or his very writing of *The Stranger* has resulted in some glaring misinterpretations. Murray Krieger's conception of "the tragic vision," for example, is remarkably similar to Camus's own notion of the form of Greek tragedy and literary form in general providing a brake on thematic chaos and despair. Yet, in discussing *The Stranger,* Krieger completely fails to see this vision embodied in it and in fact reads it as an exception to the characteristic pattern of modern novels whose form redeems the despair of their heroes' thwarted existential self-assertions.[9] He not only is unable to see that Meursault's indifference is also a mode of existential revolt but in effect equates that indifference with the novel's total statement—a surprising oversight for a prominent expounder of New Critical formalistic complexities. Krieger even more surprisingly ignores all of Camus's works except *The Stranger* and *The Fall,* thus missing the explicit statements on literary form in *The Rebel* and elsewhere that show Camus to be a perfect example of Krieger's tragic visionary. Leo Bersani and Irving Massey note that *The Stranger* points toward the assault on conventional epistemological cogency that has been carried further by structuralism and antinovelists like Robbe-Grillet and Beckett.[10] But they view its countervailing elements of coherence as an equivocation rather than a justifiable

9. "Albert Camus: Beyond Nonentity and the Rejection of the Tragic," in *The Tragic Vision* (New York: Holt, Rinehart and Winston, 1960), pp. 144–53.
10. Bersani, "The Stranger's Secrets," in *Balzac to Beckett: Center and Circumference in French Fiction* (New York: Oxford University Press, 1970), pp. 247–71; Massey, *The Uncreating Word* (Bloomington: Indiana University Press, 1970).

control that was to become Camus's guide in his conscious reversal of direction away from the antinovelists' avowed total negations of language—although Bersani does find similar controls in *these* writers.

IV

The Stranger, then, ends up saying at the same time that life is worthless and worthwhile, incoherent and coherent. To what extent was Camus aware of these self-contradictions at the time he wrote the novel? Is his position in *The Rebel* and "The Enigma"—which he had formulated as early as March 1943 in a letter replying to a critic of *The Myth* (*Essais,* pp. 1422-24)—a reversal of that in *The Stranger* or a consistent, dialectical extension of implicit attitudes that he purposely built into it? Attuned as he always was to paradox, it is doubtful that he would have been completely ingenuous here, and arguments can be made to support the assertion that he knew quite well what he was doing on both levels. On the metaphysical plane, it may be that Camus viewed his act of writing *The Stranger* as a conscious illustration of the absurd creator in *The Myth* "negating on the one hand and magnifying on the other" (*Myth,* p. 84) and that what he was magnifying was the positive side of Meursault's character, the side he would emphasize in his 1955 preface.

This argument can be countered, however, by pointing out that, whatever positive traits of the absurd hero Meursault does possess, he also undeniably embodies a certain attraction toward death not evident in *The Myth;* and if this negative trait outweighs his positive ones, as I think it does, then Camus is left in the tenuous position of saying that it is an affirmative gesture to write a novel exalting its protagonist's death wish. Of course Meursault is not Camus (an argument Camus was to invoke indirectly in "The Enigma"), and the tension between character and author can be viewed as a legitimate form of literary ambiguity; nevertheless, Camus seems only to have articulated this justification after the fact, and then only as a point of departure from his period as exponent of the absurd. In *The Rebel* he says:

The absurd, in its purest form, attempts to remain dumb. If it finds its voice, it is because it has become complacent or, as we shall see, because it considers itself provisional. This complacency is an excellent indication of the profound ambiguity of the absurdist position. In a certain way, the absurd, which claims to express man in his solitude, really makes him live in front of a mirror. And then the initial anguish runs the risk of turning to comfort. The wound that is scratched with such solicitude ends by giving pleasure. [Pp. 8–9]

And about the purportedly solitary agony of the dandy: "Rebellion puts on mourning and exhibits itself for public admiration" (p. 50). [A closer translation would be, "Rebellion decks itself out in mourning clothes and goes onstage to be admired."] Camus may have been thinking here of the accusation he had left himself open to that he had built a successful literary career out of parading absurdist despair in the character of Meursault. So if he did originally conceive *The Stranger* as a simultaneous metaphysical negation and affirmation, he later recognized that this was at best a limited conception.

On the epistemological plane, Camus's reversal in the later works of Meursault's denial of semantic signification might be said to be already implicit in *The Myth*'s recognition that reason and literature reflect a minimal degree of unity and explicability in the absurd condition. Camus could have made a natural extension even within *The Myth* to his conclusion in "The Enigma" and *The Rebel* that language—and preeminently the language of literature—also reflects a minimal degree of signification, and he could have thereby made this one more theme on which *The Myth* counterbalanced *The Stranger*. But the fact is that he did not. There is no explicit mention of the paradoxes that semantic signification poses for an absurd epistemology in any of his works up through 1941 when he had finished both *The Stranger* and *The Myth*. His first articulations of these paradoxes appear in the 1943 letter mentioned above and his 1942–43 notebook entries (*N2*, pp. 23, 72, 84) and 1944 essay "On a Philosophy of Expression" (*LCE*, pp. 228–41) about his contemporary Brice Parain, whose originality, according to Camus, is that "he makes language a metaphysical question" (p. 229). Parain's strong influence on Camus's subsequent line of thought is clear:

Parain's basic premise is that if language is meaningless then everything is meaningless, and the world becomes absurd. [P. 230]

But his books show, *at the same time,* that words have just enough meaning to refuse us this final certainty that the ultimate answer is nothingness. Our language is neither true nor false. It is simultaneously useful and dangerous, necessary and pointless. "My words do perhaps distort my ideas, but if I do not reason then my ideas vanish into thin air." . . . However uncertain language may be, Parain does does feel, in spite of everything, that it yields the elements of a hierarchy. [P. 237]

There are further indications of a marked change of emphasis, if not a complete reversal, in Camus's epistemology between the period of *The Stranger* and *The Myth* and that of *The Rebel*. While in *The Myth* he does recognize reason as a form of revolt against total meaninglessness, he extols it primarily as a lucid perception of absurd incoherence. In *The Rebel*, the epistemological rage for order becomes one of the most important forms of metaphysical revolt: "To fight against death amounts to claiming that life has a meaning, to fighting for order and for unity. . . . The rebel obstinately confronts a world condemned to death and the impenetrable obscurity of the human condition with his demand for life and absolute clarity" (p. 101). And in one of Camus's most clear-cut reversals, literature, rather than merely glorifying absurd life in its diversity as it does in *The Myth,* becomes a vital source of unity:

Man has an idea of a better world than this. But better does not mean different, it means unified. This passion which lifts the mind above the commonplaces of a dispersed world, from which it nevertheless cannot free itself, is the passion for unity. It does not result in mediocre efforts to escape, however, but in the most obstinate demands. Religion or crime, every human endeavor in fact, finally obeys this unreasonable desire and claims to give life a form it does not have. The same impulse, which can lead to the adoration of the heavens or the destruction of man, also leads to creative literature, which derives its serious content from this source. [P. 262]

v

One more dimension of meaning and value remains to be integrated into Camus's overall pattern—that dealing with language and literature as communication. One of the set of paradoxes providing the transition from the period of *The Stranger* and *The Myth* to that of *The Plague,* "The Enigma," and *The Rebel* is that, although part of the absurd condition is man's solitude in the natural universe and in society, this very solitude can become a source of solidarity between men recognizing their common condition. In the later works Camus accordingly comes to emphasize the communicative function of language and literature along with their life-affirming and unifying functions. In *The Myth* language and literature are already forms of rebellion against total meaninglessness, and in *The Rebel* Camus defines all rebellion as communal. In *The Stranger* part of Meursault's "negative truth" is his minimal linguistic communication and compassion with the other characters—although he thinks of the latter primarily in terms of the fellowship of men condemned to death. In the subsequent works Camus moves toward a more life-oriented concept of compassion between men, which he expresses in the image of "dialogue," as opposed on one hand to the silence associated with accepting the absurd and on the other hand to the verbose monologues of those who use language to set themselves above others. To the metaphysical and social ills he has been concerned with previously are added those resulting from faulty communication.

In the 1946 essay *Neither Victims nor Executioners* he expresses his postwar hopes for a pacifist, democratic socialist "civilization of dialogue":

> Yes, what it is necessary to combat today is fear and silence, and with them the separation of minds and souls that they entail. What it is necessary to defend is the dialogue and universal communication between men. Servitude, injustice, falsehood are the scourges that shatter that communication and forbid that dialogue.[11]

In *The Plague* Tarrou says of the contemporary political euphemizing of murder, "I'd come to realize that all our troubles spring from our failure to use plain, clean-cut language. So I resolved always to speak— and to act—quite clearly" (p. 230). And similarly in *The Rebel*:

> The mutual understanding and communication discovered by rebellion can survive only in the free exchange of conversation. Every ambiguity, every misunderstanding, leads to death; clear language and simple words are the only salvation from this death. [Camus's footnote: 'It is worth noting that the language peculiar to totalitarian doctrines is always a scholastic or administrative language.'] The

11. My translation from *Essais*, p. 350. Macdonald's translation here (p. 18) is very loose.

climax of every tragedy lies in the deafness of its heroes. Plato is right and not Moses and Nietzsche. Dialogue on the level of mankind is less costly than the gospel preached by totalitarian regimes in the form of a monologue dictated from the top of a lonely mountain. On the stage as in reality, the monologue precedes death. [Pp. 283–84]

The reference to misunderstanding recalls Camus's 1943 play *The Misunderstanding* and his 1957 preface to it in which he changes his interpretation of its tragedy from being that of absurd fatalism to that of faulty communication: "It amounts to saying that everything would have been different if the son had said: 'It is I; here is my name.' It amounts to saying that in an unjust or indifferent world man can save himself, and save others, by practicing the most basic sincerity and pronouncing the most appropriate word" (*CTOP*, p. vii). Here he is again noticeably influenced by Brice Parain, whom he paraphrases in the 1944 essay: "Naming an object inaccurately means adding to the unhappiness of this world. And, in fact, the vast wretchedness of man, which has long pursued Parain and which has inspired so many moving accents in his work, is falsehood" (*LCE*, p. 238).

Camus resembles George Orwell in his postwar exposures of the deceitful use of language by governments—fascist, communist, and capitalist—to justify tyranny through bureaucratic jargon, euphemism, and pure double-talk. In *State of Siege* The Secretary explains the purpose of an edict of legalistic rigmarole issued by the government of The Plague: "It's intended to get them used to the touch of obscurity which gives all government regulations their peculiar charm and efficacy. The less these people understand, the better they'll behave" (*CTOP*, p. 165).

In *The Fall* Clamence says of twentieth-century political discourse, "For the dialogue we have substituted the communiqué" (p. 45). Of course Clamence too has substituted the communiqué, or the monologue, for any real dialogue with his *cher compatriote*. Clamence is the dandy of *The Rebel*, who repudiates the despair of absurdist silence and solitude in the act of speaking but, instead of using speech to establish a dialogue with others, exploits them as an audience for a narcissistic monologue parading despair for dramatic effect. *The Fall* is Camus's warning of the threat to communion between men in this theatrical equivocation whereby speech, rather than embodying revolt against the absurd and human self-righteousness, lapses into being the accessory of both.

At this stage the communicative value of literature becomes obvious: "If he speaks, if he reasons, *above all if he writes,* immediately the brother reaches out his hand." "Even if the novel describes only nostalgia, despair, frustration, it still creates form and salvation"—salvation through compassion between men in their common nostalgia, despair, and frustration. Camus's entire development of the theme of meaning and value can be seen as culminating in his final ideal of the vocation of the writer, whose challenge is double: first, to strike a balance between negating false hopes of total metaphysical or epistemological meaning and affirming the validity and value in life's limited level of meaning; and second, to be "the artist [who] fashions himself in that ceaseless oscillation from himself to others," again striking a balance between that degree of solitude inherent in the absurd condition as well as in the artistic temperament, and that degree of solidarity attainable through literary creation.

4

A Psychoanalytic View

I

In recent years psychoanalytic interpretations of individual works by Camus have proliferated.[1] It still remains, however, to consolidate the many useful insights in these studies into a psychoanalytic perspective on the totality of his works and their relation to his personal life.

If Camus read much Freud or other psychoanalytic theory, he studiously avoids mentioning it or acknowledging its influence on his thought —which is especially curious considering that at the time of his association with them Sartre and Beauvoir were both writing extensively about Freud. I have been able to find only one significant allusion, among his 1942 notebook entries about the narcissistic theatricality of the dandy: "In the psychoanalyst's view, the ego is constantly putting on a show for itself, but the libretto is false" (*N2*, p. 8). Nevertheless, whether intentionally or unintentionally, all his work clearly reflects the modes of thought psychoanalysis deals with and reveals at least an intuitive literary use of these modes, particularly in relation to his mother's influence. In his earliest published words, the first entry in his 1935 notebooks at twenty-

1. I have found the following to be most useful: Jose Barchilon. M.D., "A Study of Camus' Mythopoeic Tale *The Fall* with Some Comments about the Origin of Esthetic Feelings," *Journal of the American Psychoanalytic Association*, Apr. 1971, pp. 193–240; Richard Geha, Jr., "Albert Camus: Another Wish for Death," *Psychoanalytic Review*, Winter 1967, pp. 106–22 (on the plays); Donald M. Kaplan, "Homosexuality and American Theatre," *Tulane Drama Review*, Spring 1965, pp. 25–55 (not primarily about Camus but draws from the discussion of dandyism in *The Rebel* to support an illuminating psychoanalytic study of theatricality); Nathan Leites, *"The Stranger,"* in *Art and Psychoanalysis*, ed. William Phillips (New York: Meridian Books, 1963), pp. 247–67 (originally published in *American Imago*, 1947); Michael A. Sperber, "Camus' *The Fall:* The Icarus Complex," *American Imago* 26 (1969) : 269–80; Julian Stamm, "Camus' *Stranger:* His Act of Violence," *American Imago* 26 (1969) : 281–90; C. Roland Wagner, "The Silence of *The Stranger,"* *Modern Fiction Studies* 16 (1970): 27–40.

two, he recognizes that "the strange feeling which the son has for his mother constitutes his whole sensibility. The latent material memory which he has of his childhood (a glue that has stuck to the soul) explains why this way of feeling shows itself in the most widely differing fields" (*N1*, p. 3).

Camus's father was killed in World War I when Albert was less than a year old. He and his brother Lucien, five years older, were brought up by their mother and her mother, whom he describes in "Irony" and "Between Yes and No" as a cruel woman who raised them with a riding whip. There is much in his writing to indicate that the absence of the father, as is frequently the case in such circumstances, intensified and prolonged the normal stage of pregenital, infantile narcissism—the mentality of the baby at his mother's breast and, according to some analytic theorists, still vividly remembering her womb before birth. At this stage the child's identity has not yet been fixed. He has not learned to perceive a difference between his own subjective being and the objective world outside. His entire universe consists only of him and his mother, an Eden of satiety, freedom, wholeness, and timelessness. The infant's fall from Eden begins with the first rejections from the mother's breast, with weaning and teething, and accelerates when he runs up against the concrete realities of the external world, when he is obliged to forge his distinct ego against the unaccommodating forces of time, physical limitations, and other people—preeminently his father and siblings as rivals for his mother's love. The boy without a father gets an extended lease on infantile narcissism, a reprieve before growing up, a sense of suspended time. At the genital, or Oedipal, stage of development, around the fifth year, when he comes to imagine his penis as the means by which he can reenter his mother's womb and become his own father, with no jealous or punitive father to oppose this fantasy he is inclined toward feelings of omnipotent self-confidence, like Jean-Baptiste Clamence before his fall.

Camus never expressed his childhood situation in such explicit psychoanalytic terms, but Sartre, whose father also died in the son's infancy, did in his 1964 autobiography *The Words,* and what he says is pertinent to Camus as well:

Actually, my father's early retirement had left me with a most incomplete "Oedipus complex." No Superego, granted. But no aggressiveness either. My mother was mine; no one challenged my peaceful possession of her. I knew nothing of violence and hatred; I was spared the hard apprenticeship of jealousy. Not having been bruised by its sharp angles, I knew reality only by its bright unsubstantiality. . . . I have the lordly freedom of the actor who holds his audience spellbound and keeps refining his role. . . .

   If one is defined only by opposition, I was the undefined in person. If love and hate are the obverse and reverse ['l'envers et l'endroit'] of the same coin, I loved nothing and nobody. . . . Am I therefore a Narcissus? Not even that. Too eager to charm, I forget myself.[2]

Unfortunately, the advantages of fatherlessness are counterbalanced by certain drawbacks that Sartre does not acknowledge here. The boy without a father is apt to become retarded in his ego development and prone as an adult toward schizoid detachment from his life, which seems provisional, inauthentic, theatrical—like Camus's Clamence and the dandy who play-acts at life in default of being able to live it or Sartre's Baudelaire, Genêt, and Kean. The son's prolonged narcissism and faulty sense of objective reality make him, like Caligula, deficient in feelings for other people (Sartre's "Other") as autonomous entities. If the absence of a paternal rival facilitates the Oedipal fantasy of becoming one's own father, creating a prototype of metaphysical and social freedom to forge one's own essence, it also foreshadows existential anxiety in the emotional and sexual responsibilities weighing on the boy's small person, with no male model to emulate. The son is likely to come to blame his mother for his father's death as well as for stifling his own male identity, adult sexual and emotional development, intellectual growth, and capacity to relate to other individuals and fulfill social obligations. Furthermore, the male child normally resents his mother on the one hand for rejecting him from her womb and breast, forcing him to grow up, and on the other hand has fantasy fears of being orally devoured by her, of smothering, strangling, or drowning in her womb, and at the Oedipal stage, of punitive castration by teeth in her vagina as he tries to reenter it. These fears will be intensified when the mother is the only Oedipal figure and has wholly taken over the threatening superego role. Thus he may long for a father, not only to provide a masculine model and relieve some of the burden of

2. *The Words* (New York: Fawcett World Library, 1966), pp. 16–17, 24–25.

male responsibility but to take a portion of the Oedipal hazard away from the mother and be an ally in fears of her.

Even for the boy without a father, then, pre-Oedipal narcissism cannot healthily be prolonged indefinitely, and Oedipal threats other than the father inevitably present themselves. Much of the dualism and ambivalence in Camus's writing can be interpreted as reflecting the equal dangers in advancing to adult, genital sexuality and in regressing to infantile narcissism.

II

Although it has not been widely recognized as such, "Between Yes and No," written in 1935-36 when he was twenty-two, is one of his most beautiful and significant pieces, both in conventional literary and psychoanalytic terms. On the manifest level, here is the origin of virtually all his key phrases: estrangement, silence, indifference, solitude and solidarity, hope and despair, lucidity, *la démesure,* the death penalty. On a subliminal level, these phrases, along with the rest of the essay's themes and images, convey a consistent, unmistakable psychoanalytic symbolism, and the structure is that of analytic free association. Yet in none of his other works does he use or theorize on this technique, in none does he reveal intense personal emotions so transparently and pointedly. That is why this extraordinarily charged nine-page piece remains an intriguing anomaly.

The essay is a Proustian exercise in nostalgic recapture of the past, specifically in memories of his mother.[3] At the beginning the adult Camus is seated meditating in an Arab café overlooking the Bay of Algiers on a starlit summer night: "An emigrant returns to his country. And I remember. The irony and tension fade away, and I am home once more"

---

3. Isn't literary nostalgia for past happiness and unity always ultimately nostalgia for the mother's breast or womb? In *The Great Gatsby,* for instance, F. Scott Fitzgerald describes Gatsby's feelings upon his youthful fulfillment in capturing Daisy: "Gatsby saw that the blocks of the sidewalks really formed a ladder and mounted to a secret place above the trees—he could climb to it, if he climbed alone, and once there he could suck on the pap of life, gulp down the incomparable milk of wonder" (New York: Charles Scribner's Sons, 1953), p. 112. On the last page Gatsby's wonder before Daisy is compared to that of the early Dutch settlers first sighting America, "a fresh, green breast of the new world." In this context the novel's familiar concluding sentence takes on a superb double significance: "So we beat on, boats against the current, born[e] back ceaselessly into the past," p. 182.

(*LCE,* p. 30). [Kennedy's translation misses several important psychological connotations in the original: 'Un émigrant revient dans sa patrie. Et moi, je me souviens. Ironie, raidissement, tout se tait et me voici rapatrié' (*Essais,* p. 23); literally, 'An emigrant returns to his fatherland. And I remember. Irony, stiffness, all becomes quiet, and here I am repatriated.']

His actual memories are preceded by a reflection on the cathartic power of memory to soften the pain of unhappy past events:

> When everything is over, the thirst for life is gone. Is this what's called happiness? As we skirt along these memories, we clothe everything in the same quiet garb and death looks like a backdrop whose colors have faded. We turn back into ourselves. We feel our distress and like ourselves the better for it. Yes, perhaps that's what happiness is, the self-pitying ['pitiful'] awareness of our unhappiness. [p. 31]

This last paraphrases a quote from Joseph Conrad that Camus cited directly in an early draft (*Essais,* p. 1187), and the essay's theme and technique are quite similar to Conrad's stories such as *Youth, Nostromo,* and *Lord Jim* in the narrator's continual jumps between present and past that impose a perspective of detached, Lucretian equanimity on events in which the narrator or other characters are emotionally involved at the moment they occur. Memory here is analogous to Camus's concept of art—paraphrasing Proust's—in *The Rebel,* where he says that even if the novel describes only nostalgia, despair, frustration, it still creates form and salvation. Memory, then, is at once an aesthetic process—as Robert Champigny sees it working in *The Stranger*—and an anesthetic one, serving the same function as art in sublimating dangerous infantile wishes, as we shall see again later.

The first three paragraphs also introduce a dualism between Camus's distinct identity in his active, adult life and a loss or transcendence of ego in his merging with the natural world outside the café at the moment of the narrative ("The world sighs toward me in a long rhythm, and brings me the peace and indifference of immortal things" [p. 31]) and earlier with his mother through love ("And if I loved then in giving myself, I finally became myself, since only love restores us" [p. 30]); he expresses the same notion of finding through losing himself, but in relation to nature, in nearly all the other essays in *L'Envers et l'endroit* and *Nuptials.* His ego is further dissipated through the aesthetic distancing of memory—he shifts from referring to himself as "I" in the present to "he" in the past, which may also signify that he had no strong sense of self-identity at the time of his childhood and now sees the child he was as a stranger.

His happy/unhappy past returns via four Proustian involuntary memories evoked by the summer night, with its beauty on the one hand and on the other its silence and indifference that leave man feeling solitary and estranged. He automatically associates these antithetical qualities with his childhood, whose poverty was balanced by its natural beauty, and with his mother—half deaf, illiterate, inarticulate almost to the point of feeble-mindedness—whom her child associated, even more than the rest of mankind does, with Mother Nature: "The indifference of this strange mother! Only the immense solitude of the world can be the measure of it" (p. 34). In the first flashback, as a young boy he returns home from school to find his mother sitting alone in the dark, as was her habit after coming home from work as a scrubwoman, staring blankly at the floor:

> He is scarcely aware of his own existence, but this animal silence makes him want to cry with pain. He feels sorry for his mother; is this the same as loving her? She has never hugged or kissed him, for she wouldn't know how. He stands a long time watching her. Feeling separate ['étranger'] from her, he becomes conscious of her suffering. She does not hear him, for she is deaf. In a few moments, the old woman [the grandmother] will come back, life will start up again [literally, 'life will be reborn']: the round light cast by the kerosene lamp, the oilcloth on the table, the shouting, the swearing. Meanwhile, the silence marks a pause ['un temps d'arrêt'], an immensely long moment ['un instant démesuré']. Vaguely aware of this, the child thinks the surge of feeling in him is love for his mother. And it must be, because after all she is his mother. [Pp. 33–34]

This moment of arrested time, suggesting a perpetuated infancy or prenatal state, is soon shattered:

> His mother has given a sudden start. Something has frightened her. He looks stupid standing there gazing at her. He ought to go and do his homework. [*Le devoir* can mean either 'homework' or 'duty.' Thus 'faire ses devoirs' here also connotes 'do his duty,' a

universal euphemism during toilet training, a momentous step in growing out of infancy.] The child has done his homework. Today he is in a sordid café. Now he is a man. Isn't that what counts? Surely not, since doing homework and accepting manhood leads to nothing but old age. [P. 34]

The wish for suspended infancy and merging of identity with his mother in this first past interlude is expanded in the second, at which time "he was already quite grown up." His mother has been sitting outside on her balcony (in the same manner as Meursault on the Sunday after his mother's death in *The Stranger*), and a strange man has leaped up, beaten her unconscious, and run away. When Albert is called home, the doctor advises him to spend the night with her, and he lies down beside her on top of the blankets, where the odor of his perspiration in the overheated room blends with that of the vinegar used to cool her brow.

> It was only later that he realized how much they had been alone that night. Alone against the others. The "others" were asleep, while they both breathed the same fever. . . . The world had melted away, taking with it the illusion that life begins again each morning. Nothing was left, his studies, ambitions, things he might choose in a restaurant, favorite colors. Nothing but the sickness and death he felt surrounded by. . . . And yet, at the very moment that the world was crumbling, he was alive. Finally he fell asleep, but not without taking with him the tender and despairing image of two people's loneliness together ['l'image désespérante et tendre d'une solitude à deux'—cf. 'la tendre indifférence du monde' at the end of *The Stranger*]. Later, much later, he would remember this mingled scent of sweat and vinegar, this moment when he had felt the ties attaching him to his mother. As if she were the immense pity of his heart, spread out around him, made corporeal and playing diligently, without need of imposture, the role of a poor old woman with a moving destiny. [I have retranslated the last sentence, which is garbled in Kennedy's version.] [Pp. 35–36]

This passage is an extraordinary collection of the classic images of fantasies of the womb: the dark, overheated bedroom, the simultaneous breathing of mother and fetus (cf. his rapport with nature outside the café: "The world sighs toward me in a long rhythm"), amniotic odors, the umbilical attachment, the surrounding body.

The affirmative tone of the essay thus far turns to negation in the next paragraph, on pages 36–37, which is surely the most amazing passage in all of Camus's writing. To begin with, packed into one paragraph are five distinct, elliptically yoked movements of thought whose interconnections on the first reading are virtually inexplicable. It begins with a return to the present in the café, whose natural surroundings continue to evoke the mood of maternal harmony from the previous episode. Then Camus stops short in the dissolving of his identity: "How far will it go, this night in which I cease to belong to myself?" As if in answer, but inscrutably, he shifts to a discussion of suicide: "And tonight I can understand a man wanting to die because nothing matters anymore when one sees through life completely"—specifically, "if a reason must really be found, he killed himself because a friend spoke to him carelessly. In the same way, every time it seems to me that I've grasped the deep meaning of the world, it is its simplicity that always overwhelms me. My mother, that evening, and its ['her'] strange indifference." From here he shifts abruptly to a later episode in his past when he was living alone with a family of cats.

> The mother cat could not feed them. One by one, all the kittens died. They filled the room with their filth. Every evening, when I arrived home, I would find one lying stiff, its gums laid bare. One evening, I found the last one, half eaten by the mother. It stank already. The stench of death mingled with the stench of urine. Then, with my hands in the filth and the stench of rotting flesh reeking in my nostrils, I sat down in the midst of all this misery and gazed for hour after hour at the demented glow in the cat's green eyes as it crouched motionless in the corner.[4]

This unpleasant memory is next offset by a pleasant one, "not long ago," when he has gone home for a brief visit with his mother. "They sat ['sit'] down facing each other, in silence. But their eyes met ['meet']."

4. Camus apparently fictionalized the story about the cats, which in his notebooks is related by someone else. (*N1*, p. 23). This leads one to wonder whether other elements in the essay might be fictitious, such as the attack on his mother, in which the assaulter's identity and motivation are extremely vague.

And the paragraph ends with a transition into a loving dialogue between them, during which, "though her lips do not move her face lights up in a beautiful smile."

The most extraordinary thing about this paragraph is that while its manifest thematic sequence is quite incoherent, in psychoanalytic terms it is perfectly coherent—and perfectly terrifying. Ostensibly, the cat and mother are contrasted, the two sides of the coin, but the structure of the whole paragraph strongly hints otherwise. The sequence of the first three movements—the pulling back from the infantile loss of identity, the shift to the man who kills himself, and the reference to the mother's "strange indifference" on the night they slept together—leaves little doubt that Camus associates the friend who has spoken carelessly to the suicidal man with the mother in her estranging indifference toward himself, an indifference that was once tender and comforting because it encompassed him but that now excludes and disheartens him to the point of suicidal despair. The next shift leaves even less doubt that he associates this indifferent mother with the cat who not only kills her kitten by rejecting it from her nipples but half eats him—an unmistakable image of the infant's fantasy fear of castration by vaginal teeth, combined with that of being orally devoured by the mother. The mixed stench of the cats' death and urine recalls the earlier association of sweat and vinegar with his mother, and the cat crouches motionless in the corner hour after hour with a demented glow in her eyes much as his mother was accustomed to sit with glazed eyes. Furthermore, the eye-to-eye confrontation between him and the cat directly anticipates the end of the paragraph where he and his mother sit with their eyes meeting, ostensibly with love. Camus was too conscious a symbolist to have been completely unaware of what the imagery of this paragraph so undeniably says; yet nowhere in his writings does he give any overt indication that he felt anything but love for his mother, and certainly not this hostility and fear. And he emphasizes that the sequence with the cats is not merely an incidental, grisly anecdote but is momentously significant, when he says of it, "The whole of life can be summed up in an image."

In the last, most recent flashback, pages 38–39, Albert asks her, " 'Is it true I look like my father?'

" 'The spitting image. Of course, you didn't know him. You were six months old when he died. But if you had a little moustache!' "

The father's "head was split open in the battle of the Marne. Blinded, it took him a week to die."

"When you think about it," she says, "it was better that way. He would have come back blind or crazy. So, the poor man . . ."
"That's right."
What is it then that keeps him in this room, except the certainty that it's still the best thing to do [literally, 'that it was still better that way,' referring to the fourth previous sentence, i.e., it's better that the father is dead], that the whole *absurd* simplicity of the world has sought refuge here.
"Will you be back again?" she says. "I know you have work to do. [Cf. her earlier order for him to go do his homework.] Just from time to time . . ."

The concluding paragraph returns to the present:

But where am I now? And how can I separate this deserted café from that room in my past? I don't know any longer whether I'm living or remembering. The beams from the lighthouse are here. [Throughout the essay, the phallic lighthouse has stood in contrast to the dark, maternal bay, its lights calling him back from the past to the present.] And the Arab stands in front of me telling me that he is going to close. I have to leave ['sortir'—more precisely, 'get out'.] I no longer want to make such dangerous descents. It is true, as I take a last look at the bay and its light, that what wells up in me is not the hope of better days but a serene and primitive indifference to everything and to myself. But I must break this too limp and easy curve. I need my lucidity. Don't let them tell us any stories. Don't let them say about the man condemned to death: "He is going to pay his debt to society," but: "They're going to chop his head off" [literally, 'They're going to slit his throat']. It may seem like nothing. But it does make a difference. There are some people who prefer to look their destiny straight in the eye.

A fairly cogent interpretation can be derived from this ending on the manifest level. He must resist the temptation to romanticize his father's death for leaving him sole possession of his mother, the temptation to re-main fixated in the past, in the indifference and intellectual lethargy he associates with her. He must, instead, go on being a man, "doing his homework," exercising his lucidity as a writer to expose the euphemizing of death, whether of cats, of men in war, or the victims of capital punishment. The passage recalls the end of *Le Cimetière marin,* when Valéry tears himself away from the hypnotizing immobility of the sea, with the resolution to meet the challenge of life—"Il faut tenter de vivre!"

On a deeper psychic level, a somewhat different interpretation suggests itself. To begin with, the question arises of precisely why Camus elliptically associates his father, blinded and eventually dying in the war, with the guillotined man. This connection is especially striking because we know retroactively that he will make it explicitly in both *The Stranger* and "Reflections on the Guillotine," in the story his mother had told him about his father coming home and vomiting after having witnessed the guillotining of a man who "had slaughtered a family of farmers, including the children" (*RRD,* p. 131). Once again, it is only in psychoanalytic terms that the association and Camus's overdetermined preoccupation with it becomes quite clear: decapitation (and the similar splitting open of the father's skull) and blinding are both classic symbols for castration. Given the earlier symbolism of the cat as a castrating mother, we can surmise that Albert became conscious of his father's death and was told the story of the execution by his mother during the Oedipal phase of his childhood when he was feeling incestuous desire for her and the consequent guilt and fears of punishment by castration. Both these stories are appalling even on the manifest level, but it is likely that they became all the more so for the child because at that stage he unconsciously imagined that it was his mother who had castrated and killed his father. He must have interpreted his father's revulsion at the execution as a reaction to seeing himself castrated, as he later in effect was in the war. Albert not only identified himself with his father as a spectator of the father's own castration but saw in it and his later real death the punishment for being the mother's lover, a warning against Albert's incestuous impulses. The image of the mother as blinder-castrator has been suggested earlier by the emphasis on the cat's and his mother's powerful eyes. The essay's last sentence forges the final link in this association: speaking specifically about decapitation, Camus resolves to look his destiny straight in the eye—clearly a reiteration of his earlier eye-to-eye confrontations with the cat and his mother.

Camus must have further associated castration with his mother's lack
of intellect. It would have been natural for him to interpret blindness, a
split skull, decapitation as symbols of antiintellectuality, along with her
deafness and near dumbness (in "The Renegade" cutting off the tongue
is explicitly associated with punitive castration). She allowed the grandmother to whip Albert and his brother, with only a feeble protest: "Don't
hit them on the head" (*LCE*, p. 33). His intellectual development ("doing
his homework") and adult premium on "lucidity" and "clairvoyance"
must have represented in large part a rejection of identity with his mother.
In fact he may have been impelled to become the only intellectual in his
family and a writer precisely because he sublimated into intellectualism
and articulateness his repressed incestuous desires and fears.

If this interpretation is accurate, then his resolve at the end to continue
an active, intellectual life in the present indicates lucid opposition not only
to current social evils (which he elsewhere comes to associate with paternal authority, as we shall see) but to the castrating threat of his mother.
If regressing to infancy entails the same fate his father met, no wonder he
has to get out before the café/womb is closed behind him by *le patron*
(who earlier has been described in a crouching, fetal position); no wonder
he no longer wants to make "such dangerous descents." He must accept
not only mature intellectuality but mature, phallic sexuality: "I must break
this too limp and easy curve," in opposition to the opening paragraph
where he has said of his regression into memory, "Irony, stiffness, all
becomes quiet."

III

Several of the symbolic implications in "Between Yes and No" cast new
light on his other works. For instance, in the story of the cat whose nipples
are insufficient to feed all her kittens there is a hint of sibling rivalry for
maternal affection. The only thing he says about his brother, who was their
father's namesake and enough older than Albert to be a substitute paternal
rival, is that their mother "loves them with a hidden and impartial
['equal'] love" (p. 33). Camus rarely mentions him elsewhere; he told an
interviewer that Lucien had stayed in Algiers and became a government
insurance agent, definitely not an intellectual[5]—in other words, his

5. Carl A. Viggiani, "Notes pour le futur biographe d'Albert Camus," *Revue des lettres
modernes*, nos. 170–74 (1968), p. 203.

mother's son. Brothers are conspicuously absent in his writing; there are no pairs of them among his characters, which is especially curious considering his frequent use of "fraternity" to speak of humanitarian solidarity, and the pervasive influence on him of *The Brothers Karamazov*. The brother of Raymond's girl friend in *The Stranger* becomes a symbolic Oedipal rival to Meursault. In *The Misunderstanding*, Jan's sister Martha may be a disguised brother-father figure; she is utterly unfeminine and dominates the mother much as Camus's grandmother paternally dominated his mother. She feels no regret over killing her brother, and Camus empathizes with her as a jealous sibling. When the mother, rather than leaving with Martha, drowns herself in the same river where they drowned Jan, she laments, "By now my mother's lying with her son, pressed to the sluice-gate. . . . First my mother cast me off, and now she is dead. I have lost her twice" (*CTOP*, pp. 129–30). Barchilon perceives further hints of sibling rivalry in *The Fall*, such as Clamence's admission that he drank the water of a dying comrade in a Nazi prison camp, his story of the mother forced by the Nazis to choose which of her two sons they should shoot, and his theory about Christ's sense of guilt over the Massacre of the Innocents.

The suggestion that Camus's mother is the "friend" whose indifference could drive a man to suicide gives a new meaning to the theme of suicide throughout Camus, particularly in three other works where the motivation is the same—a notebook sketch for *A Happy Death* contemporaneous with "Between Yes and No" (*N1*, pp. 21–22), *The Myth* (p. 4), and *The Fall* (p. 31) and a variant on p. 74: "I thought of killing myself to play a trick on them [his friends], to punish them," after which he tells the story of a girl who killed herself to "show" her father. Leites sees the same parent-spiting theme, "You'll be sorry when I'm dead," in *The Stranger*, as Geha does in *The Misunderstanding*, which he reads as a fantasy about a son who had originally been driven away from home by his mother's indifference; in failing to recognize him on his return and then inadvertently murdering him, she is symbolically repeating her rejection, but the son is vindicated when his identity is revealed and she kills herself in remorse.

That a part of Camus felt not just mild alienation over his mother's indifference but active hostility toward her and women in general is confirmed symbolically in several other early works, most notably *Caligula*, written in 1938. Caligula's murderous frustration stems from his metaphorically wanting the moon, which, as Geha notes, is an archetypal mother symbol. He even fantasies having sexually possessed her, "only two or three times, to be sure." "She was like a milky pool. . . . She crossed the threshold of my room, glided to my bed, poured herself into it, and flooded me with her smiles and sheen" (*CTOP*, p. 46). His inability to truly, permanently possess the moon is compounded by the death of his sister, Drusilla, whose incestuous lover he was. (Brother-sister incest is frequently a disguise for that between mother and son; Sartre admits to using this code in *The Flies* and *The Condemned of Altona*.) But Caligula avows that possessing a woman is worse than losing her. "When I am with the women I make mine and darkness falls on us and I think, now my body's had its fill, that I can feel myself my own at last, poised between death and life—ah, then my solitude is fouled by the stale smell of pleasure from the woman sprawling at my side" (pp. 37-38). And, "Beyond the frontier of pain lies a splendid, sterile happiness. . . . Love isn't enough for me. . . . To love someone means that one's willing to grow old beside that person. That sort of love is right outside my range. Drusilla old would have been far worse than Drusilla dead" (p. 71). He makes this speech as he is strangling his mistress, Caesonia, whose image he had earlier effaced from his mirror, as though he is trying to eliminate even the disappointing surrogate mother from his world of infantile narcissism. But the narcissistic child cannot kill his mother without killing himself; immediately after Caesonia dies, he shatters his mirror and welcomes the assassins' blinding/castrating knives stabbing at his face.

IV

In each of the works discussed so far, violence and death are associated with the mother. But whether she symbolically kills the son, is killed by him or brutalized by a surrogate third party like the mysterious assaulter in "Between Yes and No" whose attack enables Albert to sleep with her, there is usually a suggestion that the death of mother and/or son would allow him permanently to repossess her. This redemptive link between death and mother love is common in subliminal fantasies, with various explanations including death as a Lucretian reunion with Mother Nature, the similar stopping of time and aging in infancy and in death, the removal of the loved one from the grasp of rivals, or the wish that punishing one's mother or oneself will purge incestuous guilt and allow reconciliation. In Camus's personal symbolism, moreover, the silence of the tomb becomes identified with the silence of his mother.

The mother is again associated with death, but with significant differences, in *The Stranger*. Approaching the novel with "Between Yes and No" in mind, we can see the element of Camus's hostility toward his mother and toward women in general coming out in places where we might not perceive it otherwise. In this light, for instance, Meursault's collaboration with Raymond's vendetta against his Arab girl friend no longer appears completely gratuitous or passive. Camus has disguised his own misogyny by projecting it away from his hero onto a disagreeable surrogate. There is poetic justice, then, in the girl's brother threatening Meursault along with Raymond and in Meursault ending up killing the brother and being executed in place of Raymond. Leites sees Salamano and his dog resembling a sadomasochistic parent-child relationship; some similarities can indeed be seen with the relation between Camus and his mother in "Between Yes and No," and Leites's point was strikingly confirmed with the appearance in 1971 of *A Happy Death,* Camus's previously unpublished precursor to *The Stranger,* in which the character of Salamano is foreshadowed by a lonely man who had sadistically tormented his mother but who cries over her photo long after her death (the personal implications are intensified by Camus's naming the man Cardona, his own grandmother's maiden name, and making him a barrel maker like his uncle but deaf and half dumb like his mother). At one point in his interview with the examining magistrate, Meursault concedes about his attitude toward his mother, "I could truthfully say I'd been quite fond of Mother ['mama']—but really that didn't mean much ['that didn't mean anything']. All normal people . . . had more or less desired the death of those they loved" (p. 80). (The next sentence in a literal translation begins, "Here the attorney cut me off . . .") The prosecuting attorney at the trial accuses Meursault of being "morally guilty of his mother's death" (p. 128), and on one subliminal level *The Stranger* can in fact be read as the story of a man who desires his mother's death and defiantly accepts the punishment of his own death for refusing to feel remorse over it.

The element of hostility toward the mother, however, is counterbalanced and, I think, outweighed by a different symbolic tendency in the novel. Most of the threatening forces are paternalistic: the director at the home, Thomas Pérez (whose name is a play on *père,* "father"), Meursault's boss (*le patron*), the knife-wielding brother, the French fatherland (*la patrie*) in whose name Meursault is tried and executed, the judges and attorneys, and finally the priest-chaplain, who asks why Meursault doesn't call him "Father" and against whom Meursault's final purgative explosion is set off when he calls Meursault "my son" (p. 150). In clear contrast, the sympathetic forces are symbolically and verbally associated with the mother, *la mère: la mer* (the sea), Marie, Meursault's own name, *l'amour* (love)—and finally, *la mort* (death).

What this antithesis indicates is that Camus here has tried to resolve his divided feelings toward his mother by splitting off all her negative qualities and projecting them into father figures. Camus's own mother embodied both maternal and paternal elements, and it is as if when Meursault's mother dies it is only her unpleasant, paternal side that dies—the maternal continuing to live or being symbolically reborn, as we shall see. Camus's accomplishing this split may have been facilitated because in his childhood a cruel second woman, his whip-wielding grandmother, took over much of his father's role; Meursault's mother's burial is in fact modeled on that of Camus's grandmother described in "Irony." (It remains a puzzle why he gave Raymond Sintès his grandmother's married name and Marie Cardona her maiden name, unless he was also splitting the grandmother into *her* paternal and maternal components as he had intermingled these components in the Cardona of *A Happy Death*.) In this symbolic context, it becomes quite plausible that Meursault should feel little grief over his mother's death and that after passing the next Sunday in the same manner as he did when she was alive, he can observe, "Really, nothing in my life had changed" (p. 30). In the same context, Meursault's crime, ironically, is not failing to love his mother but loving her too much; it is his incestuous possession of her that must be punished by the surrogates for the father he has killed in her. The prosecuting attorney's bizarre accusation on page 128 that Meursault is guilty both of matricide and patricide is symbolically quite accurate.

The mother's agedness and indifference having died along with her paternal identity, she is free to be reborn the day after her burial in the young, nubile incarnation of Marie—the virgin mother. Naturally her rebirth takes place, like the birth of Venus, in Swinburne's great sweet mother and lover of men, the sea. Having swum around with their bodies linked in the warm, salty, amniotic water, Meursault and Marie climb onto a raft, where he plays with her breasts and lies with his head on her stomach, which he feels "rising and falling gently" (p. 22), recalling the simultaneous breathing of mother and son in "Between Yes and No."

In the first half of the novel Meursault encounters and overcomes several father-rivals. On the long, hot route to his mother's burial, old Pérez, his mother's "fiancé," collapses of exhaustion. Meursault's outlasting this rival on the way to the mother's tomb/womb reconfirms the elimination of the paternal side of his mother. He lets himself become involved in Raymond's punishing of his unfaithful girl friend, who in turn is avenged by her brother, indirectly an agent of the rival lover as well as a disguised jealous father. In the confrontation on the blazing, arid beach, the Arab blocks Meursault's path to the cool, fresh water of the stream, which might be associated symbolically either with male potency or with the mother, although the latter is usually identified with warm sea water. When the Arab brandishes his knife, "beneath a veil of brine and tears my eyes were blinded; I was conscious . . . of the keen blade of light flashing up from the knife, scarring my eyelashes, and gouging into my eyeballs" (p. 75). This is another extraordinary association of blinding and castration with the salty water of the womb, but here the blinder-castrator has become paternal rather than maternal. In response to this threat Meursault's phallic revolver, fired four times in rapid succession after the first shot like an assertion of potency, prevails over the castrating knife. (Stamm suggests a different interpretation of this scene: a subliminal homosexual attraction toward the Arab, who earlier was lying seductively on the beach blowing on a reed flute, draws Meursault away from the domesticity of Masson, his wife, and Marie, with whom he has just been seriously considering marriage. Meursault's ambivalent reactions toward his latent homosexual impulse, along with a sadomasochistic struggle for domination between him and the Arab, then motivate the shooting.)

In the second half of the novel Meursault is finally overcome by paternal vengeance, but still ends up triumphant. Part Two consists of a remarkable portrayal of Meursault's step-by-step symbolic regression from adult sexuality to all the traits of Camus's infantile sexuality in "Between Yes and No," traits which here become even more clearly identified with death. Deprived of women when first imprisoned, he begins to masturbate, playing with oneself being the adult equivalent of infantile narcissism. "Il ne faut jamais jouer," Meursault moralizes during this same period over the story of the son in *The Misunderstanding* who has played at sneaking back incognito to the bedroom of his childhood in his mother's house, his father having died in his absence. Meursault recognizes, as he will in his own case, that the price of such regression is one's life. Meursault has noted the events of Part One with precise chronological awareness; in prison, days and nights, weeks and months merge indistinguishably—as Carl Viggiani notes, he literally "kills time." [6] Previously disinclined to remember the past, he now focuses his mind on memories, to the point where past and present become intermingled, as in the indeterminate moment of the book's narration; predictably, the first object he chooses to exercise his memory on is the room where he and his mother lived together. In Part One he has been rather withdrawn from society (Leites diagnoses him as a schizophrenically affectless personality, although it can be argued that such clinical psychiatric terms have only limited validity applied to what Camus intended to be a symbolic, non-naturalistic novel and mythic hero, pertinent though they may be to the author's own psychological preoccupations), but his ego has been sufficiently intact in relation to nature, Marie, and himself. Now, estranged from nature and women, his sense of self-identity dies. After months in prison, he realizes he has been talking to himself, and using his food pan as a mirror, the symbol of narcissism, he sees his physical being as that of a stranger. Although he is understandably disconcerted over his imprisonment at first, he eventually becomes content in his cell, as though it were a substitute womb, like the hollow tree trunk he imagines himself living in on pages 95–96, which he associates with *maman*.

As noted above in chapter 2, after being convicted Meursault undergoes a similar acclimatization to the prospect of his execution. At first, of course, he is realistically repulsed, and it is at this stage that he identifies with his father's revulsion before the image of his own decapitation/castration. But in the end he becomes resigned to death, and the process by which he does so suggests that Camus has fantasied a shift in the consequences of castration by displacing blame for it from the mother, as in "Between Yes and No," to society as a superego substitute for an Oedipal father. By the same shift Camus/Meursault can fully identify and sympathize with his personal father as the victim not of the mother but of society; angered by the chaplain asking Meursault why he didn't call him

6. "Camus' *L'Etranger*," *PMLA* 71, no. 5 (Dec. 1956): 884.

"Father," "I told him he wasn't my father; quite the contrary, he was on the others' side" (p. 150). (The "he" on the others' side also implicitly refers to the vengeful Old Testament God, in contrast to Camus's concept of Christ as the compassionate and victimized son—hence the symbolism of the Crucifixion in the book's last paragraph.) Maintaining the image of the pre-Oedipal mother with castrating vaginal teeth would forever forbid dreams of reentry to her womb, but castration by a paternal figure permits fantasied reunification with her. Paternal castration removes the son's adult, genital sexuality and his male identity, making him a "castrated" female mirroring his mother. Once he has taken his punishment and paid the price of his penis and life, Meursault, happily reunited with his castrated real father as well, will be able to possess his mother guiltlessly, with the undifferentiated sexual identity and timelessness of infancy, in an eternal resurrection.

This symbolic context makes the book's enigmatic final paragraph beautifully clear. Meursault has long since forgotten Marie, but now, before death, his thoughts turn to his mother: "And now, it seemed to me, I understood why at her life's end she had taken on a 'fiancé'; why she had played at making a fresh start. . . . And I, too, felt ready to start life all over again. . . . For all to be accomplished ['consommé,' with its suggestion of Christ's last words, "It is consummated"], for me to feel less lonely, all that remained to hope was that on the day of my execution there should be a huge crowd of spectators and they should greet me with howls of execration ['cries of hatred']" (p. 154). Meursault is now his mother's fiancé. Death will be the consummation of their marriage, making him feel less lonely before the jealous, superegoistic crowd, whose noisy cries will contrast with the silent mother and whose hatred will distinguish its members from his father, who had sympathetically identified with the victim when *he* witnessed an execution.

In *A Happy Death* Camus had combined paternal and maternal elements in his hero by giving him the first name Patrice and the last name Mersault, which without the "u" is close to *mère*. Mersault's death is even more evidently than Meursault's a symbolic reunification with both mother and castrated father. An older man named Zagreus, who has lost his legs and full sexual capability—in World War I, according to one manuscript version—encourages Mersault to shoot him and use his money to live fully in his place. At the end, when Mersault himself is dying from pleurisy, his thoughts concerning Zagreus verbally echo the last paragraph of *The Stranger:* "At the limit of his strength and resistance, he joined Roland Zagreus for the first time. . . . He was overcome by a violent and fraternal love for this man from whom he had felt so distant, and he realized that by killing him he had consummated a union ['des noces' —'nuptials'] which bound them together forever" (*HD*, pp. 148–49). Mersault's last thoughts, in the presence of his wife, again suggest an association between the consuming maternal mouth or womb and the tomb: "He looked at Lucienne's swollen lips and, behind her, the smile of the earth. He looked at them with the same eyes, the same desire" (p. 151).

v

In "Between Yes and No" and *The Stranger,* Camus fantasied two opposing but equally fatal resolutions of incestuous desire. To remain with the mother without paternal rivalry leads to castration by her; to advance to adult sexuality and challenge paternal authority leads to vengeful castration by father figures. The dilemma of infantile sexuality is the human condition; as Meursault muses, "To stay or to leave . . . either way one was in for it. . . . No, there was no way out." Both fatal paths have their compensating allure, to be sure, but only in the realm of fantasy. In real life death is death, with no hope of redemptive resurrection for the agnostic like Camus. In *The Fall* Clamence indulges in another dream of redemptive castration, in the role of John the Baptist: "I would be decapitated, for instance, and I'd have no more fear of death; I'd be saved. Above the gathered crowd, you would hold up my still warm head, so that they could recognize themselves in it and I could again dominate— an exemplar. All would be consummated" (pp. 146–47). But elsewhere, after contemplating killing himself to spite his friends, Clamence recognizes: "If I had been able to commit suicide and then see their reaction, why, then the game would have been worth the candle. But the earth is dark, *cher ami,* the coffin thick, and the shroud opaque. The eyes of the soul—to be sure—if there is a soul and it has eyes! But you see, we're not sure, we can't be sure" (p. 74). (In this setting it is irresistible to find a *double entendre* in the common maxim "le jeu ne vaut pas la chandelle." "The game," in all its associations with infantile sexuality, isn't worth the loss of the phallic candle!)

If we are to avoid letting our dangerous unconscious impulses lead us to suicide, the schizophrenic death of the ego, or narcissistic solipsism, we must find means to curb them—as Camus tacitly recognized in rejecting nineteenth-century romantic necrophilia, mystical transcendence of the ego, and dandyish narcissism in *The Rebel*. His philosophy of "limits" becomes an imperative for lucid suppression and sublimation of fatal desires. His works indicate that he sublimated his incestuous cravings for and fear of his mother into rapport with nature and into "solidarity" or humanitarian love for mankind in general, his deadly defiance of father figures into the doctrine of nonviolent resistance, and all his dangerous impulses into the safely fictitious world of literary creation.

The sublimation of incestuous desires, or sexual desires in general, into nature worship is of course a mainstay of romantic literature. What is refreshingly unique in Camus is that he is virtually explicit about it and that he also acknowledges the deadly elements in nature, which closely parallel the dangerous aspects of the mother and other women:

> Here [in the ruins at Tipasa] I understand what is meant by glory: the right to love without limits. There is only one love in this world. To clasp a woman's body is also to hold in one's arms this strange joy that descends from sky to sea. In a moment, when I throw myself down among the absinthe plants to bring their scent into my body, I shall know, appearances to the contrary, that I am fulfilling a truth which is the sun's and which will also be my death's. [*LCE*, pp. 68–69]

He uses extended metaphors of sexual intercourse like a metaphysical poetic conceit to describe rapport with nature, as in the endings of "Summer in Algiers" and "The Adulterous Woman." There is no lack of lyrical descriptions of attractive women and sex in his works; still, his most extensive, detailed sexual lyricism is lavished on nature.

In *The Plague*, Rieux reluctantly concludes that when plagues strike, one has to forgo his personal happiness to side with the victims. Rambert faces the same problem in the more fleshy form of separation from his mistress, and although he argues with Rieux, he too ends up deferring his pleasure to fight the plague. Symbolically parallel to this theme, but manifestly unconnected, is the departure of Rieux's tubercular wife to a distant sanitarium before the plague begins and the simultaneous arrival of his mother. At the end of the book his wife, safely removed from the plague, dies; his mother, exposed to it all along, survives (a reversal of *The Stranger*, where the young lover, Marie, replaces the dead and previously institutionalized mother). It is as though by substituting his humanitarian love toward the plague victims for sexual desire toward his mother—previously transferred to his wife—Rieux has safely desexualized his love for the mother, permitting her to return to him, while the still sexual wife has become *de trop*.

Tarrou in *The Plague* is a pivotal but somewhat inscrutable figure in Camus's psychological scheme. Whereas in "Between Yes and No" and *The Stranger*, Camus distinguished between social authorities, especially judges, as castrating fathers and his literal father as their victim, Tarrou's father has become the castrator: a prosecuting attorney who demands the defendant's decapitation. "I," recalls Tarrou, "felt a far closer, far more terrifying intimacy with that wretched man than my father can ever have felt" (pp. 224–25). Furthermore, his mother acquiesces to the father's occupation, although she no longer sleeps with him and no longer loves him. Despite this hint of the mother siding with the father against the son, "when he died I had my mother come to live with me, and she'd still be with me if she were alive" (p. 226). As a psychological correlative to Tarrou's espousal of personal nonviolence (and, contemporaneously, Camus's), it can be surmised that Camus's previous identification with his own father as society's victim is no longer operable; the literal father has become the Oedipal rival and superego. Yet the son, in his repressed hostilities, identifies with this father too, and upon learning that revolutionaries also pass death sentences, he comes to see the Oedipal father both as castrator and castrated: "It befalls even the victim sometimes to turn executioner" (p. 263). As in more conventional Oedipal relationships, the son cannot fantasy killing his father without killing himself. Hence Tarrou's doctrine of nonviolence, of sympathy and understanding (*la compréhension*, which also denotes inclusion or encompassing) for executioners as well as victims. (There may also be a remnant here of Camus's identification of his father as a victim of his mother.)

At the time of the story, Tarrou's father and mother have both died. Even before, he had curbed his hostility toward the father, as well as toward all father substitutes, and was cool toward the mother. He has had no love life, in contrast to Rieux, Rambert, and Grand; his only personal bond has been attained fraternally with Rieux. There is a strong suggestion of homosexual love here, although, like the affection between Caligula and Scipio, it would probably more accurately be described as narcissistic, since all these characters are alter egos of one another and of Camus. In the transition between *The Myth* and *The Rebel* Camus empathetically extended metaphysical and social egoism to incorporate all humans as reflections of oneself, which would seem to be an exemplarily healthy means, psychologically and socially, of sublimating narcissistic and homosexual impulses. Despite their friendship and common humanitarianism, however, Tarrou dies but not Rieux, who has managed to maintain his love for his mother as well as for humanity (a feat doubtlessly facilitated by the absence of his father, who is never even mentioned). With an astute intuition of depth psychology, Camus appears to be saying that the sublimation of *all* libidinal drives into saintly, celibate love for one's fellow men is fatal too, that totally denying oneself even the fantasies of illicit desires, parental hostilities, and consequently purgative self-punishment, leaves one impotent, dried up—*taré*—as Tarrou's name and the following imagery suggest: "Tarrou . . . realized the bleak sterility of a life without illusions. There can be no peace without hope, and Tarrou, denying as he did the right to condemn anyone whomsoever . . . had lived a life riddled with contradictions and had never known hope's solace" (p. 263).

For Diego in *State of Siege* and Kaliayev in *The Just Assassins,* sacrificing their lives in rebellion against paternal social authorities, but in the name of solidarity with suffering humanity rather than of selfish Oedipal desires—emphasized by their forsaking sexual fulfillment—turns death into a guilt-free reunion with the mother. In *State of Siege* death is allegorically personified as a matronly woman who makes advances to Diego, calling him *chéri,* and who, after he has renounced his life and love for his fiancée Victoria in exchange for the defeat of the paternalistic personification of The Plague, consoles his survivors: "Do not weep. The bosom of the earth is soft for those who have loved her greatly" (*CTOP,* p. 230). For the revolutionaries Kaliayev and Dora, the only consummation of their love can be to imagine dying on the same gallows, umbilically united by "the same rope" (*CTOP,* p. 302). When Dora is told of the crash of Kaliayev's body at the moment of his hanging, she exults: "A hideous crash! That was enough to plunge him back into the carefree joy of childhood" (p. 302). *The Just Assassins* symbolically dramatizes one solution to the Oedipal dilemma of how to kill one's father while enabling at least a part of oneself to survive retribution. Kaliayev refuses to kill the grand duke's two children along with him. (A remnant of Camus's maternal hostility comes out when Kaliayev tells their mother that he would have thrown the bomb if she but not the children had been in the carriage.) Identifying himself with the children, and more broadly with the future generations his act will help liberate, he can envision his image in them living on after his personal death.

Camus's most conscious and effective selection of a channel for sublimating forbidden desires is the occupation of the literary artist. "The same impulse, which can lead to the adoration of the heavens or the destruction of man, also leads to creative literature" (*Rebel*, p. 262). The nature of the creative act, countervailing the artist's destructive tendencies, guarantees that every serious artist "absolves instead of condemning." Only art allows us with relative psychic impunity the hubris of repeating the past, particularly of regressing to infancy and recapturing its sense of wholeness and fulfillment. Although Camus does not explicitly make the connection, this notion corresponds with psychoanalytic theory that views the practice of art itself as a form of playing, a projection of infantile sexuality into an adult occupation. That he, like many artists, felt at least the occasional twinge of guilt over his occupation that accompanies all tendencies toward infantilism is indicated in *The Fall* when Clamence jocularly concocts a random but interesting conjunction of possible vices: "You are an evil-doer ['un pervers'], a satyr, a congenital liar ['un mythomane'], a homosexual ['un pédéraste'], an artist, etc." (p. 131). The fictional world walks the line between reality and irreality, allowing the writer to bring into the open his illicit desires and painful memories, safely insulated by aesthetic distance (the same way he describes the faculty of memory itself working in "Between Yes and No"). Artistically portraying or seeing portrayed our libidinal cravings, murderous hostilities, and self-punitive urges provides a healthier outlet than either acting them out in real life or submerging them into the unconscious in neurosis-producing repression. In the work of art we can possess our mother, be killed by our father in expiation, then repeat the whole process as often as we wish, like the actor or Don Juan in *The Myth* living a whole lifetime or repeating the perfect love affair every day. It is the author and reader who are really reborn at the end of *The Stranger;* it is the playwright, actor, and audience who can die with Caligula, yet walk out of the theater exulting, "I'm still alive!"

Camus's works of the late 1940s through *Summer* in 1954 provide an admirable model of emotional adjustment, a healthy equilibrium between maternal and paternal forces and their religious and political counterparts. (Undoubtedly a large part of his widespread appeal lies in the fact that his distinctive psychological formation and means of adjusting to it coincided resonantly with the most prevalent spiritual and social problems of his time, in much the same way that Freud saw Dostoevsky's internal conflicts recapitulating the cultural crises of his era.) His increasing sympathy for fathers, coinciding with his period of espousing nonviolent rebellion in the late forties, might be partly attributable to his becoming one in 1945. (He had a twin son and daughter—as if his male-female identity problems weren't difficult enough already. One almost suspects he willed their birth as a symbolic literary creation.) It is curious, though, that even after he becomes a father, none of his heroes is, with the exception of Jonas in "The Artist at Work," who neglects his wife and children for his art and ends up fatally withdrawing from them into a dark, womblike loft.

The effects of fatherhood on him remain conjectural, but other propaternal influences from the late 1940s onward are more verifiable. He saw filial, French-colonized revolutionaries becoming more murderous than *la patrie*. Heretofore he had viewed mainland France as paternal, Algeria as maternal and filial, and had seen the cause of reform in Algeria as one of antipaternal justice, without sharply distinguishing between Arabs and poor European people there. But with the outburst of revolutionary Arab nationalism and racial violence in the mid-fifties, he and his mother suddenly were lumped together with the paternal oppressor. In 1957 he admits, "I believe in justice, but I will defend my mother before justice" (*Essais*, p. 1882). These events associating him parentally with European France may have created a psychological block that would explain the uncharacteristic, overdetermined rigidity of his increasing opposition to colonial revolutionary violence.

By the mid-1950s *The Fall* and *Exile and the Kingdom* portray emotional forces threatening to disrupt Camus's earlier equilibrium by tipping the scale of his identity unhealthily toward the Oedipal father, not as a figure deserving compassion but as a vindictive tyrant. Clamence is hopelessly torn apart by his ambivalent loyalties and hostilities to both mother and father. The hostility toward father figures, especially judges, is manifestly evident, but the aggression and fear toward the mother, although at its strongest here since "Between Yes and No," is almost entirely subliminal. Clamence reveals little about his family background, but Barchilon, in his brilliant study of *The Fall,* deduces from his character type that like Camus he is a fatherless child who resents the excessive influence of his mother, as is indicated by numerous traits including his Don Juanlike need to dominate women, his preference for ten-minute adventures—for one of which "I'd have disowned father and mother" (*Fall,* p. 58)—to any long-term involvement, his fear of caves, and most importantly his failure to jump into the dark river to join and save the young woman, whose black dress identifies her with Camus's own widowed mother (this may seem a farfetched association at first, but it is confirmed by all the images in Camus of the mother and son united by water—most prominently their drowning together in the river in *The Misunderstanding*—as well as by Clamence's earlier description of himself on page 17 as the legal defender of "widows and orphans" [literally translated, 'the widow and the orphan']).

Barchilon acutely analyzes Clamence/Camus's unconscious yearning to be relieved of the burden of being his own father:

> A child needs both parents, not only to modulate and balance each other's influence, but to learn to tolerate primary love and hate towards loved ones and eventually develop the full spectrum of secondary, "tamed" affects, in short, to develop out of a narcissistic matrix a mature identity. . . .
>
> The father not only dilutes the mother's influence but, as an object for identification, he can facilitate the development of dialectic thought and eventual conversation between the mother, father, and self-representations; without triangular relations no reliable sense of reality or mature object relationships can develop. Thus the father's presence becomes both the embodiment of the child's inadequacy and the *means* by which the son can develop realistic object representa-

tions thereby undoing the narcissistic wound of not being acceptable to the mother as a *genital* object. . . . The far-reaching consequences of the absence of an important father image in the life of the little Clamence is the curse that could not be undone. . . .

These two episodes [the paternal laughter on the Pont des Arts and his humiliation by the little man on the motorcycle] speak of an overwhelming unconscious need to have a father put him back in his place, allow him to be the child which he never allowed himself to be ("I already knew everything at birth"); punish, humiliate him perhaps, *but be there* to curb his unsatisfiable desires and the unopposed influence of the mother.[7]

Clamence's fall, then, represents the failure of his antipaternal, Oedipal ambitions. In a violent reaction against his incestuous impulses and fears, he opts for strong paternal identification, craving any punitive father substitute before whom he can play the contrite, submissive son. He expresses a concise fantasy of Oedipal sexuality: "Do you know what I used to dream of? A total love of the whole heart and body, day and night, in an uninterrupted embrace, sensual enjoyment and mental excitement— all lasting five years and ending in death. Alas!" But now, "for want of betrothal or interrupted love, it will be marriage, brutal marriage with power and the whip. The essential is that everything should become simple, as for the child. . . . So hurray for the master, whoever he may be, to take the place of heaven's law, 'Our father who art provisionally here . . .'" (pp. 135–36).

In Camus's last fictional work, *Exile and the Kingdom,* is found his most orthodox Oedipal fantasy (if one may put it so), "The Renegade." The runaway missionary, who has fled Europe in hatred of his parents— "one really ought to kill one's father" (*EK*, p. 36)—to domineer the Algerian natives, instead becomes the slave of the savage Taghâsans. Imprisoned in the dark, hot hall of the Fetish ['fétiche'='foetus'?], he is repeatedly forced to watch the Sorcerer beat and ravish women slaves— a symbolic primal scene in which the child spies on his parents having intercourse. One day he is left alone to take one of the women himself:

But, immediately afterward, *gra,* the Sorcerer was lying in wait for me, they all entered and tore me from the woman, beat me dreadfully

7. Barchilon, pp. 217, 221.

on the sinful place, what sin, I'm laughing, where is it and where is virtue, they clapped me against a wall, a hand of steel gripped my jaws, another opened my mouth, pulled on my tongue until it bled, was it I screaming with that bestial scream, a cool cutting caress, yes cool at last, went over my tongue. [Pp. 52–53]

Camus is all but explicitly portraying a willing punitive castration by and repentant submission to the Oedipal father, after which it is significant that the tongueless slave continues a babbling interior monologue, in contrast to earlier associations of castration with restoration to the silent mother. The renegade's bondage to brutal males, both the natives and their French conquerors, continues to the moment of his death. The handful of hard, dry salt that finally silences him reiterates the suggestions of sterility and sadomasochistic homosexuality, contrasting with previous images throughout Camus of maternal salt water as well as the metaphorical, fecund waters of the desert in "The Adulterous Woman" (see chapter 11, section 11 below).

Camus of course intended *The Fall* and "The Renegade" to be negative portraits, cautionary tales of deviation from the healthy balance depicted in his earlier works. And despite the temptations toward harsh paternal identity in these late works, in the 1958 preface to *L'Envers et l'endroit,* less than two years before his death, he avows that his work will be incomplete until he writes a book that returns to the subject and setting of "Between Yes and No":

Nothing prevents me from dreaming that I shall succeed, from imagining that I shall still place at the center of this work the admirable silence of a mother and one man's effort to rediscover a justice or a love to match this silence. In the dream that life is, here is man, who finds his truths and loses them on this mortal earth, in order to return through wars, cries, the folly of justice and love, in short through pain, toward that tranquil land ['patrie'] where death itself is a happy silence. [P. 16]

And, "If I have come a long way since this book, I have not made much progress. Often, when I thought I was moving forward, I was losing ground" (p. 14). So we beat on, boats against the current . . .

PART TWO

5

The Artist and His Time

Camus's essays on the social responsibility of artists and intellectuals are of special importance today because this subject has provoked increasingly intense debate in France and the United States since the time of his death and was a crucial point on which he was opposed to Sartre and subsequent revolutionary ideologists. His ideas on the topic are found mainly in "The Artist as Witness of Freedom" (1948), the section "Rebellion and Art" in *The Rebel,* "The Artist and His Time" (1953) in *The Myth of Sisyphus and Other Essays,* "Bread and Freedom" (1953) and "The Wager of Our Generation," "Create Dangerously," and "Socialism of the Gallows" (all 1957) in *Resistance, Rebellion, and Death,* the Nobel Prize acceptance speech of 1957, and an untranslated 1955 newspaper article titled "Sous le signe de la liberté" (*Essais,* pp. 1746–49).

As previously indicated, his literary theory is most distinctive as a middle path between two opposite extremes prevalent in twentieth-century aesthetics. On the one hand, in Camus's analysis, nineteenth-century notions of pure art for art's sake have led to ahistorical formalism and social isolation or dandyism in the artist, who by abdicating public responsibility leaves mass culture the exclusive realm of trivial entertainers and mass politics that of unscrupulous professionals. In an interview with the American journal *Venture* shortly before his death, he observed, "The error of modern art lies, most often, in giving priority to the means over the end, to form over content, to technique over subject matter." [1]

On the other hand, he asserts, the realistic tradition has also had its excessive offshoots. Naturalism, as for example in Hemingway or the "tough" American detective that was an intellectual fad in France during

1. *Venture,* Spring–Summer 1960, p. 38.

the 1940s, claims to record life impassively, in its totality, without the artist interposing selection, arrangement, or judgment—an impossible claim to begin with, in Camus's view. It binds the writer, at least in theory, to an isolated historical moment and impersonal themes and style. Because these two extremes either totally ignore or accept the world as it is, neither serves rebellious art's purpose of "correcting creation":

> The realist artist and the formal artist try to find unity where it does not exist, in reality in its crudest state, or in imaginative creation which wants to abolish all reality. On the contrary, unity in art appears at the limit of the transformation that the artist imposes on reality. [Literally, 'Unity in art surges from the terminal of the transformation . . .'; Bower's erasure of the electrical metaphor typifies the way his translation deadens and muddles Camus's style.] It cannot dispense with either. This correction which the artist imposes by his language and by a redistribution of elements derived from reality is called style and gives the re-created universe its unity and its boundaries. [*Rebel,* p. 269]

Realism is distorted in another way by didacticism, particularly in Sartrean "littérature engagée" and "socialist realism," which according to Camus subordinate the artist's unhampered creativity—to his mind, the truly revolutionary function of art—to a prescribed revolutionary party line. Socialist realism, as propounded by the Soviet Union, contradicts itself by demanding that the artist realistically and in totality portray socialist society; but since no present society is totally socialist, to portray it as such is unrealistic. In a play on words that is not entirely convincing, Camus claims that because of this insistence on total depiction of an untotal reality, "now we understand why it should be the official aesthetic of a totalitarian revolution" (*Rebel,* p. 270). Confronted with this contradiction, the proponents of socialist realism shift their ground to say that the artist must then select those aspects of present society that foreshadow or dialectically lead toward the total socialism of the future. But since this future state is not yet real, "Finally, that art will be socialistic insofar as it is not realistic" (*RRD,* p. 199)—and realistic insofar as it is not socialistic.

Camus's own ideas on the authentic relationship between the artist and the reality of his times begin with the impossibility of remaining apolitical in today's world in which, as Orwell said, all issues are political issues:

> Until the present moment, remaining aloof has always been possible in history. When someone did not approve, he could always keep silent or talk of something else. Today everything is changed and even silence has dangerous implications. The moment that abstaining from choice is itself looked upon as a choice and punished or praised as such, the artist is willy-nilly impressed into service. "Impressed" seems to me a more accurate term in this connection than "committed" ['engagé']. Instead of signing up, indeed, for voluntary service, the artist does his compulsory service. [*RRD,* p. 190]

But, continuing the military metaphor, "The only really committed artist is he who, without refusing to take part in the combat, at least refuses to join the regular armies and remains a free-lance" (*RRD,* p. 205).

The artist must draw from his time for the raw material on which he will impose order. Our time consists of unprecedented, incessant bloodshed and mass injustice, "collective passions and historical struggle," in which the artist must immerse himself, to his personal sacrifice and risk: "To create, today, is to create dangerously" (*Rebel,* p. 274). Furthermore, the complexity and confusedness of contemporary history present him with an overwhelmingly difficult task in trying to make order of it. Like Camus himself, the artist or intellectual may not feel personally inclined or exceptionally well qualified to meddle in politics; yet it is exactly his instinctive passion for order and understanding that morally obliges him to involve himself in political issues rather than leaving them to illiterate or expediently motivated "specialists." Similarly, his capacity for observing and articulating makes it his responsibility to act as witness and spokesman: "The miner who is exploited or shot down, the slaves in the camps, those in the colonies, the legions of persecuted throughout the world—they need all those who can speak to communicate their silence and to keep in touch with them" (*Myth,* p. 150).

As a craftsman in words, the literary artist again is obliged to fight for the clear and truthful public use of language. "The intellectual's role will be to say that the king is naked when he is, and not to go into raptures over his imaginary trappings" (*RRD*, p. 128). Art is by Camus's definition communal, so lies are antiartistic in separating men: "Because his vocation is to unite the greatest possible number of men, it cannot countenance falsehood and slavery, which breed solitudes wherever they prevail" (*NP*, p. 34).

Liberation, internal and external, is equally intrinsic to art. "The aim of art, the aim of a life can only be to increase the sum of freedom and responsibility to be found in every man and in the world. . . . There is not a single true work of art that has not in the end added to the inner freedom of each person who has known and loved it" (*RRD*, pp. 184). So the artist is bound to defend political freedom, all the more so if he has the good fortune to be personally free to create while other men are enslaved: "How could an artist justify his privileges (if he has them) other than by taking part, on the level of everyone, in the long struggle for the liberation of work and of culture?" (*Essais*, p. 1748). He similarly links the freedom of workers with that of culture in "Bread and Freedom," a speech delivered at the Labor Exchange of Saint-Etienne expressing solidarity between intellectuals and trade unions.

Against Marxist arguments that artists and intellectuals should subordinate their individual creative inclinations to those that expressly advance revolutionary doctrine, or that they should give up the bourgeois privilege of culture altogether to join in direct action until all men are liberated and have equal access to culture, Camus replies that "suppressing creative liberty is perhaps not the right way to overcome slavery and that until they can speak for all it is stupid to give up the ability to speak for a few at least" (*RRD*, p. 200). Moreover, "Tyrants know there is in the work of art an emancipatory force, which is mysterious only to those who do not revere it. . . . This is why it is not true that culture can be, even temporarily, suspended in order to make way for a new culture" (p. 206). The artist, then, should seek his revolutionary justification not in doctrinally condemning the old order—"No great work has ever been based on hatred or contempt" (*RRD*, p. 184)—but in affirmatively creating his personal, exemplary images of beauty, clearsightedness, liberty, and brotherhood. "Without culture, and the relative freedom it implies, society, even when perfect, is but a jungle. This is why any authentic creation is a gift to the future" (*Myth*, p. 151).

II

Camus's position on art for art's sake was formulated mainly in reference to the French parnassian and symbolist poetic traditions, whose major twentieth-century spokesman was Paul Valéry, but his ideas are equally applicable to the American and English formalistic artists and theorists enumerated in my first chapter. Actually, his and their theoretical positions are not as far apart as they at first appear to be. Although T. S. Eliot, I. A. Richards, and the New Critics stress the distinctive quality of literary discourse and the self-contained world literature creates, nearly all of them end up acknowledging, in varying degrees, that this "autotelic" creation does ultimately have meaning and value for other areas of experience or intellect and is in turn subject to evaluation in their light (Eliot, for example, at least partly subordinates literary values to religious ones). Like Camus, most of them in principle deny a dichotomy between form and content; they regard formal technique not as an end in itself but as a mode of structuring and concentrating experience or emotion.

Richards and some of his followers emphasized the capacity of literature to educate a sensibility attuned to order in life as well as art. None of them, however, went as far in practice as Camus did with his insistence that the artist's "rage for order," in Wallace Stevens's phrase, should commit him to the struggle for social justice. W. H. Auden, in his jaundiced post-Marxist mood of the 1950s, diametrically opposed Camus's position (although Camus recognized the same danger in it when pushed to excess):

A society which was really like a good poem, embodying the aesthetic virtues of beauty, order, economy and subordination of detail to the whole, would be a nightmare of horror for, given the historical reality of actual men, such a society could only come into being through selective breeding, extermination of the physically and mentally unfit, absolute obedience to its Director, and a large slave class kept out of sight in cellars.

Vice versa, a poem which was really like a political democracy—

examples, unfortunately, exist—would be formless, windy, banal, and utterly boring.[2]

The Anglo-American formalists also often acknowledge the power of literature to broaden our intellectual scope toward the greatest possible comprehensiveness and maturity. Thus they admit that literature may—though it *need* not—encompass political ideology and historical actualities. Still, there is no denying that in the applied criticism of these theorists, the weight falls more on the *how* of literary expression than on the *what,* more on the poetic sensibility in isolation (and they do tend to equate poetry with the totality of literature, while Camus thinks more in terms of fiction and drama, genres that have had far wider social influence in our time) than on the kind of integration Camus achieved through placing his aesthetic reflections within the historical and political context of *The Rebel* and the *Actuelles*.

The case of Eliot provides several further striking contrasts to Camus's notions on the responsibility of the artist to his time. (Other practicing disciples of art for art's sake as opposed to historically committed art, such as Yeats, Pound, Stevens, Forster, or Joyce might provide similarly instructive comparisons, but Eliot both as poet and theorist probably exerted the largest single influence on twentieth-century American literary aesthetics.) Eliot's concept of tradition and the individual talent accorded with Camus's aesthetic to the extent that both men believed that the artist's role involves discovering in his own age's unique experience reenactments of past archetypes and values. In Eliot's poetic vision, however, our age falls contemptibly short of the past, with democracy dissipating established values. In contrast to Eliot's scorn for the contemporary common man, and closer to Joyce's affectionately ironic view of Leopold Bloom as the modern Ulysses, Camus could reincarnate Sisyphus in Meursault or glorify Algerian workers sporting on the beach as avatars of the athletes of ancient Delos, classical measure in their harmony with nature.

Moreover, in the poetry of Eliot and his associate Pound, homage to the past takes the form of erudite allusions fully comprehensible only to a steadily dwindling percentage of readers steeped in classical scholarship. Although Camus equally respected the wisdom of antiquity, as he ma-

2. "The Poet and the City," in *The Dyer's Hand* (New York: Vintage, 1968), p. 85.

tured he believed increasingly that today's artist must translate the experience of the past into popularly accessible forms, that art, without vulgarizing itself in mass-cultural commerciality, should be "a means of stirring the greatest number of men by providing them with a privileged image of our joys and woes."

The values that Camus admired in classical antiquity and in their revival by Renaissance humanism were those least emphasized by Eliot— Socratic ignorance, skeptical agnosticism and pluralistic tolerance, epicurean tempered hedonism, and stoic contemplation of mortality unredeemed by an afterlife. Camus's application of these values to present-day society in democratic-socialist political attitudes was sharply opposed to Eliot, who, following the New Humanists Irving Babbitt and Paul Elmer More earlier in the century, invoked the classical tradition to support conservatism, elitism, and a general retreat from modern political realities. (As we shall see, however, Camus did come to echo Eliot's conservatism somewhat in the late 1950s when he rallied in defense of the Western cultural tradition against the threat he saw posed to it by Third World peoples' assertion of their own identity in Algeria and elsewhere.)

Eliot and several of the New Critics following him advanced a Christian version of tragedy in which man's fallen state blights historical aspiration and necessitates looking to the hereafter for redemption. For Camus tragedy lay in the innocence and joy of living here and now that make life's inevitable loss more poignant: "Only one thing is more tragic than suffering, and that is the life of a happy man" (*LCE,* p. 91). It is this joy in life that impels us to commit ourselves to combatting the political forces that deprive men of its full realization. Eliot repudiated all the major twentieth-century ideological movements—fascism, capitalism, communism, and socialism—in a rearguard defense of the ideal of a Christian society but admitted that his social program was an unrealistic one in today's world.

Thus when Eliot and New Critically–oriented American aestheticists after him attempted to coordinate their literary and political visions, the outcome usually fell quite short of their own standards for the intellectual sophistication supposedly engendered by literature. Their revered literary "tradition" was highly restricted, including few irreligious writers or political egalitarians; they were blatantly prejudiced against Marx and other thinkers in the socialist tradition. To the terrors of the atomic age they could only oppose the genteel conservatism of Christian quietism or Southern agrarianism. From the mid-1940s until the mid-1960s, their voices were virtually inaudible on vital issues like the nuclear arms race, McCarthyism, racism, gross extremes of wealth and poverty, and America's movement toward monopoly capitalism and imperialism supported by a military-industrial complex and service-station multiversities. By the criterion of intellectual integration, then, Camus's aesthetic proved to be the more effective guide for applying literary sensibility to the historical problems of our time.

III

Camus's aesthetic has provoked less open opposition from advocates of art for art's sake than from the other direction, the literary-political left. His most vocal opponent on the left was Jean-Paul Sartre, especially beginning with their argument over *The Rebel* in 1952. The primary difference between their concepts of the artist's social responsibility is Sartre's more heightened sense of historical and class situation. For him Camus's defense of cultural freedom is formulated *hors situation,* valid perhaps from the viewpoint of the bourgeois intellectual but not applicable to every historical circumstance or segment of society. In Sartre's view the freedom to create or enjoy high culture is a privilege of the bourgeoisie— including those living on its margins, who are nonetheless bourgeois in the eyes of the proletariat even if, as Camus advocates, they scrupulously refuse to exploit their prerogatives. Consequently, for objective purposes Camus's defense of political freedom in the name of cultural values serves a class interest, the freedom of the bourgeoisie at the expense of the working class and colonial subjects. Those in poverty, denied freedom and culture, cannot be expected to applaud or endorse the social utility of the bourgeois artist's affirmations of beauty, even when he, like Camus, has been born in poverty and, having had the good fortune to escape it, devotes his art (patronizingly, according to Sartre) to describing its deprivations and compensations. As Sartre says in "Reply to Albert Camus":

> We *know* that if not wealth, then at least culture, that priceless and inequitable treasure, is needed in order to find luxury in the midst of poverty. . . . All the value that an oppressed man can still have in

his own eyes, he puts into the hatred that he bears his enemies. Neither your books, nor your example, can do anything for this man. You teach an art of living, a "science of life," you teach us how to rediscover our body, but when this man discovers his body at night, after it has been stolen from him all day, it is nothing more than a huge ache which weighs upon and humiliates him.[3]

Sartre's earlier theoretical work *What Is Literature?*, published in 1948, agreed on many points with Camus's aesthetic, for instance, that every great work of art ultimately affirms freedom and opposes hatred, but even then his view was more astringently qualified:

One can imagine a good novel being written by an American Negro even if hatred of the whites were spread all over it, because it is the freedom of his race that he demands through this hatred. And, as he invites me to assume the attitude of generosity, the moment I feel myself a pure freedom I can not bear to identify myself with a race of oppressors. Thus, I require of all freedoms that they demand the liberation of colored people against the white race and against myself insofar as I am a part of it.[4]

Sartre came increasingly to disagree with Camus's belief that the vocation of artist enables one to avoid implication in judgment and murder, since even when the bourgeois artist or intellectual propounds nonviolent ideals he is still objectively acquiescing to the violence being perpetuated in actuality by his class and country. While Sartre does not name Camus in his 1961 preface to Frantz Fanon's *The Wretched of the Earth,* his remarks there are unmistakably pointed:

A fine sight they are too, the believers in non-violence, saying that they are neither executioners nor victims. Very well, then; if you're not victims when the government which you've voted for, when the army in which your younger brothers are serving without hesitation or remorse have undertaken race murder, you are, without a shadow of doubt, executioners. And if you choose to be victims and to risk being put in prison for a day or two, you are simply choosing to pull your irons out of the fire. . . . But if the whole regime, even

3. "Reply to Albert Camus," in *Situations,* p. 74.
4. *What Is Literature?* (New York: Washington Square Press, 1966), pp. 40–41.

your non-violent ideas, are conditioned by a thousand-year-old oppression, your passivity serves only to place you in the ranks of the
oppressors." [5]

Camus's defense of Western culture was even more vehemently contradicted by Fanon himself, a black French psychiatrist born in Marti-
nique who served in an Algerian hospital during the civil war. He wrote
The Wretched of the Earth shortly before his premature death in 1961
to justify Arab revolutionary violence as well as the necessity for colonized
and colored peoples throughout the Third World to repudiate European
and white culture in the assertion of their own cultural identities. From
Fanon's perspective, a statement by Camus in 1957 such as "There is no
culture without legacy, and we cannot and must not reject anything of
ours, the legacy of the West" (*RRD,* p. 207) takes on imperialist and
racist overtones.

In 1946 Camus had written prophetically, "Everywhere the colonial
peoples are asserting themselves. Perhaps in ten years, perhaps in fifty,
the dominance of Western civilization itself will be called into question.
We might as well recognize this now, and admit these civilizations into
the world parliament, so that its code of law may become truly universal"
(*NVNE,* p. 13). By the time of "The Wager of Our Generation," the
actualities of that subsequent decade, including Dien Bien Phu and the
Algerian uprising, have made him less sanguine about Third World
self-assertion. This interview suggests that he was uneasily shifting
ground from his earlier pan-Mediterraneanism to an affirmation of his
French national identity and of the European cultural tradition (although even as early as his 1937 lecture "The New Mediterranean Culture," it had been the Greco-Roman heritage he invoked, with only
taken acknowledgment of the Moslem contribution). His defenses of
cultural independence here and in his other statements on aesthetics at
the time of the Nobel Prize apparently did not extend to the notion of
self-determination for Algerian Arabs. He pays tribute to a number of
Arabs there who "have taken their place among European writers" (*RRD,*
p. 187), but the prospect of an Algeria independent politically *or* cul-
turally from France and Europe would, understandably, have involved
such a painful denial of his own identity that he evidently could not

5. *The Wretched of the Earth* (New York: Grove Press, 1968), p. 25.

even imagine it. (Another possible indication of conservative leanings in "The Wager of Our Generation" is his citing of Ortega y Gassett, "perhaps the greatest of European writers after Nietzsche" [p. 186], as an exemplar of pan-Europeanism. There are no prominent references to Ortega in Camus's previous writings, and this high praise for a cultural elitist and advocate of formalistic dehumanization of art, in the middle of a refutation of these notions, is difficult to explain, except perhaps as a polite eulogy for Ortega, who had recently died.)

IV

A final limitation in Camus's aesthetic lies in his reduction of all Marxist literary ideology to the most heavy-handed Stalinist party-line notions of socialist realism and the subordination of art to revolutionary doctrine. He indicates little awareness of more sophisticated Marxist critics like the Hungarian Georg Lukács, Ernst Fischer and Walter Benjamin in Germany, Lucien Goldmann (and for that matter, Sartre, in works like *What Is Literature?*) in France, or of others who, though not avowedly Marxists, draw extensively upon Marxist thought, such as Roland Barthes in France, Raymond Williams in England, and Conor Cruise O'Brien in Ireland. Many of the important works of these writers, to be sure, were only appearing at about the same period as Camus's works on the artist and his time, and he might not yet have read or assimilated them; still, in retrospect they appear to have more in common with his theories than with the Stalinist line.

Camus's assertion that socialist realism claims to portray unselectively the totality of experience is a travesty of the doctrine as formulated by Marxists like Lukács and Fischer.[6] (Lukács in fact attributes such unselectivity to naturalism in contrast to socialist realism.) For them the contemporary writer's selective and organizational principle should be socialist consciousness—as independently arrived at, not dictated by party bureaucrats. This perspective is "total" in the sense that it strives toward a comprehensive analysis of life that distinguishes its historically situated aspects from immutable existential ones. The historical variables

6. See Lukács, "Critical Realism and Socialist Realism," in *Realism in Our Time*, pp. 93–135; and Fischer, "Socialist Realism," in *The Necessity of Art: A Marxist Approach* (Baltimore: Penguin Books, 1963), pp. 107–15 (original German edition, 1959).

that socialist writers or critics see reflected in literature include class and racial relations; local and large-scale socioeconomic forces influencing characters' motivation and consciousness; authors' unconscious biases imposed by their class interests or conditioning; and progressive or regressive ideological implications. Lukács acknowledges that not every work of an author can or should embody the total socialist vision. In a formulation reminiscent of Camus's aesthetic in *The Myth,* Lukács writes, "Of course, neither socialist realism nor critical [bourgeois] realism are able to portray the totality of a society in the crude sense of the word. Even Balzac, who set out to do this in his *Comédie Humaine,* made this claim only in regard to the whole cycle. Each part, novel or short story, contains only a small segment, though complete in itself. But the greatness of his conception is that the whole is constantly present in the parts. Each individual novel is organically related to that whole." [7] (This principle should have averted Lukács's own misreading of *The Plague* outside the context of Camus's total work.) The Marxist perspective, then, is not essentially opposed to Camus's ideal of the artist aspiring toward comprehensive understanding of his time or, for that matter, to Matthew Arnold's conception of the poet, exemplified by Sophocles, viewing life steadily and whole. From the viewpoint of Marxist criticism, however, Camus's artistic practice fell somewhat short of his own theoretical standard of inclusiveness, as we shall see in subsequent chapters.

On the issue of subordination of artistic or intellectual freedom to revolutionary party discipline, Sartre, in his exposition of *la littérature engagée* in *What Is Literature?,* did not approve of party control of thought, although he did assert that a comprehensive analysis of today's world would be bound to commit the artist to a socialist perspective through his independent discernment. Only with the Third World revolutionary struggles beginning in the 1950s did Sartre gradually become convinced that in some extreme situations intellectual submission to collective discipline is necessary.

During the 1960s other intellectually responsible literary critics also reformulated the case for cultural subordination. Conor Cruise O'Brien, for instance, in a 1967 article on "Politics and the Morality of Scholarship," wrote:

7. *Realism in Our Time,* p. 99.

Scholars and artists are likely to reprobate both the theory and practice of revolutionary subordination. We might do well, however, to consider also how our reprobation must look to those whose theory and practice we reprobate. If we say we cannot accept the need for revolutionary subordination, they can reply that the reason for this is obvious: that since we belong among the principal beneficiaries of the social *status quo* in the world, our assertion of higher values is just a way of expressing, in the language of our mandarin caste, an economically based antagonism. It would not be very easy to refute this. One reason why the doctrine of revolutionary subordination is likely to seem so repulsive to most of us is that most of us do not conceive of revolution as being desirable at all, and therefore *a fortiori* we cannot conceive of its being worth great moral, intellectual, and other sacrifices. . . . Few of us have known conditions such as those that created, in China, the conviction, more strongly held among intellectuals than even among others, that revolution was worth any sacrifice —one's own life, one's family, one's artistic or professional integrity. . . . The revolutionary, if we can assume him to have adequate reasons to be candid, might well declare that the right kind of bad novel or bad poem can strengthen the revolutionary will to fight: that the exposure of the badness of such works can weaken such will and lead to revolutionary defeats—for example, to restoration of landlordism in a province, with all the conditions that go with it, including starvation among the children of peasants. And if all these factual, and not implausible, assertions are true, then an honest book review can indeed in certain circumstances kill children.[8]

At the same time, however, Cruise O'Brien acknowledges the counterargument that in practice it is difficult to prove that a mendacious book review has caused children's deaths "and that all the reasoning will *certainly* result in is a spate of mendacity; in short, the children may or may not be saved, but they will certainly be systematically misinformed." Camus would undoubtedly have held the latter opinion, but he never did fully come to grips with the first.

A similar leftist line of opposition to Camus's position has been that his and other Cold War liberal intellectuals' insistence on the inviola-

8. In *The Morality of Scholarship*, ed. Max Black (Ithaca: Cornell University Press, 1967), pp. 61–63.

bility of ideological independence and their support of the West because
it tolerates such independence are attributable at least partially to their
marginal sociological and psychological perspective. Camus, with his
fatherless childhood, his proletarian birth and bourgeois education and
later career, his mixture of Mediterranean and French culture, was a
classic case of what Raymond Williams has identified as the intellectual
"exile" or "vagrant." Williams's analysis of George Orwell as this type
can be equally well applied to Camus: "The vagrant, in literary terms,
is the 'reporter,' and where the reporter is good, his work has the merits
of novelty and a certain specialized kind of immediacy. The reporter is
an observer, an intermediary: it is unlikely that he will understand, in any
depth, the life about which he is writing (the vagrant from his own society, or his own class, looking at another, and still inevitably from the
outside)." [9] About the exile's premium on independence, Williams continues:

> His attacks on the denial of liberty are admirable: we have all,
> through every loyalty, to defend the basic liberties of association and
> expression, or we deny man. Yet, when the exile speaks of liberty, he
> is in a curiously ambiguous position, for while the rights in question
> may be called individual, the condition of their guarantee is inevi-
> tably social. The exile, because of his own personal position, cannot
> finally believe in any social guarantee: to him, because this is the
> pattern of his own living, almost all association is suspect. He fears it
> because he does not want to be compromised (this is often his virtue,
> because he is so quick to see the perfidy which certain compromises
> involve). Yet he fears it also because he can see no way of confirming,
> socially, his own individuality. . . . To belong to a community is to
> be a part of a whole, and, necessarily, to accept, while helping to de-
> fine, its disciplines. To the exile, however, society as such is totali-
> tarian; he cannot commit himself, he is bound to stay out. [10]

Williams elsewhere explicitly criticizes Camus along the same lines,
pointing out the ideological limitations in works such as *The Plague* and
The Just Assassins: "Thus while the suffering is genuinely collective, the
revolt is inevitably individual. . . . The capacity of history to change the

9. *Culture and Society, 1780–1950* (New York: Harper & Row, 1958), pp. 289–90.
10. Ibid., p. 291.

common condition, in any essential way, is implicitly denied. Thus revolt is sharply distinguished from revolution."[11] In Williams's analysis, then, if intellectual submission to revolutionary party discipline *were* justifiable, Camus's temperamental bias would probably prevent him from admitting it. Although Williams does not formulate his characterization of the exile in psychoanalytic terms, his observation that "alongside the tough rejection of compromise, which gives the tradition its virtue, is the felt social impotence, the inability to form extending relationships"[12] inevitably recalls to us the influences in Camus's psychological formation that might have inclined him toward these traits. In my preface I stated that it is not legitimate to imply that an author's psychological biases negate the objective validity of his ideas. On the other hand, our concept of what is objective is itself not entirely objective, as recent criticisms of "value free" scholarship have revealed. There may be such a thing as objective truth, but it is certain that we can only aspire toward it after becoming fully conscious of everyone's tendencies toward subjective bias. The Freudian and Marxian viewpoints both provide important controls for taking account of the way an individual's psychological and sociological formation—an author's or our own as readers—unconsciously predisposes him toward beliefs he has ostensibly arrived at objectively.

These disagreements over the social role of the artist and intellectual found their way tacitly into Camus's fictional works, most notably *The Plague* and *The Fall,* and we will encounter them again in subsequent discussions of those works. His position on this issue has lost some ground since the time of his death. The late 1960s brought an increased atmosphere of crisis in Western culture, a loss of identity and confidence among middle-class intellectuals. Too many of them had turned their intelligence toward technocratic support of the status quo. In this age of relative cultural affluence, their defenses of artistic independence or academic freedom were too often colored by the self-serving motives Camus warned against in "Create Dangerously": "The freedom of art is not worth much when its only purpose is to assure the artist's comfort. . . . And I cannot agree, for example, with those who complain today of the decline of wisdom. Apparently they are right. Yet, to tell

11. *Modern Tragedy* (Stanford: Stanford University Press, 1966), p. 183.
12. *Culture and Society,* p. 289.

the truth, wisdom has never declined so much as when it involved no risks and belonged exclusively to a few humanists buried in libraries" (*RRD*, pp. 207–8). In a period of worldwide revolutionary ferment and antiwar resistance, even those who professed to leftist politics were accused of being dilettantes so long as they continued to pursue middle-class careers. Sartre, for his part, increasingly disdained purely literary achievement because of its bourgeois taint, to the extent of refusing the Nobel Prize in 1964. He left his projected fictional tetralogy, *Roads to Freedom,* unfinished, and after his last play, *The Condemned of Altona,* in 1960, devoted himself almost exclusively to revolutionary political theory and polemics, attempting to reconcile existentialism with Marxism in the *Critique of Dialectical Reason, The Words,* and his massive study of Flaubert. If Camus's position has lost viability, however, it is still uncertain whether the major cause has been the irreversible dialectic of history or simply the absence of enough intellectuals with his integrity to validate it in theory and practice.

6

The Artist as Essayist:
Lyrical and Journalistic

I

If Camus had never written any fiction or drama he would still be likely to rank among the outstanding authors of the twentieth century solely as a literary essayist. Indeed, while his fiction, plays, metaphysical and social philosophy may have their weaknesses or at least limitations as such, one of their strongest redeeming virtues is always the exemplary quality of his prose, which is distilled in its purest, most autonomous form in the essays.

Because of their individual brevity and occasionality, the essays in *L'Envers et l'endroit, Nuptials,* and *Summer* are too often regarded as minor works, thematic corollaries to *The Myth* and *The Rebel* (not until fourteen years after publication of *L'Eté* in 1954 did a complete translation of the three volumes appear here, in *Lyrical and Critical Essays*). Artistically, however, both individually and as a collective unit, the lyrical essays often surpass the "major" essays and stand among his very finest works. Here Camus is most fully, comprehensively himself, in contrast to the ironic personae of his fictional narrators and to the single lines of formal argument that he isolates in *The Myth, The Rebel,* and the political journalism. The personal essay is the medium in which he is most at home—that is to say, in the world of immediate, concrete experience. Here he relaxes and speaks in his own voice of the actual settings and personal relationships of his life, the flesh-and-blood inspirations of the abstract themes of *The Myth* and *The Rebel*. Here too he reveals the compassion, the warmth of personality and zest for living, the amused affection for the details of everyday life that he subordinates in his fiction and plays—perhaps regrettably—to the creation of mythic settings and

117

characters and crisis-pitched action. Suspending his usual principle of keeping his private life out of his writing, he comes close to autobiography in talking about the poverty of his youth in Algiers, his pathetic mother and family life, the first attack of tuberculosis that threatened his life at seventeen, early travels to Czechoslovakia and Italy, and the later discomforts of living in Paris and becoming a literary celebrity. He writes compassionately about old people left behind by the young with nothing to think about but death; about the minor humiliations of traveling alone in a foreign country (not knowing streetcar fares, eating repeatedly in the same awful café because it's the only place they "know" you); about the parochial rivalry between Algiers and Oran (a boxer from the other town is ostentatiously applauded "so that he won't be able to say *back there* that we of Oran are savages" [*Myth*, p. 124]); and about pretty girls dancing all night in necklaces of jasmine or flowering yearly on the Algerian beaches (later he is to reflect with Proustian nostalgia, "The young girls in the flower of their youth still laugh and chatter on the seashore, but he who watches them gradually loses his right to love them, just as those he has loved lose the power to be loved" [*Rebel*, p. 267]).

Dominating all else is his rhapsodic love affair with the Mediterranean sun, sea, and flower-covered landscape. He succeeds in elevating intensity of sense experience into a rationalist metaphysic and in exalting the communion of man with nature in overtly sexual imagery without ever lapsing into mysticism, pantheism, or the pathetic fallacy. After the first autumn rains in Algiers, "the whole earth lies, its belly moistened with a bitter almond-scented seed, at rest from having yielded all summer long to the sun. And once again this fragrance consecrates the nuptials of man and earth, and gives rise in us to the only truly virile love in this world: one that is generous and will die" (*LCE*, p. 92).

Thematically and stylistically, the individual lyrical essays—even the earliest ones in *L'Envers et l'endroit*—contain his most concise, integrated expressions of his ideal of keeping life's paradoxes and antithetical possibilities in balance, as I have indicated by drawing extensively from them for examples in chapter 1, section IV. Moreover, their stylistic homogeneity and the current of his central themes and variations through the different essays tie the three volumes together into what is in effect a single work with its own internal cohesion. Countless dialectical relationships can be found between various pieces. For instance, "Summer in

Algiers" (1939), "Helen's Exile" (1948), and "Return to Tipasa" (1953) form a thesis, antithesis, and synthesis on the theme of hedonistic self-fulfillment, beauty, and freedom against social commitment and the joyless struggle for justice.

In "Summer in Algiers" he praises the natural beauty of Algiers and the Algerians' love of life, while making the qualification, "it is true that a certain intensity of living involves some injustice" (*LCE*, p. 89). One indication, perhaps unconscious on Camus's part, of the kind of injustice involved is the fact that the avatars of ancient Greek athletes swimming in the harbor seem to be exclusively European: "Everybody's skin changes at the same time from white to gold, then to brown, and at last to a tobacco hue, the final stage the body can attain in its quest for transformation." Yet, in a striking juxtaposition heightening the implication of segregation, "From water level, people's bodies form a bronzed frieze against the glaring white background of the Arab town" (p. 83). The oxymoronic reversal of skin colors is telling, although probably unintentional.

"Helen's Exile" describes the opposite pole from Algiers, a Europe that has lost sight of beauty in its immoderate preoccupation with justice: "We have exiled beauty; the Greeks took arms for it" (*LCE*, p. 148). (O'Brien's translation, "the Greeks took up arms for her" [*Myth*, p. 134], more wisely maintains the French feminine pronoun, with its suggested personification of beauty in Helen of Troy.) In "Summer in Algiers" he has said paradoxically, "In the Algerian summer I learn that only one thing is more tragic than suffering, and that is the life of a happy man" (*LCE*, p. 91); in other words, the man who has enjoyed life fully has the most to lose. He reiterates this theme at the beginning of "Helen's Exile," suggesting that the beauty of the Mediterranean contributed to the Greeks' conception of tragedy, then contrasts Europe: "We turn our back on nature, we are ashamed of beauty. Our miserable tragedies have the smell of an office, and their blood is the color of dirty ink" (p. 150).

In "Return to Tipasa" he briefly revisits Algeria for a rejuvenating exposure to natural beauty that will enable him to continue the fight for justice. The wintry weather and unlaughing faces in Algiers at the beginning of this essay might be taken as an indication of the darkening political situation there, but it is not mentioned explicitly, and the locus of injustice here is still Europe. When the rainy weather finally breaks,

"In the depths of winter, I finally learned that within me there lay an invincible summer" (*LCE,* p. 169). Despite the barbed wire now enclosing Tipasa, the timeless beauty of its natural surroundings enables him in conclusion to resolve to maintain a just medium between the two extremes: "Yes, there is beauty and there are the humiliated. Whatever difficulties the enterprise may present, I would like never to be unfaithful either to one or the other" (pp. 169–70). He then recapitulates this summation—somewhat redundantly—in the image of a coin with a worn "tails" and a "heads" depicting the face of a beautiful woman which again evokes Helen of Troy from "Helen's Exile."

Structurally, the essays follow a typical pattern of a passage of straight narration or description that evokes a meditation that is in turn elaborated into a paradoxical metaphor or aphorism, as for example in the image of the two-sided coin just cited from "Return to Tipasa" or in the passage quoted above in chapter 1, section v, from the preface to *L'Envers et l'endroit* concluding "Solitudes unite those society separates." They are further characterized by a rise to poetic diction in the closing paragraphs, as in the three essays previously discussed. The last paragraph of "Summer in Algiers" personifies the earth after the first September rains as a contented woman after intercourse. "Helen's Exile" ends with the extended metaphor of the Trojan War used as an exhortation to restore love and beauty to contemporary society. The coda of "Return to Tipasa" on pages 170–71 is a series of oxymorons mingling speech and silence and live and dead cities: the "lipless mouth" of the beautiful woman depicted on the coin echoes his own internal voice recalling his twenty years of wandering over the landscape near Tipasa "questioning dumb goatherds, knocking at the door of empty ruins." In contrast, his "family" of Europeans, reigning over rich and hideous cities that are more dead than Tipasa, constantly shouts but is "deaf to all [nature's] secrets," and he too, having forgotten nature amid "our shrieking tombs," is both "a noisy accomplice who has cried out among the stones" and "deaf and active." Summing up his meditative theme that we forget the lessons of nature as soon as we are exiled from it and must periodically come back in order to relearn them, he closes with one more paradox: his resolution to return permanently to Tipasa (in death, perhaps?) to "learn for one last time what I know."

The lyrical essays have the expository form of tightly knotted prose poems, challenging the reader with complex extended figures of speech, obliquely expressed themes, elliptical jumps in narration and thought, and cryptic motifs that reveal their meaning bit by bit as they recur with variations from essay to essay—such as silence, indifference, black sun and dark flame, or the seaside cemetery near Algiers. Each piece demands close explication, and to illustrate I will use "The Enigma," although I might equally well have chosen any of the three discussed earlier or "The Wind at Djémila," "Death in the Soul," "L'Envers et l'endroit," or "The Desert."

II

"The Enigma" (*LCE,* pp. 154-61) presents the familiar antitheses of society against nature, speech against silence, dark against light, modern Europe against ancient Greece, but in an unusual context: one of Camus's rare discussions of his public image as a literary celebrity.

The essay opens with the description of a sunny Mediterranean landscape characteristic of the earlier pieces in *L'Envers et l'endroit* and *Nuptials*—but now, in 1950, the scene is near Camus's home in Provence, on the plain below Mount Luberon, which is paradoxically "a vast block of silence that I listen to unceasingly." The first paragraph further develops the mixture of visual and oral imagery: "I listen carefully, someone is running toward me in the distance, invisible friends call to me, my joy grows, just as years ago." The "happy enigma" of the scene will help him clarify the meaning of the absurd in face of the public's distortion of his position in *The Myth:*

> Where is the absurdity of the world? Is it this resplendent glow or the memory of its absence? With so much sun in my memory, how could I have wagered on nonsense [i.e., epistemological meaninglessness as an aspect of the absurd]? People around me are amazed; so am I, at times. I could tell them, as I tell myself, that it was in fact the sun that helped me, and that the very thickness of its light coagulates the universe and its forms into a dazzling darkness.

Facing the sun will help him explain the absurd, and "the very fact of talking about it [the absurd], after all, will lead us back to the sun."

His attention shifts from the Mediterranean to Paris literary society, and he speaks with a mixture of amused irony and annoyance about the popular press's prurient interest in his personality rather than his work, readers' simplistic identification of him with his characters, and above all, his stereotyped label as an author of the absurd and of nihilistic despair. To the latter he responds with the argument discussed in chapter 3 about semantic sense and nonsense and about a literature of despair being a contradiction in terms. Here he reiterates the earlier paradox of mute objects speaking: "Despair is silent. Even silence, moreover, is meaningful if your eyes speak."

Moving from metaphysical and epistemological absurdity to that of history, he disavows optimism in our murderous century, "but real pessimism, which does exist, lies in outbidding all this cruelty and shame." He himself has sought to transcend nihilism, not through virtue but through instinctive fidelity to the Mediterranean sunlight, "in which for thousands of years men have learned to welcome life even in suffering." He metaphorically equates the challenging enigma of modern history both with that of the sun as it epitomizes nature's ambiguity and with that of the world view of Greek tragedy:

Aeschylus is often heartbreaking; yet he radiates light and warmth. At the center of his universe, we find not fleshless nonsense but an enigma, that is to say, a meaning which is difficult to decipher because it dazzles us. Likewise, to the unworthy but nonetheless stubborn sons of Greece who still survive in this emaciated century, the scorching heat of our history may seem unendurable, but they endure it in the last analysis because they want to understand it. In the center of our work, dark though it may be, shines an inexhaustible sun, the same sun that shouts today across the hills and plain [again, the synesthesia of the visual and oral].

In other words, Camus as a writer faces up to the absurdity of modern history as Sisyphus surmounts metaphysical absurdity through the pride of endurance, as the rebel "obstinately confronts a world condemned to death and the impenetrable obscurity of the human condition with his demand for life and absolute clarity," and as the true artists of the Nobel Prize speech "force themselves to understand instead of judging."

Camus leads into his peroration with another Greek allusion, Plato's cave allegory, in which the habitués of Paris literary society have turned their backs on the sun to pursue the shadows of fleeting renown. "But we have learned, far from Paris, that there is a light behind us, that we must turn around and cast off our chains in order to face it directly, and that our task before we die is to seek through any words to identify it." In this task we can only be aided by others with creative attitudes, whether artists or lovers, not by literary gossips. (The reference to lovers recapitulates the mention of his friends in paragraph one and his defense of writing as a denial of despair: "If he speaks, if he reasons, above all if he writes, immediately the brother reaches out his hand, the tree is justified, love is born.") And in contrast to Paris *bavardage,* loving and writing are silent enterprises: "Yes, all this noise . . . when peace would be to love and create in silence!" As he has said it would, talking about the absurd has led him back to the silent sun and the writer's equally silent struggle to decipher its enigma: "But we must learn to be patient. One moment more, the sun seals our mouths."

An afternote remained to be added to "The Enigma": Camus is now buried in the same countryside described here, in a cemetery within sight of Mount Luberon.

III

As a journalist Camus was one of the few in the midcentury to produce a substantial body of daily and weekly articles of lasting literary value, only a small number of which have been translated into English. (Emmett Parker's thoroughly documented study of Camus's journalism, *The Artist in the Arena,* contains a full compilation of his contributions to the periodical press.)[1] He was superlative not only as a reporter and columnist for *Alger-Républicain* before the war and *Combat* during and after it but as the wholly dedicated daily editor of *Combat* from 1944 to 1947 and as a critic of the press. In the latter role he repeatedly called attention to a fact of capitalist society that has been shamefully ignored in America: the debasement of news reporting by profit-maximizing sensationalism and by its being turned into a filler between advertising and publicity handouts. At the same time he kept equal watch on the propagandistic distortions of the French leftist press. A. J. Liebling, his closest American counterpart as a press watcher, admired Camus's idea for a daily "control

1. *The Artist in the Arena* (Madison: University of Wisconsin Press, 1966), pp. 185–203.

newspaper" that would report on the lies and distortions in the others.[2]

His own journalistic ideals and practice exemplified what the periodical press can and should be: the application to daily events of a refined humanistic sensibility, long-range historical perspective, and a radical integrity whose task in the atomic age is "to speak out clearly against the Terror and at the same time to define the values by which a peaceful world may live" and to "consistently oppose to power the force of example; to authority, exhortation; to insult, friendly reasoning; to trickery, simple honor" (*NVNE*, pp. 15–16). He had a rare capacity to get above the restrictions in viewpoint imposed on most of us by our emotional involvement in the historical moment and by our nationalistic and ideological parochiality (although he too was to fall victim to parochially restricted vision on the Algerian problem). He tried to make the reader understand the human factors on the opponent's side as well as the follies on his own, as in "Letters to a German Friend" or *Neither Victims nor Executioners,* where he denounces the reciprocity of lies and murderous self-righteousness between communist and capitalist governments. He was tough minded in cutting through sentimentality and abstraction to get to reality on the level of human flesh and blood: after the 1956 Hungarian revolt he writes with irony echoing *The Fall,* "I am not one of those who long for the Hungarian people to take up arms again in an uprising doomed to be crushed under the eyes of an international society that will spare neither applause nor virtuous tears before returning to their slippers like football enthusiasts on Saturday evening after a big game" (*RRD,* p. 117). His judgments might have been faulty on occasion, but they nearly always, at least before the Algerian War, reflected the most scrupulous effort toward clarity, exactitude, fairness, and compassion.

Unfortunately, from today's perspective the sense his earlier journalism conveys that his responses could be trusted to ring true on any given issue diminishes somewhat in the mid-1950s. In his Algerian chronicles, excerpted in *Resistance, Rebellion, and Death,* he continued to defend the French colonial presence even as it became more and more evident that the course of history and justice was in opposition. His position was that independence would mean the persecution or expulsion of Frenchmen whose families had been native Algerians for generations and that Arab rule would cause Algeria to be drawn into the orbit of the United Arab

2. *The Press* (New York: Ballantine Books, 1964), pp. 21–22.

Republic and, indirectly, of Russia. His alternative, however, was a program of liberal reforms that in retrospect sounds quite paternalistic. When civil war broke out, he condemned the use of torture and repression by the French forces but refused to recognize the legitimacy of the Front for National Liberation or to acknowledge the same justification for Arab revolutionary violence that he did for Hungarian freedom fighters. In spite of—or perhaps because of—his principle of opposing violence on either side, his position in effect leaned toward support of the status quo, which entailed violent government efforts to put down the revolutionary movement. (His policy does continue to have its defenders, including Germaine Brée, who in *Camus and Sartre: Crisis and Commitment* [3] argues that he supported the more responsible Arab factions struggling for self-determination. Brée marshals numerous references in support of his general stance on Algeria, in rebuttal to his critics on the left such as Simone de Beauvoir [4] and Conor Cruise O'Brien.)

Camus's previous equal criticism of both sides in the Cold War lost its balance as he became increasingly apologetic for the West. This movement was largely understandable in light of the historical circumstances, following the Russian development of nuclear weapons, Berlin, Korea, the French defeat in Indochina, and Hungary, although other French intellectuals of the period including Sartre and his circle continued to place equal blame on the West for provocation and counterrevolutionary reactionism. Camus, like most American liberals of the period, was incredulous toward this position, but subsequent historians have tended to support it. Sartre's words to Camus today sound far more creditable than when he wrote them in 1952: "The Iron Curtain is only a mirror, where each half of the world reflects the other. Each turn of the screw *here* corresponds to a twist *there,* and both here and there, to finish, we are all both the screwers and the screwed. An American freeze, which is translated by an outburst of witch-hunting, provokes a Russian freeze, which perhaps will be translated by intensifying arms production and increasing the number of slave laborers." [5]

By the time of the Nobel Prize discourses in 1957 his rhetoric was tend-

3. *Camus and Sartre: Crisis and Commitment* (New York: Delta, 1972), pp. 151–53, 212–18.
4. See Beauvoir's *Force of Circumstance* (New York: G. P. Putnam's Sons, 1965), pp. 381–84; translation of *La Force des choses* (Paris: Gallimard, 1963).
5. "Reply to Albert Camus," in *Situations*, p. 65.

ing toward the self-righteous, pompous abstractions he had always condemned. This is most evident in "The Wager of Our Generation," one of several interviews that give the impression the questions were prefabricated by Camus, where he writes, "One may even have to fight a lie in the name of a quarter-truth. This is our situation at present. However, the quarter-truth contained in Western society is called liberty" (*RRD*, p. 189). Here he seems to be supporting all the simplistic propaganda about "the Free World," as though liberty was total in all capitalist countries and the degree of its absence invariable in all communist countries regardless of changing degrees in the Western threat. Yet, a few months later he contradicts himself: "For a hundred years a society of merchants ['has'] made an exclusive and unilateral use of liberty, looking upon it as a right rather than as a duty, and did not fear ['has not feared'] to use an ideal liberty, as often as it could ['has been able'], to justify a very real oppression" (*RRD*, p. 194). (Was O'Brien, in changing Camus's present perfect to simple past tense, waging the Cold War on the grammatical front?) In other words, the quarter-truth in Western society is, for all practical purposes, the freedom of the bourgeoisie to oppress others. His point here, as in the related piece "Bread and Freedom," is that Marxists misplaced their words when they claimed that freedom was a bourgeois hoax, "for it should have been said merely that bourgeois freedom was a hoax—and not all freedom" (*RRD*, p. 66)—but that bourgeois society's lip service to freedom at least leaves open more of a possibility for its true attainment than communist society's explicit disavowal of it. He might have said somewhat more accurately, then, that it is sometimes necessary to fight total slavery in the name of a quarter-liberty (so far as these glib percentage games have any value at all). The question he never satisfactorily answered, though, is whether defending that constantly varying partial degree of liberty also unavoidably entails defending the three quarters of lies and injustices that Camus acknowledged in bourgeois society, as well as the imperialism and counterrevolutionary aggression he was increasingly loath to acknowledge.

IV

It is important to note in Camus's favor that, while on international affairs his reasoning was becoming strained and his rhetoric hollow by the late fifties, on a domestic issue he could still, in 1957, write his most radically incisive political statement, "Reflections on the Guillotine." [6] First published as part of a book, *Réflexions sur la peine capitale,* alongside the French translation of Arthur Koestler's more documentary study of the problem in England, *Reflections on Hanging,* this is the single work that probably best epitomizes Camus's journalistic style, and indeed his entire art and thought. Here Camus marshals all his powers of novelistic and dramatic description and of straightforward journalistic exposition, heightened literarily by bristling irony, paradox, and aphorism and supported philosophically by his most maturely refined and concisely articulated metaphysical, political, and moral principles. The result is one of the most devastating polemics against capital punishment ever written.

Fifteen years after *The Stranger* he recapitulates the novel's motifs: his father's nausea after witnessing an execution, the agonies of the condemned man in the death cell, the arbitrary theatricality of courtroom rhetoric and variability of the verdict; then he continues beyond the end of *The Stranger* to describe actual executions, juxtaposing their barbaric reality to the euphemisms in which society inconsistently shrouds this purportedly exemplary ritual.

After supporting the visceral physical descriptions with a review of criminological data citing judicial errors and refuting defenses of capital punishment based on deterrence, he moves to the political plane, where in large part he follows a traditional socialist line of argument attributing blame for crime to the inequities of bourgeois society; however, he avoids the extreme of completely exonerating the criminal through Rousseauan sentimentality or rigidly Marxist determinism. With classical exactitude he delineates between social and individual responsibility:

> The instinct of preservation of societies, and hence of individuals, requires that individual responsibility be postulated and accepted without dreaming of an absolute indulgence that would amount to the death of all society. But the same reasoning must lead us to conclude that there never exists any total responsibility or, consequently, any

6. Beauvoir reports that Camus refused requests to read from "Reflections on the Guillotine" as a plea for clemency at the trial of an Arab revolutionary assassin in 1957 (*Force of Circumstance,* p. 381). Roger Quilliot, however, presents evidence that Camus did privately appeal to the court for clemency in this case and similarly interceded, publicly or privately, for several other condemned revolutionaries throughout the Algerian War (*Essais,* pp. 1844–47).

absolute punishment or reward. . . . The death penalty, which really neither provides an example nor assures distributive justice, simply usurps an exorbitant privilege by claiming to punish an always relative culpability by a definitive and irreparable punishment. [*RRD,* pp. 160–61]

In a second, more conservative, political line of argument he condemns the death penalty as an evil of statism:

In relation to crime, how can our civilization be defined? The reply is easy: for thirty years now, State crimes have been far more numerous than individual crimes. . . . Those who cause the most blood to flow are the same ones who believe they have right, logic, and history on their side.

Hence our society must now defend herself not so much against the individual as against the State. . . . Justice and expediency command the law to protect the individual against a State given over to the follies of sectarianism or of pride. "Let the State begin and abolish the death penalty" ought to be our rallying cry today.

Bloodthirsty laws, it has been said, make bloodthirsty customs. But any society eventually reaches a state of ignominy in which, despite every disorder, the customs never manage to be as bloodthirsty as the laws. [Pp. 174–75]

These lines were urgently applicable in the America of the late 1960s and early 1970s, not only to capital punishment but to military brutality in Vietnam and to the conflict between right-wing "law and order" and leftist appeals for restraint of police authority to kill.

Camus makes his most profound arguments when he puts his criminological and political points into a metaphysical perspective. (I am taking liberties with the essay's expository sequence, which is rather carelessly organized—one of its few faults.) He echoes the epistemological skepticism of *The Myth* and *The Stranger* in asserting that beyond the purely pragmatic aspects of judicial error and arbitrariness, a court surpasses the bounds of human wisdom in presuming to know, with the absolute certainty implied by the death sentence, what was in a man's mind and heart at the moment of crime (a tacit theme in *The Brothers Karamazov, An American Tragedy,* and *Native Son,* as well as *The Stranger*) or to judge irrevocably that he is incapable of rehabilitation or repentance: "There is a solidarity of all men in error and aberration. Must that solidarity operate for the tribunal and be denied the accused?" (p. 166).

He reiterates Dostoevsky's opposition to the death penalty on the grounds that it is a blasphemy against Christ: "The unbeliever cannot keep from thinking that men who have set at the center of their faith the staggering victim of a judicial error ought at least to hesitate before committing legal murder" (p. 171). The Church-State at least believes it is deferring final judgment of the criminal to God, but the State that no longer believes in God becomes a rival to both the murderer and the absurdity of nature in definitively cutting short his life. Whereas the Christian Dostoevsky condemns society for presuming to a level of judicial wisdom that only God possesses, Camus the agnostic condemns it precisely because in the apparent absence of a God no such level of wisdom is to be found anywhere in this absurd universe. In one of the many memorable aphorisms that sum up the essay and his entire work, he concludes, "Capital judgment upsets the only indisputable human solidarity—our solidarity against death" (p. 170).

7

The Myth and *The Rebel*: Diversity and Unity

I

The Myth of Sisyphus is Camus's most difficult work, particularly in the first, forty-eight-page sequence, "An Absurd Reasoning," which presents stylistic challenges similar to the lyrical essays—dense construction, digressive asides, elliptical jumps between sentences, cryptic aphorisms—and compounds them with a lengthily sustained, involved line of argument in a combination of philosophy and literary essay reminiscent of Kierkegaard or Nietzsche. The book is filled with nearly as many points of ambiguity as *The Stranger,* which would undoubtedly be a defect from a purely philosophical point of view but which makes it all the more engrossing as an aesthetic creation, embodying in its own structure the epistemological pluralism that comprises one aspect of the absurd.

Despite these difficulties, however, *The Myth* makes a strong initial impression, even on casual readers who may simply be struck by the incisiveness of many individual passages. Readers who are mature enough to have experienced a measure of disenchantment with life are also likely to feel the shock of recognition in the author's enumeration of the absurd's various aspects, which are nonspecific enough to prompt everyone to fill in examples from his personal brushes with absurdity. Perhaps you see a man killed (a rare event for well-insulated, middle-class American whites between World War II and the rash of violence initiated in the 1960s with the assassination of President Kennedy, the Vietnam War, ghetto riots, and college campus rebellion) or hear about the sudden death of a youthful friend or relative. A jarring auto accident on the way to a party or sports event wipes out your anticipation of it and exposes the triviality of such diversions. One day you are overwhelmed by the superhuman magnitude of mountains or the sea and by the indifference to human existence of this natural world that you have been accustomed to viewing as a stage set existing for purposes of your recreation. You witness abdominal surgery and see human life reduced to an animal organism, a slab of beef on the butcher's block. You suddenly perceive a sign of aging in yourself, with its chilling premonition of what you will look like at seventy—or when you are dead. You feel the eerie sensation of perceiving yourself as an Other when you see your picture on film or hear your recorded voice. You find yourself deserted in sickness or adversity, realize the indifference of most people to anyone else's suffering but their own, and make the infuriating discovery that the rest of society goes on doing business as usual, oblivious to your personal calamities.

Another factor contributing to the book's emotional power is its dramatic techniques like the buildup of narrative tension and dynamic modulations in tone. Camus displays his flair for drama in the startling opening —"There is but one truly serious philosophical problem, and that is suicide" (*Myth,* p. 3)—and in the way he systematically demolishes all the illusory values that sustain conventional life, then amid this seeming wasteland builds a new scale of values consistent with the absurd in which "everything resumes its place and the absurd world is reborn in all its splendor and diversity" (p. 48). *The Myth* shares with the fiction and lyrical essays Camus's characteristic of rising in climactic paragraphs to a rhapsodic tone and intensely poetic diction, as for example in the descriptions of the absurd man's lucid, polar night on page 48 or Sisyphus's pride in his fate and in his underworld memories of the beauties of this world on page 91, which recall Meursault's scene with the chaplain.

A dramatic shift in tone comes again when, after the relative abstractness and impersonality of "An Absurd Reasoning," Camus brings his themes down to human scale, in the manner of Kierkegaard or Gide, in the character sketches of Don Juan, the actor, the conqueror, and later Sisyphus. His Don Juan, an absurd hero in the guises both of seducer and blasphemer, ranks with his most appealing fictional characters. Camus, obviously a kindred male soul, rescues Don Juan from his associations by the romantic movement with insatiable questing and by modern psychiatry with misogyny: " 'At last,' exclaims one of [his women], 'I have given you love.' Can we be surprised that Don Juan laughs at this? 'At last? No,' he says, 'but once more' " (pp. 51–52). ['Enfin? non, dit-il, mais une fois de plus' (*Essais*, p. 152).] Camus adds to the legend a touching end: the commander's statue fails to keep his dinner date, and Don Juan is damned not to fire and brimstone but to a ripe old age in a senior citizen's home.

The Myth's ambiguities begin with the central term itself, "the absurd," partly because Camus isn't entirely consistent in its usage, partly because he considers it essentially an indefinable, emotional quality, such as beauty: "Solely appearances can be enumerated and the climate make itself felt" (p. 9). Still it is puzzling, when the climate unquestionably does make itself felt, that it is so difficult to define even a common denominator covering this complex of appearances. One might venture to say, in the broadest possible terms, that the various aspects enumerated in "Absurd Walls" are all experienced as an alienation from or breakdown in our habitual patterns or expectations of life. These patterns and expectations, then, are absurd in the sense of being illusory, ephemeral, or parochial. And the absurd man is one who lucidly recognizes that his normal routine is subject to collapse at any moment and is steeled to go on living after that collapse—indeed, to see it become his routine and to thrive in a permanent state of alienation.

The book's expository structure also contributes to several ambiguities, some doubtlessly intentional, some probably not, that tend to mislead unwary readers. The shock opening leads one to expect a discourse on suicide in general, despite Camus's subsequent qualification that he is only dealing with suicide as a response to the absurd. The expectation of a comprehensive discussion of suicide is furthered by the statement in the 1955 preface to the American edition, "Even if one does not believe in God, suicide is not legitimate" (p. v), which also leads one to expect that the question of God's existence will be more central than it is. In the essay itself the question does not arise until pages 24–25, where Camus sneaks it in by the back door in describing Jaspers's and Chestov's leap to faith as an evasion of the absurd. Considering the importance of God's existence in the subsequent discussions of Kierkegaard and Dostoevsky, in "Absurd Freedom" and the appendix on Kafka, Camus could have placed the problem more effectively in the book's organizational framework by including it among the aspects of the absurd in "Absurd Walls."

There are several more organizational weaknesses that make the line of argument unnecessarily difficult to follow while lacking sufficient literary merit to redeem them: the jumps back and forth between metaphysical and epistemological absurdity in "Philosophical Suicide" and "Absurd Freedom"; Camus's failure to expand the reference to Heidegger in "Absurd Walls" into "Philosophical Suicide" as he does with the other philosophers he refers to there; the digressions on the existential philosophers and Husserl in "Philosophical Suicide," which are too sketchy to do justice to any of them but long enough to distract from the main line of argument; and finally, the circuitous exposition of the argument in favor of preserving the absurd centered in "Philosophical Suicide" and "Absurd Freedom," which is one of the most ambiguous and difficult points in the book even when it is reassembled into a more straightforward order—as I shall now attempt to do.

II

This argument can be interpreted in at least two distinct ways. The first centers on the paradox that the absurd is an evil, but that in order to oppose it we must preserve it: "What seems to me so obvious, even against me, I must support" (*Myth,* p. 38). The human condition is inextricably tied to the absurd, like Sisyphus and his rock; there is no escaping the absurd without destroying life itself. The paradox can perhaps best be clarified by comparing the absurd to a disease, which can only be treated so long as the patient remains alive. Killing the patient eliminates the disease rather than directly combating it and in fact signals its victory. Suicide, then, is a surrender to the disease of the absurd, eliminating the absurdity of one's particular life instead of keeping it alive so that it can be opposed: "It may be thought that suicide follows revolt—but wrongly. For it does not represent the logical outcome of revolt. It is just the contrary by the consent it presupposes" (p. 40).

If one decides that it is worthwhile to combat the absurd (only a hypothetical proposition at this point in the argument, since the value of revolt has not yet been established), he must, first, do everything he can to stay alive. Second, he must fully acknowledge the truth of life's absurdity rather than evading it through the existential leap to faith in God (Chestov, Kierkegaard, Dostoevsky, Jaspers) or through a total irrationalism that destroys the intellectual faculties necessary to perceive the absurd. Finally, since the absurd is by definition a state of mind, existing only through the mental act of perceiving it, one must not only acknowledge the absurd on principle but must apply this acknowledgment by constantly either thinking explicitly about the absurd or making his every action consistent with its terms, without giving in to the temptation toward mindless distraction, Pascal's *le divertissement*. To stop thinking about the absurd is to kill it, the intellectual equivalent of suicide: "Living is keeping the absurd alive. Keeping it alive is, above all, contemplating it. Unlike Eurydice, the absurd dies only when we turn away from it" (p. 40).

These, then, are the conditions one must meet *if* he judges that the absurd is worth preserving. Its worth still remains to be established at this point, when the question becomes "whether I can live with what I know and with that alone" (p. 30). The answer comes in "Absurd Freedom" with the affirmation of the values of revolt, freedom, and passion summarized in chapter 3 above. This interpretation, then, simply establishes maintaining awareness of the absurd as a precondition for revolting against it, whose value is established elsewhere—in contrast to the alternate interpretation, which follows, according to which maintaining absurd awareness becomes a value, even an ethical necessity, in itself.

A second dimension to the foregoing argument, more complex and ambiguous logically, originates on page 5: "The principle can be established that for a man who does not cheat, what he believes to be true must determine his action. Belief in the absurdity of existence must then dictate his conduct." Camus in effect is making intellectual truthfulness into a moral imperative and another value to be found within the boundaries of the absurd. Since the absurd is not inherent in the objective world but survives only as an attitude within the human mind, adhering to the truth of the absurd entails keeping both the mind and its awareness of the absurd alive:

And it is by this elementary criterion that I judge the notion of the absurd [which he has distinguished on page 21 from the unarticulated, emotional experience of it] to be essential and consider that it can stand as the first of my truths. . . . If I judge that a thing is true, I must preserve it. If I attempt to solve a problem, at least I must not by that very solution conjure away one of the terms of the problem. For me the sole datum is the absurd. [O'Brien's translation inexplicably leaves out the following sentence here: "The problem is where to proceed from it and if suicide must be deduced from this absurd" (*Essais,* p. 121).] The first and, after all, the only condition of my inquiry is to preserve the very thing that crushes me, consequently to respect what I consider essential in it. I have just defined it as a confrontation and an unceasing struggle. [P. 23]

He repeats the same argument on page 38, concluding, "And what constitutes the basis of that conflict, of that break between the world and my mind, but the awareness of it? If therefore I want to preserve it, I can through a constant awareness, ever revived, ever alert."

This apparent attempt by Camus to demonstrate the logical necessity of preserving the absurd has provoked refutations by several critics and philosophers, including John Cruickshank and Herbert Hochberg. Hochberg claims that Camus makes an "unfortunate play on the notion of preserving, or alternatively, denying a truth or a fact. Need one do more than point out that it is quite one thing to deny that some one has a wart by stating that it is not so; it is quite another thing to 'deny' that fact by removing the wart. Of course, in Camus' case one removes the disease by removing the patient, but the point is still the same."[1] I do not think that the point *is* still the same or that Camus does in fact fall into this fallacy, even though he at times appears to.

If Camus meant his assertion "If I judge a thing is true, I must preserve it" to be categorical, as Hochberg takes it to be, it would obviously be fallacious: although a wart really exists, nothing obliges one not to remove it. We can infer, however, that Camus's assertion is not universal, but applies only to the unique truth of the absurd. The wart still exists even if one stops thinking about it or denies that it exists, but the absurd continues to exist only through thinking about it. It lies, for example, not in the irrationality of the natural world or fate alone, which would continue to be facts even if I were not aware of them, but in the tension between "my appetite for the absolute and for unity and the impossibility of reducing this world to a rational and reasonable principle" (p. 38); it does not lie in the imminence of my death alone, which likewise will still be fact even if I stop thinking about it, but in the anxiety created between my recognition of that inevitability and my innate sense of and craving for immortality. All I need to do to end the absurdity of my particular

1. "Albert Camus and the Ethic of Absurdity," *Ethics,* Spring 1965, p. 92.

life is to stop thinking about it—intellectual suicide. But doing so is to betray Camus's earlier principle of always acting in accordance with what reasoning consciousness judges to be true, i.e., that the authentic mental state is that of the absurd.

This syllogistic argument, more formally contrived than most of Camus's thought, does have an aura of being sophistic even if it isn't, and its conclusion barely carries enough emotional force to make it worth the mental gymnastics demanded to grasp it. Assuming that the argument is logically sound, all it really ends up saying is that intellectual honesty favors maintaining the absurd consciousness, all other things being equal. Intellectual integrity alone, however, would be a shaky basis for remaining alive if the absurd condition were so painful, or even barren, otherwise that it eclipsed the gratifications of integrity. What really redeems his argument is his subsequent affirmation of the values within the absurd —freedom, revolt, and passion—which provide reasons for not committing suicide that are emotionally far more persuasive.

Logicians may challenge Camus's line of reasoning, or at least my account of it, and I confess that having wrestled with this book about once a year for a dozen years I have changed my interpretation and evaluation of Camus's argument—sometimes agreeing with Hochberg—with every rereading, often several times during one rereading. But all of this only indicates that from a literary viewpoint it is only secondarily important whether we finally judge his logic to be completely valid or not. What is most important is the argument's—and the book's—enigmatic power to engage the reader's mind protractedly over a span of years. Camus has once again constructed an aesthetic labyrinth, a verbal objective correlative for that absurd world which "resembles the data of experience in that it is both infinitely simple and infinitely complicated" (p. 23).

III

After what we have already seen of Camus's practice of balancing metaphysical with sociopolitical themes in different works, it should scarcely be necessary to reiterate that the most common criticism of *The Myth* by left-wing critics, that it deals with existence only on the metaphysical plane to the neglect of social reality, is based on an ill-informed consideration of this work, and sometimes *The Stranger,* in isolation from

Camus's total creation. In a footnote near the beginning of the book, Camus makes it clear that he is purposely restricting his present scope: "Let us not miss this opportunity to point out the relative character of this essay. Suicide may indeed be related to much more honorable considerations—for example, the political suicides of protest, as they were called, during the Chinese revolution" (p. 5). Nevertheless, it is necessary to ask whether *The Myth* is consistent with radically critical political thought even while excluding it.

As his aesthetic theory has indicated, Camus's writing generally does not convey a highly developed sense of specific social or historical situation. Although in his reportage he did criticize the inequities of class society, in his fiction, drama, and literary and philosophical essays he purposely strove for universal truths even when he located them in recognizable social settings. The price he paid was a certain loss of fidelity to those specifics of existence that vary enormously between different social strata and historical moments. The gap left by the absence of these specifics can be remarked even in the ostensibly asocial, ahistorical world of *The Myth*. The very awareness of metaphysical absurdity, resulting from a breakdown in habitual routine and expectations, is a bourgeois privilege, even with all its attendant anxieties. Exploited or unemployed workers, colonized or ghettoized peoples, the victims of war cannot even afford the luxury of habits and expectations to be alienated from; absurd alienation is their habitual condition. Thus Norman Mailer, in "The White Negro: Superficial Reflections on the Hipster," describes the Negro as the American existentialist:

> Any Negro who wishes to live must live with danger from his first day, and no experience can ever be casual to him, no Negro can saunter down a street with any real certainty that violence will not visit him on his walk. The cameos of security for the average white: mother and the home, job and the family, are not even a mockery to millions of Negroes; they are impossible.[2]

On the other hand, there are more implications for social reality in *The Myth* than granted by critics like the German Marxist Ernst Fischer, who chastises "writers, ranging from Camus to Beckett, who set out to divorce man from society, to dissolve his identity and to wrap him in

2. *Advertisements for Myself* (New York: G. P. Putnam, Berkeley Medallion, 1966), p. 314.

mystery as the agent of 'eternal being' and 'formless original forces.' Any man is more than the mere mask of a social character. But the tendency to turn him into a hieroglyphic in a play of cosmic mysteries, to blot out his social as well as his individual face in a mystical archaic fog, leads to nothingness."[3] I find Fischer's characterization wholly appropriate to Beckett but not Camus. As indicated in my previous chapters, *The Myth* and *The Stranger* (which Fischer seems to be referring to more specifically) already contain implications that, followed to their logical conclusions, lead directly to the social philosophy of *The Rebel, The Plague,* and *The Just Assassins.*

The Myth first points out the absurd insignificance of each individual's subjective consciousness, then asserts its irreplaceable importance. Once we affirm every individual consciousness as an absolute value, we become bound to seek a social system that promotes maximal length, intensity, and freedom for each individual's life. Hence we must oppose war, capital punishment, and any ideology that subordinates human flesh and blood to abstractions such as nationalism or bourgeois propriety. On its epistemological level, *The Myth*'s exhortation for the absurd man constantly to follow the dictates of truth and to challenge the inscrutability of the universe with his utmost capacity for lucidity carries over into Camus's later notions of the artist's and intellectual's responsibility to pit their understanding against the equally absurd enigmas of contemporary politics and to oppose political lies and euphemisms that obfuscate carnal truth and separate those whom absurd solitudes should unite. *The Stranger,* too, tacitly criticizes bourgeois verbal abstractions and arbitrary restraints on individual life and liberty, notwithstanding Meursault's utter lack of political consciousness as such. The primacy of fleshly reality in *The Myth* and *The Stranger* constitutes the matrix for the explicit anticapitalism of "Create Dangerously":

> For about a century we have been living in a society that is not even the society of money (gold can arouse carnal passions) but that of the abstract symbols of money. The society of merchants can be defined as a society in which things disappear in favor of signs. When a ruling class measures its fortunes, not by the acre of land or the ingot of gold, but by the number of figures corresponding ideally to a certain

3. *The Necessity of Art: A Marxist Approach,* p. 99.

number of exchange operations, it thereby condemns itself to setting a certain kind of humbug at the center of its experience and its universe. A society founded on signs is, in its essence, an artificial society in which man's carnal truth is handled as something artificial. [*RRD*, pp. 193–94]

This far in his thinking, Camus is quite at one with Marxist denunciations of bourgeois society for its wage slavery, verbal mystifications, alienating separation of individuals in lonely crowds, reification of human beings and their subordination to commodity fetishism that rationalizes war, capital punishment, and police shooting of petty larcenists. His disagreements with what he considered doctrinaire Marxists and the Communist party come at later stages of his political philosophy, in *The Rebel*. Camus's thought, in sum, is more authentically dialectical than Fischer's in his fragmentary account of Camus, although their general aesthetics are quite similar. The sophisticated Marxist should be able to see in *The Myth*, as well as *The Stranger*, the generation of theses and antitheses that will be resolved in the syntheses of *The Rebel*.

IV

Although *The Rebel* is three times as long as *The Myth* and demands more historical and literary background from the reader, it is easier to follow because Camus holds to a straight line of exposition and strives on principle for clarity rather than ambiguity—a principle that is betrayed by Bower's clumsy, obfuscating translation. Camus does maintain the customary ambiguity of his titles in *L'Homme révolté*, which translates either as "Man in Revolt" or "The Revolted [or 'disgusted'] Man." The essay's artistic complexity is mainly contained in its monumental structure and a world view synthesizing metaphysics, political and literary history and theory. In lieu of his projected 1500-page "The System," it is the closest approximation to his *summa*, encompassing virtually all aspects of his formal thought and all the stages in the dialectical development of his themes.

Critical appreciation of the book's total scope has been impeded because its appearance in 1951, at the height of the Cold War, resulted in a nearly exclusive focus by Francis Jeanson and Sartre in *Les Temps modernes* and other critics on Camus's attack against Hegelian-Marxian dialectical philosophy and the political history of communism, which takes up only seventy-five of three hundred pages. The Jeanson-Camus-Sartre exchange matched three highly intelligent and farsighted opponents on the central political issues of our time and still retains its urgent importance for Americans today (although unfortunately at this writing only Sartre's reply has been translated here; Camus's letter to *Les Temps modernes* was reprinted as "Révolte et servitude" in *Actuelles II* and *Essais,* pp. 754–74). The political themes, however, will be considered here only in their due proportion to the complete work as a literary essay.

In some ways *The Rebel*'s ideological weaknesses are literary strengths. Jeanson, in fact, charged that its structure was so elaborate and its style so elegant that the political issues became subordinated to a literary virtuosity calculated to win approval in bourgeois literary circles. Camus in turn objected to the implication that a polished style must be a sign of cultural reactionism. Undoubtedly, Camus's vast syntheses, categories, and polarities indicate intellectual oversimplifications, especially in contrast to the essay style of the more recondite Sartre, who is less inclined to reduce ideas to clear-cut dualities. Sartre's counterstatement to *The Rebel* in political theory, *Critique of Dialectical Reason,* required the projection of two large, densely written volumes; the one volume that has appeared, however, like much of Sartre's writing and that of his associate Beauvoir, is open to the opposite criticism, that it is excessively protracted, with repetitious and obscure stretches. Camus's clarity, conciseness, and judicious editing in almost all his works at least constitute a persuasive case for his belief in the autonomous value of artful literary style.

One recent American critic, Leo Bersani, has gone so far as to say that *The Rebel* "makes no sense at all except as a bizarre and unsuccessful stylistic exercise in the lyricism of abstract antinomies." [4] Even as hyperbole, this is an extremely glib dismissal of a work that can be profitably studied over many years for its unique application in our times of a classical humanistic perspective to the most pressing modern literary and political disorders. (Bersani compares Camus disadvantageously to Samuel Beckett, Alain Robbe-Grillet and other French New Novelists, as well as to recent structuralist critics. These writers may well have superseded Camus in abstruse thought or literary technique—they are often, in

4. *Balzac to Beckett: Center and Circumference in French Fiction,* p. 262.

fact, far more abstract than Bersani claims Camus is—but they have not invalidated his common-sense fidelity to the immediate, fundamental truths of individual existence.) Whatever the drawbacks of *The Rebel*'s massively symmetrical structure, it effectively underscores the theme of man's perpetual passion for unity, forming an organizational counterpart to the reflection of absurd pluralism in *The Myth*'s fragmented exposition.

The introduction is one of the key passages of his entire works, encapsulating the transition between the phase of the absurd and that of rebellion. Picking up from where *The Myth* leaves off, Camus moves from the problem of suicide to that of murder. Although he does not mention the titles of his earlier works, he implicitly contrasts the nihilistic implications of the absurd, those followed by Meursault and Caligula, with the affirmative implications in *The Myth,* whose line of argument, if followed accurately and to its end, rejects nihilistic suicide and now by extension rejects nihilistic murder as well: "To say that life is absurd, the conscience must be alive. How is it possible, without making remarkable concessions to one's desire for comfort, to preserve exclusively for oneself the benefits of such a process of reasoning? From the moment that life is recognized as good, it becomes good for all men" (*Rebel,* p. 6).

As a corollary to Camus's thesis of the inconsistency of deducing nihilism from the absurd, he adds the self-contradictions implicit in metaphysical and epistemological absurdity discussed in chapter 3 above, the point of which in this context is that if absurdist despair neither ends in suicide nor is surpassed it runs the danger of turning into a pleasure-giving pose in which "the absurd, which claims to express man in his solitude, really makes him live in front of a mirror" (p. 8). Two pages later he expresses the necessity of transcending the absurd similarly: "The mirror, with its fixed stare, must be broken." (The mirror imagery, of course, alludes back to *Caligula* and ahead to *The Fall,* although the connotations are slightly different in the various contexts. Caligula's mirror symbolizes his nihilistic moral solipsism and is shattered at his death. In "The Dandies' Rebellion" it represents not only the narcissistic *Schadenfreude* of the romantic agony but also the dependence of the dandyish rebel on an audience: "He can only be sure of his own existence by finding it in the expression of others' faces. Other people are his mirror" [*Rebel,* p. 51]. The latter description also fits Clamence, who uses other people, especially the confidant of his confession, as a mirror for his self-satisfaction before the fall and his self-laceration afterward.)

Absurdist narcissism itself can lead to murder, either actively, through "tragic dilettantism" in which "human lives become counters in a game" (*Rebel,* p. 5), or passively, through self-absorbed paralysis: "not to act at all, which amounts to at least accepting the murder of others, with perhaps mild reservations about the imperfection of the human race" (p. 5). Furthermore, in the mid-twentieth century nihilism not only is an individual creed but has been institutionalized by governments, which commit murder on a wider scale than ever before in history. If the absurd man is to rebel against death, then his revolt must be not only metaphysical but political, directed against legalized murder by the State. The detailed history of how nihilism evolved and turned from an individual, metaphysical philosophy into a collective, political one and the problem of how to revolt against a murderous history without becoming a murderer oneself will comprise the main substance of *The Rebel.*

v

"Metaphysical Rebellion" (*Rebel,* pp. 23–104) stands by itself as a significant work of literary criticism, a cogent history of this theme from the Prometheus of Aeschylus through the surrealist movement. Camus's criticisms of individual authors are sometimes biased or superficial, but they are all interesting for the insights they give into his own thought.

"The Sons of Cain" outlines the values of moderation he admired in classical Greece, in contrast to the excesses of modern romanticism. He denies that rebellion in Greek literature was truly metaphysical, since it was directed only against individual gods who were themselves fallible, not against the whole of creation or nature, which was impersonal: "The acme of excess to the Greek mind was to beat the sea with rods—an act of insanity worthy only of barbarians" (p. 27). Furthermore, the tragic hero's outrage against the capriciousness of destiny is ultimately tempered by his enlightened resignation to the world's fatality: "The Greek mind has two aspects and in its meditations almost always re-echoes, as counterpoint to its most tragic melodies, the eternal words of Oedipus, who, blind and desperate, recognizes that all is for the best. Affirmation counterbalances negation" (p. 27). For the romantics, on the other hand, fatal-

ism dictates all-or-nothing total negation. Qualifying his affinities to epi-
cureanism and stoicism in his other works, he remarks that Epicurus,
Lucretius, and the Roman stoics, in their ascetic minimizing of life's
pleasures, mark a transition toward the modern disbalanced preoccupation with death over life.

He touches only lightly on most of the Christian era, then focuses on
the eighteenth to twentieth centuries, the same period he will cover at
length in "Historical Rebellion." The Marquis de Sade in "A Man of
Letters," the romantic hero in "The Dandies' Rebellion," Ivan Karamazov
in "The Rejection of Salvation," and Maldoror in "Lautréamont and Banality" are, like Caligula, "compelled to do evil by [their] nostalgia for
an unrealizable good" (p. 48). Revenge against the absurdity of the universe or a murderous God impels them all to become rivals in murder,
and while Nietzsche, in "Absolute Affirmation," replaces the very concepts of good and evil with his great yea-saying to all of creation, "to
say yes to everything supposes that one says yes to murder" (p. 76). Furthermore, romantic rebellion tends to become a platform for poseurs who,
congenitally deficient in normal emotions, can only fulfill themselves in
excessive ones: in a love that is perverse, as with Sade, or ill fated, as
with "the Byronic hero, incapable of love, or capable only of an impossible love" (p. 49); in paroxysms of narcissistic despair; in mystical tran-
scendentalism or apocalyptic destruction that purports to transfigure the
world but actually leads only to annihilation, as with Lautréamont, Rimbaud, and the more extreme expressions of surrealism. He does acknowledge that some writers recognized the sterility of the romantic pose and
turned from narcissism toward political commitment, in a passage that
is worth quoting as another example of Bower's loose and confusing
translations: "Between the times of the eighteenth-century eccentric and
the 'conquerors' of the twentieth century, Byron and Shelley are already
fighting, though only ostensibly, for freedom" (p. 53). [More accurately,
'Between Rameau's nephew and the "conquerors" of the twentieth century, Byron and Shelley are already fighting, even though ostentatiously,
for freedom.']

The title of "The Dandies' Rebellion" alludes to Baudelaire's 1853 essay
"The Dandy," one of the subjects of the engravings of Constantin Guys
that he interprets in *The Painter of Modern Life*. Baudelaire's essay coins
the term "the cult of oneself" to describe romantic narcissism, as well as

perceiving the paradoxical theatricality of dandyism's nonconformity—
"It is, above all, a burning need to acquire originality, within the apparent bounds of convention"—and its exaltation of what Camus calls
tragic dilettantism—"A dandy can never indulge in anything vulgar. If
he committed a crime, he would perhaps not be too upset about it; but
if this crime had some trivial cause, his disgrace would be irreparable."[5]
While Guys's and Baudelaire's dandy is the vestigial aristocrat in bourgeois society, Camus applies the idea to the romantic movement in general
as well as to absurdist nihilism. Since anguish is the strongest emotion
that the romantic rebel's peculiar temperament enables him to feel—or is
at least a more dramatic one than positive forms of revolt—he develops
a vested interest in maintaining it: "Pain, at this stage, is acceptable only
if it is incurable" (p. 50). If the spontaneous overflow of powerful
feelings can only be inspired by death and despair, so be it, whether one
participates in the carnage actively or only vicariously. While the romantics' taste for apocalypse is expressed only in literature, theirs are
"desires that a later generation will assuage in extermination camps"
(p. 51). Thus, for all the distortions in the Nazis' preemption of romantic
Geist, their nihilism can be seen as a logical though perverse extension of
this tendency in the romantic literary tradition.

Although the unhealthy tendencies that Camus criticizes may only be
deviations rather than the essence of romanticism, this analysis remains
one of his most astute points, appearing as it did in the America of the
mid-1950s when it was applicable to a neoromantic revival in the American drug cult, beat writing, and Actors Studio theater, and in French
New Wave cinema. His attack follows lines similar to Irving Babbitt's
Rousseau and Romanticism (a book that strongly resembles *The Rebel*
in its style and classical humanist viewpoint, aside from Babbitt's conservative social philosophy), Denis de Rougemont's *Love in the Western
World,* and Leslie Fiedler's *Love and Death in the American Novel.* Out
of these works emerges a pattern of insights to the romantic psychology:
idealized or unattainable love may conceal an incapacity for real love,
replacing palpable objects of desire with infinite, indeterminate longing.
An excess of sexual or other emotions is likely to stem not from satiation
with normal ones but from a deficiency of them, the frustrated passions
frequently being channeled perversely into necrophilic violence. The

5. In *The Essence of Laughter* (New York: Meridian Books, 1956), p. 48.

longing for apocalyptic transformation of the world can become an
indolent evasion of the effort necessary to make intellectual distinctions
and value judgments or to revolt directly against clear and present evils.
And the quest for mystical transcendence of the ego may be a form of
intellectual suicide, leading only to annihilation of the ego or a vegetable
mentality as banal as the conformist mentality against which it rebels.

VI

The parallel between metaphysical and historical rebellion in Part Three
is an elaboration on a theme from *The Brothers Karamazov,* expressed in
a passage that Camus quotes on page 60: "If Aliosha had come to the
conclusion that neither God nor immortality existed, he would immediately have become an atheist and a socialist. For socialism is not only a
question of the working classes; it is above all, in its contemporary incarnation, a question of atheism, a question of the tower of Babel, which
is constructed without God's help, not to reach to the heavens, but to
bring the heavens down to earth."

The anti-Church-State revolutions that, since 1789, have been aimed
at establishing earthly justice and freedom have, like nihilistic metaphysical rebellion, lost sight of their affirmative origins and ended up reestab-
lishing tyranny and murder on an even wider and more institutionalized
scale through capital punishment and total war. In the Western European
democracies, Camus claims, this has happened for the same reasons he
has given in the lyrical essays: the life-denying bureaucracy of industrial
capitalism and the hubris of governments that, arrogantly believing themselves capable of attaining total justice, have stifled individual liberty.
Under communism he attributes the suppression of freedom to betrayal
of the revolution by nihilistic leaders, to Soviet Russia's aping of capitalist
technocracy, and most importantly to Marxist-Leninist utopianism that
sacrifices present liberties toward the end of a classless society in a future
that turns out to be perpetually receding. He regards the Soviet five-year-
plan mentality as the direct offshoot of Hegelian and Marxian dialectical
theory. Although he largely agrees with Marx's critique of bourgeois
society and, as we have seen, has certain affinities to Marxism in the
dialectical turn of his mind, he considers dialectical materialism equivocal
in claiming to be at once deterministic and messianic, scientific and

hortatory, thus lending itself to the expedient, self-contradicting shifts in Communist party line under Stalin.

What emerges from this analysis is in effect a theory of historical absurdity parallel to the metaphysical absurdity of *The Myth,* in which the course of history is unpredictable and capricious and in which aspiration for political progress is virtually doomed to frustration if not to utter betrayal or reversal. What path is left open, then, for the authentic historical rebel that is comparable to the absurd man's life-affirming options for revolt?

Before answering this question, or perhaps on the way to answering it, he makes a detour into "Rebellion and Art," Part Four. This apparent disruption of the book's expository development becomes justified as art and the vocation of the artist emerge as one model for antinihilistic revolt. "Rebellion and the Novel" and "Rebellion and Style" respond to "Metaphysical Rebellion"; here the writer, rather than simply venting his spite against the disunity and obscurity of the universe, corrects creation through literary form, style, and lucidity. And "Creation and Revolution" is a delineation of the artist as historical rebel that anticipates the "Artist and His Time" interviews and Stockholm speeches. Against bloodshed and bureaucratic dehumanization the creator opposes his love of life and beauty. Camus gives art wider significance by using the figure of the artist, somewhat in the manner of Pater, Wilde, or Gide, to exemplify a creative attitude in all realms of life, in the same way that he equates the artist and lover in "The Enigma." He reiterates the theme common in Marxist literary criticism (although, perhaps with a touch of Cold War squeamishness, failing to acknowledge it) that the integration of form and content in art can provide a model for an organic society reversing the division of labor imposed by industrial capitalism. He again echoes Marx in his ideal of a postindustrial society that will erase capitalism's alienating distinctions between manual and mental labor, work and artistic creation: "Industrial society will open the way to a new civilization only by restoring to the worker the dignity of a creator; in other words, by making him apply his interest and his intelligence as much to the work itself as to what it produces" (p. 273).

From *The Myth, Neither Victims nor Executioners,* and Tarrou's monologue in *The Plague,* one could deduce that Camus's conclusion in Part Five, "Thought at the Meridian" ['La Pensée de midi'], would express a philosophy of resistance to historical absurdity, an opposition of absolute nonviolent revolt against murder, whether sanctioned by individual nihilism, the State, or revolution. But what we get is a modification of his earlier pacifism. Whereas in 1946 he avowed, "I could no longer hold to any truth which might oblige me, directly or indirectly, to demand a man's life" (*NVNE,* p. 3), now he concedes, "In the world today, only a philosophy of eternity could justify non-violence" (*Rebel,* p. 287) and "Absolute non-violence is the negative basis of slavery and its acts of violence" (p. 291). Complicity in killing in a just revolt or war of self-defense cannot be completely avoided without lapsing into a quietism that acquiesces to killing by the prevailing powers, but limits can be set that establish a reasonable culpability: "Authentic acts of rebellion will only consent to take up arms for institutions that limit violence, not for those that codify it. A revolution is not worth dying for unless it assures the immediate suppression of the death penalty; not worth going to prison for unless it refuses in advance to pass sentence without fixed terms" (p. 292).

One point on which his position does follow directly from *The Myth* is his rejection of communist (as well as Christian) messianism that defers social gratifications until the millennium of the classless society: "Real generosity toward the future lies in giving all to the present" (p. 304). As practical alternatives to present political establishments and revolutionary movements, he suggests the models of the Scandinavian republics, syndicalism, the trade-union movement—broadly, a democratic, decentralized socialism similar to that advocated by other mentors of the New Left in the late 1950s and 1960s such as C. Wright Mills, Erich Fromm, Herbert Marcuse, and Paul Goodman. And as a precondition to any specific program he urges a regenerated political ethic scaled to humane principles rather than expediency, to individuals rather than masses, plus a renaissance of the classical sense of proportion and limits without which both established powers and revolutionaries are fated to continue the cycle of violence and counterviolence until it ends in the apocalypse of nuclear war. Differences between the ideologies of capitalism, communism, and socialism are secondary; no ideology can be valid unless its exponents have the capacity to exercise a measured balance between means and ends, present and future needs, justice and freedom, the individual and the community.

Within a broad, humanistic perspective, Camus's analysis retains several valuable lessons. First, the course of history can be mercurial and inscrutable, which should serve to caution though not completely discourage revolutionary proponents. (This argument can, incidentally, also be applied to established powers and thus turned against Camus's own anticommunism and that of the more rigid Cold Warriors who failed to take adequate account of the possible flux in the communist world after the death of Stalin.) No matter how frustrated revolutionary hopes may be, men will always retain the freedom to resist political tyranny even if they cannot overthrow it. Finally, his call for a revival of classical temperance reasserts precious values that, simple as they may seem, are indeed woefully absent from the prevailing political and cultural mentality of the twentieth century. While his appeal for a sense of restraint in governmental violence may appear on the face of it to be a rather vague or mild prescription, going into the 1970s one had only to look around at Indochina, the Middle East, Czechoslovakia, American police actions in ghettos, prisons, and college campuses, or listen to the theoreticians of nuclear overkill and a perpetually escalating arms race, to recognize that governments on all sides, far from having heeded Camus's program, were still prone to use violence as a first rather than last resort.

The Rebel's overall political perspective, however, in its association of all contemporary revolution with the U.S.S.R., has become somewhat dated since the late fifties with the breakup of communism as a monolithic world power and the shift in the focus of the Cold War to Third World liberation fronts. These changes have lent support to the position of Jeanson, Sartre, and subsequent leftist critics of Camus, which may be briefly summarized as follows. His understanding of Hegelian and Marxian dialectical philosophy is rather shallow. Sartre tells him, "I have at least this in common with Hegel. You have not read either of us."[6] While his account of Stalinist manipulations of dialectical thought is accurate, it is highly disputable whether Stalinism is the logical consequence of Marxism or a perversion of it. Camus closed himself off from the possibility that some aspects of dialectical materialism were still viable. In this, he may have had the bias of the marginal bourgeois and colonial who feels his life to be relatively free from class determination, hence is reluctant to acknowledge an element of dialectical inexorability

6. *Situations*, p. 66.

in the economic necessity for European and American capitalism to expand imperialistically into Africa, Asia, and Latin America—and in the consequent violent revolt of the colonized. Instead, he would prefer to believe that these forces might be reversed by hortatory appeals for liberal humanitarianism.

It is all very well, say Camus's opponents, for intellectuals to exhort those in power to exercise restraint, but the latter are little inclined to be influenced by humanitarian appeals. This being the case, it is even less meaningful to prescribe moderation to the rulers' victims who have no alternative to fighting for their lives or liberation by any means possible. Herbert Marcuse, in his controversial 1965 essay "Repressive Tolerance," approvingly quotes Sartre's preface to Fanon's *The Wretched of the Earth* and adds, "Non-violence is normally not only preached to but exacted from the weak—it is a necessity rather than a virtue, and normally it does not seriously harm the case of the strong. . . . To start applying [ethical standards] at the point where the oppressed rebel against the oppressors, the have-nots against the haves is serving the cause of actual violence by weakening the protest against it."[7] While Camus's prognosis of the vicious cycle of revolutionary violence may be accurate, it, like his aesthetic theory, is formulated outside the flux of historical situation and consequently is largely irrelevant to the actual circumstances of "men who for example would be hungry," as Jeanson says sarcastically, "and who would try, following their very inferior logic, to struggle against those responsible for their hunger."[8]

In the end, Camus's exhortations are only fully applicable to volunteer rebels, especially intellectuals, within the bourgeoisie—one of whom, as Sartre reminded him, Camus himself had become. Camus's political theory in general is most meaningful as a program for middle-class intellectuals and artists involving themselves and their distinctive sensibility in historical struggle. These men, however, are apt to play only a marginal political role at best. Camus recognized this and at times gives the impression in *The Rebel* that he is trying mainly to formulate an ethic of minimal nonviolence for himself while conceding, like Tarrou, that other men must go on murderously making history. In this light, *The*

7. Robert Paul Wolff, Barrington Moore, Jr., and Herbert Marcuse, *A Critique of Pure Tolerance* (Boston: Beacon Press, 1969), p. 103.
8. "Albert Camus or l'âme révoltée," *Les Temps modernes,* May 1952, p. 2077.

Rebel stops short of proposing a universal political program, which is undoubtedly a grave limitation. On the other hand, perhaps the reader can best do it justice by approaching it with the understanding that its title applies mainly to the intellectual *engagé* and perhaps even more specifically to Camus himself.

8

The Ambiguities of *The Stranger*

I

In his chapter on Kafka in *The Myth,* Camus writes:

> The whole art of Kafka consists in forcing the reader to reread. His endings, or his absence of endings, suggest explanations which, however, are not revealed in clear language but, before they seem justified, require that the story be reread from another point of view. Sometimes there is a double possibility of interpretation, whence appears the necessity for two readings. This is what the author wanted. [P. 93]

This is what Camus too wanted in his art and achieved preeminently in *The Stranger.* He says in a notebook entry on it in 1942, "Conclusion: society needs people who weep at their mother's funeral; or else one is never condemned for the crime one thinks. Moreover, I see ten other possible conclusions" (*N2,* p. 19). Many more than ten possible conclusions have been discovered by critics around the world who, since this 154-page *récit* (narrative) appeared in 1942, have devoted far more commentary to it than to any other work of Camus, and indeed more than to nearly any other work of literature. It has inspired four book-length studies,[1] a 250-page collection of essays,[2] and hundreds of articles in journals and chapters in books, to which every year sees many additions (in

---

1. M.-G. Barrier, *L'Art du récit dans "L'Etranger" d'Albert Camus* (Paris: A. G. Nizet, 1962); Pierre-Georges Castex, *Albert Camus et "L'Etranger"* (Paris: Librairie José Corti, 1965); Robert Champigny, *A Pagan Hero: An Interpretation of Meursault in Camus' "The Stranger"* (Philadelphia: University of Pennsylvania Press, 1969), original French edition published 1959; Brian T. Fitch, *Narrateur et narration dans "L'Etranger" d'Albert Camus* (Paris: *Archives des lettres modernes,* 1960, rev. 1968).
2. *Autour de "L'Etranger." Revue des lettres modernes,* nos. 170–71 (1968).

the 1969 number of an annual collection of Camus studies published by *La Revue des lettres modernes,* Brian T. Fitch reviewed twenty-two articles on it published in the previous two years[3]). While recognizing that the book's ambiguities are inexhaustible, we can at least survey several of them, in addition to those discussed in previous chapters, that have contributed to making this brief first novel by a twenty-eight-year-old author the subject of such an extraordinary diversity of interpretations.[4]

The ambiguities begin with the title. In what sense is Meursault a stranger—or, literally, a foreigner, or an "outsider," as the British edition translates the title? Camus's use of the word in *The Myth* to describe various aspects of the absurd can be confusing in relation to the novel. He first uses it in describing on one hand man's longing for immortality and a sense of purpose in the universe and on the other hand the disrupting recognition that life is finite and purposeless: "In a universe suddenly divested of illusions and lights, man feels an alien, a stranger" (*Myth,* p. 5). (Camus uses only the single word "étranger"; O'Brien's translation conveys both of its senses in French, the first of which is uncommon in English.) Another aspect of metaphysical absurdity is the indifference, even the hostility, of the natural universe: "A step lower and strangeness ['l'étrangeté'] creeps in: perceiving that the world is 'dense,' sensing to what a degree a stone is foreign and irreducible ['étrangère'] to us, with what intensity nature or a landscape can negate us" (p. 11). The reference is obvious to the Sartrean "nausea" of man encountering the "thing-ness" of objects in the physical world, a sensation that arises as well out of those occasions when other human beings, even familiar ones, appear to us as objects—"Just as there are days when under the familiar face of a woman, we see as a stranger her we had loved months or years before" (p. 11)—and when one feels a disparity between his conscious being and his own body—"Likewise the stranger who at certain seconds comes to meet us in a mirror, the familiar and yet alarming brother we encounter in our own photographs is also the absurd" (p. 11). Epistemologically, "Between the certainty I have of my existence and the content I try to give to that assurance, the gap will never be filled. For-

3. *Revue des lettres modernes,* nos. 212–16 1969), pp. 149–61.
4. For a somewhat similar review of the novel's ambiguities see Ignace Feurlicht, "Camus' *L'Etranger* Reconsidered," *PMLA* 78, no. 5 (Dec. 1963): 606–21.

ever I shall be a stranger to myself" (pp. 13-14). Many readers and several critics have assumed that these passages in *The Myth* describing the undermining effect of recognizing the absurd apply directly to Meursault. They have related Meursault's daily routine in Part One and its disruption by the murder to the famous passage in *The Myth:* "It happens that the stage sets collapse. Rising, streetcar, four hours in the office or the factory, meal, streetcar, four hours of work, meal, sleep, and Monday Tuesday Wednesday Thursday Friday and Saturday according to the same rhythm—this path is easily followed most of the time. But one day the 'why' arises and everything begins in that weariness tinged with amazement" (p. 10). An identification of this quotation with *The Stranger* would seem to be supported by its resemblance to Meursault's work week and by his reflection just after shooting the Arab, "and so . . . it all began" (*Stranger,* p. 76).

The trouble with this whole interpretation is that Meursault is in fact the opposite of the stranger described in *The Myth.* He has never had any illusions of immortality or a transcendent purpose or order in life to be deprived of, for a premonition of death throughout his life has precluded such illusions. Indeed, it is his immunity to others' illusions that turns them against him; his denial of God before the examining magistrate questioning him about the murder, and later before the prison chaplain preceding his execution, threatens to undermine *their* lives. If Meursault's daily routine resembles in its superficials the "Rising, streetcar . . ." sequence, he does not use his working day as a source of distraction or of a sense of importance. In contrast to the officious involvement of his employer and the director and concierge at the old people's home in their work, Meursault knows his job is not worth taking seriously. He only continues this routine because he knows that in face of the hard fact of mortality "one never changed his way of life; one life was as good as another" (p. 52). In the avowal of the absurd tacit in his attitude toward his work, he does embody one point in *The Myth:* "A sub-clerk in the post office is the equal of a conqueror if consciousness is common to them. All experiences are indifferent in this regard" (*Myth,* p. 51). The "it all began" at the end of Part One announces the fatal change in the course of his life in Part Two, but not any radical change in his attitude.

In his 1943 explication of *The Stranger,* Sartre mistakenly applies to it the passages in *The Myth* about man's sense of estrangement as a subjective consciousness from the natural world, other people, and his own body: "This explains, in part, the title of our novel; the stranger is man confronting the world. Camus might as well have chosen the title of one of George Gissing's works, *Born in Exile*. The stranger is also man among men. . . . The stranger is, finally, myself in relation to myself, that is, natural man in relation to mind."[5] But Meursault is not in the least disturbed by his subjectivity. Indeed, he is more an object than a subject; that is, his consciousness is primarily one of animal sensuousness rather than intellectual self-awareness, and he has a strong impulse toward returning to unconscious union with nature, through swimming, sleeping, and ultimately death. He feels more affinity with nature than with men; far from being nauseated by natural objects, like Sartre's Roquentin, he shows a benevolent curiosity toward them, as in his preoccupation with the physical surroundings at his mother's burial. Rather than feeling that the natural universe is hostile, he proclaims at the very end, "I laid my heart open to the benign indifference of the universe. To feel it so like myself, indeed, so brotherly, made me realize that I'd been happy, and that I was happy still" (p. 154). (A literal translation would read "tender indifference of the world," but this is one instance where Gilbert's license might be said to have improved on the original; "benign indifference of the universe" is certainly a felicitous phrase, one that readers of the English version most frequently remember and quote.)

Nor is he bothered by the Sartrean subject-object barrier between himself and other people, for he does not expect anything more than a physical bond or elementary companionship from other people. On this undemanding level he does not feel in the least alienated from others: "I was just like everybody else; quite an ordinary person" (p. 80). Indeed, one of Camus's tentative titles for the book was "Un Homme comme les autres" (*TRN*, p. 1908). Meursault is only strange in the eyes of those who have deluded themselves into believing in a transcendent spiritual union between people—Marie with her sentimental talk of love, the people at his mother's funeral who expect Meursault to be overwhelmed with grief, and those who are indignant because he had institutionalized a mother with whom he no longer had anything in common. Again, Meursault is not as a rule estranged from his own body, for his un-self-

5. In *Camus: A Collection of Critical Essays,* ed. Brée, p. 110.

conscious physicality prevents him from feeling any great breach between consciousness and physical being. At only one point does *The Stranger* recall the image in *The Myth* of a man encountering a stranger in a mirror—when, after his long imprisonment, he encounters a strange face reflected in his food pan (p. 101). This schizophrenic split in his personality, signaling his regression from adult sexuality to infantile narcissism, has resulted because his physical being has been denied its gratification in prison and he has had to lean inordinately on his mental resources.

Finally, Meursault is little concerned about the absurdity in the limitations of human understanding of the world and self. He takes these limitations for granted, knowing that the course of events is not rational or explicable, and so accepts whatever happens without asking any questions. He is not a "stranger to myself," for the simple reason that he does not introspect: "Of recent years, I'd rather lost the habit of noting my feelings" (p. 80). Here again, it is not Meursault whose suppositions are absurd in their dissociation from reality but the examining magistrate and later the attorneys at the trial who spuriously believe that everything can be rationally explained. His inability to verbalize or interpret his sense experience makes him almost literally a foreigner among men of factitiously analytical language.

It is the others, then, not Meursault, who are subject to the absurd collapse of their complacency and to estrangement from the world and themselves. He is the only native in a country of foreigners. As Sartre recognizes: "He lives among outsiders ['strangers'], but to them, too, he is a stranger."[6] Roger Quilliot confirms that Camus did not conceive Meursault as estranged from nature, but from society: "In the course of one of our discussions, Camus specified that this was the point of departure for his book: a man who is a stranger to his life, to life such as it is ordinarily conceived—adapted to nature, but unadapted to society" (*TRN*, p. 1907).

Conclusion

II

In addition to the title, Camus leaves other key words, names, phrases, and whole passages open to two or more possible interpretations. Carl A. Viggiani has examined the connotations of the names Masson (*massif—*

6. Ibid., p. 111.

"massive"), Salamano (*sale main*—"dirty hand"), and Cardona (Italian, *carne donare*—"flesh-giving").[7] Cardona, however, also happened to be Camus's grandmother's maiden name, and any systematic theory of name symbolism in the novel would have to cope with Camus having given the most unsavory character, Raymond Sintès, the maiden name of his own mother. Furthermore, Camus had used several of the same names in *A Happy Death,* arbitrarily giving them to quite different characters in most cases.

Meursault's name has provided open game for symbol hunters: *meurs seul*—"I die alone"; *mort saut*—"death leap"; *mer-soleil*—"sea-sun"; *meurtre soleil*—"kill the sun," and so on. Camus told Viggiani that he had simply picked the name off a bottle of Meursault wine but probably had tongue in cheek, especially since he had changed the name of his hero from Patrice Mersault in *A Happy Death,* evidently to open the name to greater ambiguity. Camus interestingly revealed his thinking on this point and on literary symbolism generally in a letter responding to American critic Gerald Kamber's article "The Allegory of Names in *L'Etranger*":

> From the instant an author chooses to illustrate a certain symbol in a novel, many facts, names, turns of speech, even the most fugitive of images, come irresistibly to arrange themselves around that symbol and receive from it like a reflection. Melville, for example, didn't will all the symbolic correspondences that can be found in *Moby-Dick,* and yet they are undeniable, as is undeniable his will to create a sort of myth. . . . You can in effect defend the point of view that, as for Meursault, proper names influenced me unconsciously.[8]

One of Camus's favorite forms of word play is to use a banal expression in an ironically literal sense: "That doesn't mean anything," "It's all the same to me," "It's not important," "One never knows," "You can never be sure." This device an be illustrated at the same time as another, that of leaving the meaning of key passages ambiguous, with the famous opening paragraph (here quoted in the original and a more literal translation than Gilbert's):

> Aujourd'hui, maman est morte. Ou peut-être hier, je ne sais pas. J'ai reçu un télégramme de l'asile: "Mère décédée. Enterrement demain.

7. "Camus' *L'Etranger*," PMLA 56, no. 5 (Dec. 1956): 865–87.
8. *Modern Language Quarterly* 22, no. 3 (Sept. 1961): 292–301.

Sentiments ditingués." Cela ne veut rien dire. C'était peut-être hier.
[*TRN*, p. 1125]

> Today, mama died. Or maybe yesterday, I don't know. I have re-
> ceived a telegram from the rest home: "Mother deceased. Burial
> tomorrow. Yours sincerely." That doesn't mean anything. Maybe
> it was yesterday.

"That doesn't mean anything" here has at least five possible connotations.
On the most obvious level it refers to the uncertainty of which day his
mother died, thus opening the book with one note of ambiguity already.
But it might also mean that it doesn't matter which day she died (which
foreshadows Meursault's later conclusion that it doesn't matter in the
long run whether one dies at thirty or seventy); or that death itself does
not mean anything, that life is ultimately meaningless; or that the complimentary closing "Sentiments distingués" is emotionally meaningless
or that it is verbally meaningless in the semantic sense discussed in chapter 3 above.

The last two sentences in the first half of the book, on page 76, and the
last sentence at the end balance the first paragraph in their ambiguity.
Why does Meursault first shoot the Arab, then why does he fire four
more shots into his inert body after the first? Perhaps the best explanation for the first shot, if there is *any* valid explanation beyond the psychoanalytic one suggested above in chapter 4, is provided by Meursault's
friend Céleste at the trial: "To my mind, it was just an accident, or a
stroke of bad luck ['un malheur']" (p. 116). Similarly, the last sentence
of Part One in the French text ends with the word *malheur*—misfortune,
unhappiness, or bad luck: the shots are "like four brief blows that I was
knocking on the door of misfortune." The killing, then, is just one of
those things that happens in a fatal universe, the four additional shots
Meursault's fatalistic affirmation that he is prepared to accept the consequences of this stroke of bad luck. The wording, "But I fired four shots
more into the inert body, on which they left no visible trace," recalls a
line in *The Myth*, "From this inert body on which a slap makes no mark
the soul has disappeared" (p. 12), suggesting perhaps that Meursault sees
that the man is dead after the first shot and is compelled to fire again by
the strangely fascinating physiology of death.

The novel's last sentence, in which Meursault paradoxically hopes for
a large crowd of hateful spectators to reduce the loneliness of the execu-

tion, has provoked a wide variety of critical interpretations. Again, as we have seen, a psychoanalytic perspective provides one possible key, but on the manifest level no single explanation can be definitive. Perhaps Meursault's wish for cries of hatred expresses defiance of society, while his desire to feel less lonely indicates that to the last he will know that his fate will soon be shared by all the others there, that their jeers are a pitiable defense reaction against their own fears of death. His will be an ironically sacrificial, exemplary death, a principled denial of a God, an afterlife, and Christian morality. In *The Myth* Camus discusses Kirilov in Dostoevsky's *The Possessed,* who imagines that Christ on the cross realized he had been duped, that he was not the son of God and would not be resurrected but kept his secret so as to allow men a deluded hope of immortality. Kirilov sees himself as an Antichrist who will kill himself explicitly to deny the existence of God and immortality, thus freeing men of their delusions. Meursault's death will be like Kirilov's: "It is a pedagogical suicide. Kirilov sacrifices himself, then. But if he is crucified, he will not be victimized ['duped']" (*Myth,* p. 81). Other hints of what Camus may have had in mind here can be seen in a 1938 notebook draft of the passage, "As long as there are a lot of them, as long as they greet me with cries of hatred. As long as there are a lot of them, and I am not alone" (*N1,* p. 117), and in "Reflections on the Guillotine," where in criticizing the secrecy of executions he says that if they were conducted in public, at least "the actor in every man could then come to the aid of the terrified animal and help him cut a figure, even in his own eyes" (*RRD,* p. 156).

III

Camus's expository technique embodies further ambiguities. First there is the problem of the complex sequence of verb tenses and the related one of the moment at which the narration takes place. Meursault's narrative in the first four chapters of Part One and the last chapter of Part Two begins in the present tense and then switches to the past. The switch is most striking at the beginning of chapter 1, where Meursault, in the second paragraph, refers in the future tense to events expected to occur later the same day—the only time in the book he does so: "With the two-o'clock bus I should get there well before nightfall" [literally, 'I will take the two-o'clock bus and will arrive in the afternoon']. This gives the impression that the narration is taking place at the very moment of the events narrated. But in the fourth paragraph (the third in the French edition; Gilbert frequently makes paragraph breaks not in the original), Meursault switches to past tense, "I took the two-o'clock bus" (*Stranger,* p. 2), and so continues to the end of the chapter, thus creating the impression that the moment of narration either is continually shifting to stay a step behind the moment of action or is set at the end of the same day, looking back on its events. The following three chapters all begin with a reference to "today" or "yesterday" and then soon switch to past tense. It seems most likely here that the moment of narration is at the end of the day, especially in chapter 3, which begins, "['Today'] I had a busy morning in the office" (p. 30). It might be that Camus wanted to write a novel in which the narration would seem nearly simultaneous with the action, but, thinking that an entire novel in the present tense would become too monotonous, he put the first sentences of the first chapters in the present to establish a sense of present-tense-ness, then slipped subtly into past tense.

The tense sequence is further complicated by Camus's exceptional use throughout most of the novel of the French *passé composé,* the approximate equivalent of the present perfect in English, in contrast to the simple past tense nearly always used in written French (although the *passé composé* is used like a simple past in speaking). Instead of "I received a telegram . . . I took the bus," a more faithful translation might read, "I have received a telegram . . . I have taken the bus." The auxiliary verb "have," which when used by itself is a present tense, helps bridge the jumps between Meursault's present- and past-tense passages.

In addition to the two possibilities of a moment-to-moment and a day-to-day narration, there is a third: that Meursault is narrating the entire book from the vantage point of the very end, just before his execution. We get indications of this viewpoint from time to time throughout the story, such as his comment about the mourners at his mother's wake in the first chapter: "I even had an impression that the dead body in their midst meant nothing at all to them. But now I suspect that I was mistaken about this" (p. 13), or his reflection just after he has shot the Arab, "And so . . . it all began" (p. 76).[9] In *A Pagan Hero,* Robert Champigny develops an ingenious case for this interpretation, saying that Meursault at

9. For more detailed analysis of the moment of narration, see the works by Barrier, Champigny, and Fitch mentioned in n. 1 to this chapter.

the end is literally "ready to start life all over again" (p. 154), by mentally reliving and reaffirming the value of the life he has led, in all its
meaninglessness, against any other way of life or anything that he might
have done differently. When the chaplain asks Meursault how he would
picture an afterlife, he replies, "A life in which I can ['could'] remember
this life on earth" (p. 150). (Gilbert gratuitously adds, "That's all I
want of it," which along with the indicative rather than conditional verb
gives the false impression that Meursault believes there *is* such an afterlife.) And indeed he chooses to spend his few remaining hours remembering this one, without regrets. According to Champigny, Meursault's jumps
between present and present perfect tenses embody his simultaneous
affirmation of the value of his immediately lived experiences and of his
"perfect" or completed past which now forms an aesthetic whole, however shapeless and insignificant.[10]

IV

   Dualities pervade the novel in theme and structure. We have seen in
chapter 2 above the parallels between God's and society's judgment and
between natural death and capital punishment. There is another important thematic parallel between the absurdity of nature or fate and that
of society. The sun is the source both of Meursault's greatest pleasures
when it is comfortably warm, as in the swimming scenes, and of his
downfall when it is too hot, as in the two moments that it becomes the
agent that incriminates him. At his mother's funeral his dizziness in the
blazing sunlight exaggerates the air of indifference that the witnesses
at his trial will condemn, and later, on the beach in front of the Arab,
"the same sort of heat ['the same sun'] as at my mother's funeral" (p. 75)
blinds and disconcerts him so that he pulls the trigger. "I knew I'd shattered the balance ['equilibrium'] of the day, the spacious calm ['the exceptional silence'] of this beach on which I had been happy" (p. 76)—the
equilibrium of high noon, the meridian between pleasure and misery, the
precarious balance of nature in which life hangs.
   Capricious, ironic twists of fate are another aspect of nature's duality.
(Like Montaigne and Pascal, Camus had a penchant for chronicling such

---

10. Champigny, pp. 94–100. Also see his essay "Ethics and Aesthetics in *The Stranger*,"
in *Camus: A Collection of Critical Essays*, ed. Brée, pp. 122–31.

twists; in his notebooks, for example, he remarked on the irony of T. E. Lawrence being killed in a peacetime motorcycle accident after having survived numerous scrapes with death in battle and in the desert—a notation that is doubly ironic in light of the fate that awaited Camus himself.) Fate can catch anyone by surprise at any moment, turning the most harmless pastime into a threshold to tragedy. Thus Meursault's carefree day at the beach ends in violent death; and later in the book, when he is being driven from the courtroom back to his prison cell during his trial, he reflects, "And so I learned that familiar paths traced in the dusk of summer evenings may lead as well to prisons as to innocent, untroubled sleep" (p. 123). The fickle turn that his fate has taken enables the imprisoned Meursault to appreciate the news clipping he finds in his cell about the Czech who, having made his fortune during a long absence from his home town, returns without revealing his identity to the inn run by his mother and sister, only to be murdered by them for his money. "To my mind, the man was asking for trouble; one shouldn't play fool tricks of that sort" (p. 101), concludes Meursault, who has similarly tempted fate by getting involved needlessly with the gunplay on the beach and who will also pay with his life.

Society as Camus portrays it is as duplicitous, capricious, and lethal as fate, with one vital difference: fate makes no claim to rationality, while society does make one. Once Meursault has been labeled a "criminal," all of his previous actions that have seemed merely eccentric are brought against him as evidence of a heinous personality by the witnesses who gave no indication of judging him so harshly before his crime. There is implicit in *The Stranger* the theme that no matter how innocent a life one may have led, once he has been judged guilty of a crime, society sanctimoniously hastens to reinterpret all his past actions in a guilty light. It would be a mistake, however, to interpret the novel, as the jacket note of the American translation does, merely as the story of "an ordinary little man . . . helpless in life's grip." Although Meursault does describe himself as being "just like everybody else," this represents a certain irony on Camus's part—Meursault means that everybody is equally privileged to live and equally condemned to death—for it is clear that Camus meant Meursault to be something more than a normal citizen whose minor eccentricities are turned against him because a freakish stroke of fate has caused him to commit a crime. Meursault *is* a social rebel. Nature has gratuitously led him to murder, but society has its reasons for condemn-ing him to death, albeit spurious reasons. Camus writes in the 1955 fore-word, "I summarized *The Stranger* a long time ago, with a remark that I admit was highly paradoxical: 'In our society any man who does not weep at his mother's funeral runs the risk of being sentenced to death.' I only meant that the hero of my book is condemned because he does not play the game. In this respect, he is foreign ['étranger'] to the society in which he lives" (*LCE*, pp. 335–36). The irony of society's judgment, of course, is that underneath the superficial rationality of its workings it is based on ridiculously arbitrary values; the courtroom is more offended by Meursault's failure to cry at his mother's funeral than by his having killed a man.

   In spite of his awareness that the court's guilty verdict is absurdly arbi-trary, he is eventually able to resign himself to it because he recognizes that every death is an arbitrary guilty verdict, whether decreed by society or by nature. One of the possible conclusions Camus said could be drawn from *The Stranger*, "One is never condemned for the crime one thinks," recalls James M. Cain's *The Postman Always Rings Twice,* one of the melodramatic American detective novels that superficially influenced Camus's style here. There a man and woman murder the woman's hus-band in a perfect crime, only to have retribution catch up with them ironically when she is killed in an accident and her lover unjustly con-victed and executed for murdering her. Camus turns the idea that Cain uses for purely melodramatic purposes into a profound commentary on the duality of man's destiny in nature and in society. A man is just as likely to be condemned for the wrong crime as the right one—or for no crime at all, since the innocent and the guilty alike are subject to the caprices of destiny and, sooner or later, to natural death. In the first chapter, during the burial procession, a nurse remarks to Meursault, "'If you go too slowly there's the risk of a heatstroke. But, if you go too fast, you perspire, and the cold air in the church gives you a chill.' I saw her point; either way one was in for it ['She was right. There was no way out']" (p. 21). In Part Two, after Meursault has been imprisoned for many months, he recalls the incident: "And something I'd been told came back; a remark made by the nurse at Mother's ['mama's'] funeral. No, there was no way out, and no one can imagine what the evenings are like in prison" (p. 101). "There is no way out" is a refrain that haunts the entire novel. Shortly before he kills the Arab, when Raymond first hands him the revolver on the beach, Meursault thinks, "One might fire, or not fire—and it would come to absolutely the same thing" (the clause after the dash is not in the French version), and a few lines later, "To stay, or to make a move ['to leave']—it came to much the same" (pp. 73-74). It all comes to the same thing in the end—death.

Thus fate ironically links incidents that would seem to have no logical connection (e.g., Meursault's behavior at his mother's funeral and his trial for murder), and a foresight of death, by reducing all actions to the same level of importance, creates an identity between the most disparate events. Instead of mystical doctrines in which all objects and events are identified with one another in their equal significance, Camus presents the reverse: all are identified in their equal *in*significance: "The same thing for Salamano's wife and for Salamano's dog.['Salamano's dog had the same value as his wife']. That little robot woman was as 'guilty' as the girl from Paris who had married Masson, or as Marie, who wanted me to marry her. What did it matter if Raymond was as much my pal as Céleste, who was a far worthier man?" (pp. 152-53).

Camus's observations on the duality of nature, society, fate, and the ironic identification that death effects between diverse events mold the novel into a highly symmetrical structure. Camus remarks in the 1942 notebooks, "The meaning of the book lies precisely in the parallelism of the two parts" (*N2*, p. 19). In addition to the foreshadowings of the second part in the first already mentioned, others include Meursault's momentary impression that the mourners at the wake are a jury judging him, and his distractions to pass the time on an idle Sunday and readjustment to life without his mother, which anticipate his adaptation to prison and, later still, to the prospect of dying. Viggiani [11] and Germaine Brée [12] have both contrasted the time scheme of Part One, in which events are noted meticulously within a well-defined chronological span, with Part Two, in which Meursault's days and months in prison melt into one another indistinguishably. Most of Part Two, in fact, consists of reexamination of the events of Part One, and the ironic contrast between the actual events and their later interpretation by the authorities provides a dynamic organizing force for the whole novel. Camus, then, like

11. "Camus' *L'Etranger*," p. 868.
12. *Camus* (New Brunswick: Rutgers University Press, 1959; rev. 1961), p. 105.

Kafka, entices the reader to go back to the beginning and consider the overtones that retrospection has imposed on events that originally seemed disconnected and unambiguous.

v

Two thematic ambiguities that evoke sharply differing interpretations are the questions of whether Meursault shows any contrition for having killed a man and whether he undergoes a basic change of attitude toward life in general over the course of the book. Some critics, including Viggiani, Emmett Parker, and Louis Rossi,[13] have interpreted *The Stranger* in the light of Camus's later preoccupation with personal responsibility for murder. They have gone on to conclude that Meursault's ultimate resignation to his execution signifies that he acknowledges the justice, or at least inevitability, of having to pay for a life with a life. This interpretation can be countered by arguing that Meursault actually gives little thought to having taken another's life. At no time does he think of any connection between the murder and his condemnation; he believes in fact that he has been condemned, not for murder but for failing to cry at his mother's funeral. When Meursault tells the chaplain that he too is a condemned man, that all the other characters in the book are equally guilty, there is no implication of *their* complicity in causing anyone's death. In *The Stranger,* as in *The Myth,* Camus is more concerned about every man's condemnation to death merely for being alive than about culpability for others' deaths.

Viggiani, who is generally one of Camus's most perceptive and provocative critics, goes far astray here in trying retroactively to view Meursault as an example of the socially conscientious rebel of *The Just Assassins* and *The Rebel:* "The true rebel, however, is distinguished from the nihilist by his willingness to give life for life. . . . Like Kaliayev, Meursault affirms this fundamental value by accepting from the start the necessity and logic of paying with his life."[14] This is plainly mistaken. Meursault is far more similar to the nihilistic rebel, like Ivan Karamazov or Nietzsche in *The Rebel,* than to Kaliayev. He does not kill for the sake of any

13. Louis Rossi, "Albert Camus: The Plague of Absurdity," *Kenyon Review* 20, no. 3 (Summer 1958): 399–422.
14. "Camus' *L'Etranger*," p. 884.

social cause, and his utter lack of concern over having killed is the ultimate expression of his social rebelliousness. From his point of view, then,
what necessity or logic is there in having to pay with his life?

Emmett Parker goes to still more preposterous lengths in this kind of
liberalistic retroactive attempt to rehabilitate Meursault. Parker is answering French leftist critics who at the time of the Algerian War charged
that Camus had the racist attitudes of the "pied noir," or "poor white"
Algerian, and that this attitude is reflected consciously or unconsciously
in Meursault's aggression toward the Arab and lack of remorse over having killed him. In refutation, Parker first claims like Viggiani and Rossi
that Meursault does develop a sense of responsibility "after his trial when,
in prison awaiting execution, he admits his guilt." He then goes on to
say, "The problem of Meursault's innocence is closely related to the problem of the innocence of the European Algerians who asked no questions
and who failed to see a manifestation of the absurd in the face of a starv-
ing Moslem."[15] Parker fails to clarify or support this bizarre implication
that Meursault's alleged contrition is somehow, symbolically or analo-
gously, "closely related" to the awakening of French-Algerian conscience
toward the Arabs that Camus was striving for in his journalism of the
same period. Parker subsequently concludes, *"L'Etranger* is in no way a
disguised rationalization of the 'poor white's' fear of losing his identity.
It is rather a statement, in artistic form, of the need for awareness of a
human solidarity that transcends national and racial differences."[16]

This last is a nice account of Camus's writing in general, but it hasn't
the remotest application to *The Stranger.* The only human solidarity
Meursault becomes aware of is that between condemned men whose particular ways of life and death are unimportant. This solidarity transcends
national and racial barriers only in the sense that Meursault would probably have been little more remorseful over shooting a European than an
Arab. It would be ingenuous, however, to believe that Camus's choice of
an Arab for the victim was gratuitous. Meursault's attitudes are indeed
those of the poor white, as Conor Cruise O'Brien has amply documented.
The social and sexual tensions between French Algerians and Arabs in
fact add substantially to the verisimilitude of atmosphere and motivation
not only for Meursault but for Raymond, the Arabs themselves, and

15. *The Artist in the Arena* (Madison: University of Wisconsin Press, 1966), p. 43.
16. Ibid., p. 45.

later the court officials. It would be a novelistic inconsistency for Meursault to develop regrets over the Algerian Arab problem when he does not do so over manslaughter or any other moral or political issue.

The question of the extent to which Meursault reflects Camus's own conscious or unconscious racism is important within the pattern of racial attitudes in Camus's writing as a whole but is irrelevant to our evaluation of *The Stranger* as a first-person fictional narrative. For leftists to criticize Camus because he does not convey disapproval within the novel of his narrator's racism is to make the same mistake Parker does, that of expecting any single work to express Camus's own viewpoint completely or directly. Critical political analysis is simply not part of his intention here as it will be in *The Plague,* where his failure to treat the Algerian Arab problem adequately does become a serious artistic flaw.

The most disputable issue in *The Stranger* is whether its final implication is really that "life isn't worth living." Meursault's meditation shortly before being executed, "From the moment one dies, how and when has no importance," can be regarded as the key to his whole character. Camus may be asking us to consider the startling hypothesis of a man who in the midst of life is as indifferent to his fate as he will be after death. At no time does Meursault do anything to avert his doom, despite ample opportunities. Throughout his questioning and trial, all he need do to save himself is feign remorse; yet he does not. The reason, according to Camus's 1955 foreword, is that he has too much integrity to recant his actions and attitudes, that he does value his life but would rather die than lie. In the novel itself, however, Meursault's failure to lie appears to result less from scruples than from a lack of expedient foresight and an indifference toward saving himself even if he had this foresight. Indeed, by the end of the scene with the chaplain he has despaired of his appeal—which, as the chaplain *twice* reminds us, is still pending—and looks forward to death eagerly.

This interpretation of Meursault's indifference toward his fate contradicts a more common critical analysis according to which Meursault undergoes a radical change of mind as a result of his imprisonment and impending execution and, shaken out of his indifference, becomes aware of life's value and realizes that he should not have destroyed his happiness. The latter interpretation has a great deal to support it, but it is usually formulated under the assumption that Camus meant *The Stranger* to be a mirror of his affirmation of life in *The Myth* rather than an alternative to it, and I do not think it holds up under a close analysis of the novel's text. A typical expression of the more positive reading is found in the introduction to the American college edition by Germaine Brée and Carlos Lynes, Jr., who seem to be cosmeticizing the novel somewhat for student consumption, as they do in censoring the scene where Meursault masturbates. They write, "In a moment of self-realization [his explosion against the chaplain] Meursault's indifference vanishes; he knows that he has been happy in his life, that he is still happy, even though death is imminent. Life has a more poignant value because it is fragile and nearing its end." [17] There is no denying that toward the end of the book Meursault does come to appreciate the happiness he has lost. His imprisonment makes him bitterly miss his liberty, and between his condemnation and the chaplain's visit he is highly reluctant about giving up his life. But just as he eventually becomes reconciled to prison life, he later talks himself, rationally if not emotionally, into resignation in his death cell, and although his passions still cling to life despite his reasoning, his rage against the chaplain finally swings the balance, leaving him emotionally as well as intellectually indifferent to life. Thus Meursault's newfound appreciation of life is his penultimate, not ultimate, attitude. Yes, he has been happy, but this happiness has obviously not been important enough to make him take the necessary steps to preserve it, nor is it important enough to try to recapture—as he shows by abandoning his appeal. His attitude, then, does not undergo a radical change; his indifference only wavers, then becomes reaffirmed, more strongly than ever, at the end.

Brée and Lynes continue: "In the final pages of the novel, the sudden shift to a sustained dramatic tone suggests the important change that has come over Meursault. The emotion-charged style makes us realize that he is not resigned to his fate but will rather make his death itself an affirmation of the supreme value of life." [18] Does a man who is not resigned to his fate forget about his appeal? Does a man who thinks of his death as an affirmation of the supreme value of life hope for a crowd of spectators at his execution to greet him with cries of hatred? Brée and Lynes conclude, "*L'Etranger* is not a completely 'negative' book, however, for at

17. *L'Etranger* (New York: Appleton-Century-Crofts, 1955), p. 9.
18. Ibid., p. 10.

the end of his adventure Meursault undergoes a kind of spiritual awakening; if life were granted him he could begin to construct a new system
of values and perhaps discover vital links between himself and other
men." [19] But there is absolutely no indication that if he had his life to
live over, Meursault would try to change his fate. On the contrary: "I'd
been right, I was still right, I was always right. I'd passed my life in a
certain way, and I might have passed it in a different way, if I'd felt
like it. I'd acted thus, and I hadn't acted otherwise; I hadn't done *x*,
whereas I had done *y* or *z*. And what did that mean? That, all the time,
I'd been waiting for this present moment, for that dawn, tomorrow's or
another day's, which was to justify me. Nothing, nothing had the least
importance . . ." (pp. 151–52).

This evidence notwithstanding, a good case can be made for both interpretations, and many passages can be read in accordance with either.
The following, for example:

> Then, just on the edge of daybreak, I heard a steamer's siren. People
> were starting on a voyage to a world which had ceased to concern me
> forever. Almost for the first time in many months I thought of my
> mother ['mama']. And now, it seemed to me, I understood why at
> her life's end she had taken on a "fiancé"; why she'd played at mak-
> ing a fresh start. There, too, in that Home where lives were flickering
> out, the dusk came as a mournful solace ['respite']. With death so
> near, Mother ['mama'] must have felt like someone on the brink of
> freedom, ready to start life all over again. No one, no one in the
> world had any right to weep for her. And I, too, felt ready to start
> life all over again. [Pp. 153–54]

A first reading might well support the Brée-Lynes interpertation. The
world that has become indifferent to Meursault is the one of society's
artificial values. His mother has felt ready to start life again because
being surrounded by death has freed her from society's values and awakened her to full consciousness of her remaining days. Similarly, Meursault's tirade against the chaplain has broken his last bonds to conventional morality and inspired him to appreciate fully every minute of the
short time left him. On the other hand, perhaps it is toward *all* of life
that he has become forever indifferent. Perhaps, as I have speculated
previously, it is the anticipation of death itself that liberates Meursault

19. Ibid., p. 13.

and his mother; their death will be both a nuptial and a rebirth, a Lucretian union with the benign indifference of the universe.

These opposing interpretations might be reconciled to some degree by
an intermediate one that views Meursault as the absurd man who has
reached the end of a fully lived life and is therefore ready to die without
regrets. Meursault, irrevocably turned toward death, has become indifferent toward his particular life (like the hero of Sartre's "The Wall,"
who, reprieved after having conditioned himself to dying, cannot cope
with being returned to life), but the ending is not a universal negation
of life, for we the readers are still alive and can benefit from Meursault's
exemplary death by seeing in it an injunction to appreciate *our* life while
we still have it.

In the end, it is likely that Camus intended to leave open the possibility of at least two contradictory conclusions to make the book illustrate
that "this world is nothing and this world is everything—there is the
contradictory and tireless cry of every true artist." The only unequivocally
affirmative theme is to be found, not explicitly in Meursault's narrative
but in the novel's literary structure and in the author's having remained
alive and choosing to write that novel, as discussed above in chapter 3.
Those critics who have taken such pains to search for more overt indications of positive thinking in *The Stranger* (perhaps there is some significance in their being found in America for the most part) have almost
invariably been unconvincing. Foremost among them is Germaine Brée,
who as late as 1972, in the most recent of her now countless works on
Camus, was still straining not only to redeem Meursault morally but,
even more gratuitously, to dredge up direct current political relevance out
of *The Stranger:* "At the time of the shooting [Meursault] feels instinc-
tively he has transgressed some deep-seated, cosmic law. . . . We are not
far from incidents such as My Lai."[20] The proponents of this critical
line often sound like the wistful characters in the novel itself who simply
cannot bring themselves to face the unregenerate indifference of Meursault's world view.

VI

Of all Camus's works *The Stranger* is undoubtedly filled with the most
paradoxes, both internally and in relation to his life and other works. The

20. *Camus and Sartre: Crisis and Commitment,* p. 143.

ending ironically reverses conventional notions of innocence and guilt. When Meursault says that the little automatic woman, Masson's wife, and Marie are all as guilty as he is, he implies that universal guilt—our common condemnation to natural death—is equivalent to innocence in all particulars. Roger Quilliot describes Meursault as "a primitive whose greatest sin is precisely not believing in sin."[21] He is an ironic, Nietzschean Christ indeed, coming to wash away the whole Christian concept of sin. Yet Camus clearly regards society as sinful for taking Meursault's life, in the same paradox he later perceives in Ivan Karamazov's philosophy of crime as a revolt against a criminal God: "Every indulgence is allowed the murderer, none is allowed the executioner" (*Rebel,* p. 58). René Girard, in an article called "Camus' Stranger Retried," has in fact accused Camus of pleading a prejudiced case in favor of Meursault and against society.[22]

The accusation against Meursault of indifference toward his mother is paradoxical because it is both less and more than just. On the psychoanalytic level he is *too* loving toward her, incestuously so. Even on the manifest level, he is fond of her in his way but simply incapable of going through the theatrical rituals of filial devotion that society expects. He still calls her "mama" throughout the French edition and often recalls her ideas sympathetically, most significantly when he is about to die. On the other hand, the subliminal hostility in the book toward mother figures runs far deeper than Meursault's superficial indifference toward her. In any event, considering that Camus himself professed unusually strong devotion toward his mother, who was neither institutionalized nor dead when he wrote the novel—in fact, she outlived her son but died later the same year—his going to such lengths to create a fictional hero so opposed to himself is a curiosity that is perhaps explicable only in terms of the circuitous workings of the unconscious.

In other respects as well, it is striking how much of himself Camus studiously refined out of the novel, especially in light of his more personal writings of the same period such as *L'Envers et l'endroit, Nuptials,* the journalism collected in the first and third volumes of *Actuelles,* and the notebooks, which express a *joie de vivre,* intellectual intensity, and po-

21. *The Sea and Prisons* (University, Ala.: University of Alabama Press, 1970), p. 74 (original French edition, 1956).
22. *PMLA* 79, no. 5 (Dec. 1964): 519–33.

litical involvement almost wholly absent from *The Stranger*. The same
can be said for the way he transformed the highly personal *A Happy
Death* into *The Stranger,* which ended up bearing little resemblance to
its precursor beyond the name of its hero and a few other similar characters, scenes, and phrases which get eerily transmuted into quite different contexts between the two works. Patrice Mersault is closer to the
absurd man of *The Myth* and the Camus of the lyrical essays than to
Meursault—the settings and some passages from "Death in the Soul" and
"Nuptials at Tipasa" are repeated here. Mersault has Camus's own positive, lucid passion for life, and his death, of pleurisy—the harrowing description of which is obviously drawn from Camus's near-fatal tubercular
attacks—is happy because he has lived at full intensity. Patrice had also
lived with his mother but continued to do so until she died and had a
devoted relationship with her resembling that in "Between Yes and No."
Mersault is far more outgoing socially than Meursault; at one point he
shares a hilltop house with three young women, all his platonic friends,
a situation based on a similar episode in Camus's life as a student. By
inventing the murder, imprisonment, trial, and execution in *The Stranger,*
Camus set the stage for Meursault's indifference to his fate, as well as
introducing the parallel of social judgment to natural death and the irony
of Meursault's ingenuousness against society's artificial rituals.

Stylistically, *A Happy Death* is a third-person narrative with a tone
strongly influenced by Gide in its lyricism and effusively self-conscious
individualism. As Roger Quilliot notes, "The style, if it already carries
the mark of classical purity, only announces in flashes the short and deliberately toned-down sentences of *The Stranger*" (*TRN,* p. 1905). Camus
worked negatively in stripping down tone and characterization in order
to distance himself from *The Stranger,* but the emergence of Meursault
as a credible, sympathetic character and the resulting dynamic effect of
the tension between author and hero testify to an impressive creative
accomplishment.

By conceiving a story and a novelistic structure that epitomize the
pluralistic nature and internal contradictions of the absurd, by enriching
the novel with multiple meanings and paradoxes on every level, Camus
infused *The Stranger* with a distinctive vitality that makes this slim
récit unique among his works and those of any other author. He was
never again to attain its richness in any of his later works, although this

is not to deny their own distinctive virtues or justification for being less complex. *The Stranger* is one of those rare, fertile inventions like *Hamlet, Moby Dick, The Brothers Karamazov, Ulysses,* or *The Great Gatsby* that even the greatest of writers are seldom fortunate enough to create more than once in a lifetime: a combination of will, in the author's felicitous original conception, and of good fortune in the way this conception quickens and expands to take on a life of its own. All the elements coalesce to form a simple, yet infinitely intricate pattern, and the levels of meaning proliferate to produce an artistic organism that is as protean, enigmatic, and endlessly tantalizing as the human condition itself.

9

The Plague: Naturalistic Allegory

I

While *The Stranger* is one of the unqualified masterpieces of the twentieth century, *The Plague* is, like Father Paneloux, a doubtful case. Certainly it has many strong points and has deservedly been one of the few novels since World War II to gain worldwide recognition as a standard. Its technique culminates nearly a hundred years of novelistic experimentation. Since the generation of Melville, Flaubert, and Dostoevsky, novelists had been combining realism and symbolism, to the degree that the distinctive mode of modern fiction can be termed symbolic realism. In *The Plague* Camus audaciously synthesized the ultimate extension of both of the opposing techniques into an allegorical naturalism. He had previously demonstrated his native mastery of the metaphysical plane in fiction and drama, on which plane the plague allegorizes the absurd, natural death, the problem of evil. We sense the familiar climate of Camus's fictional world in high points such as Father Paneloux's two harrowing sermons, Rieux's refutation of the priest and of God's creation, and the memorable scene in which an opera performance turns into a morality play when Orpheus literally drops dead, shattering the delusion that "evening dress was a sure charm against plague" (*Plague,* p. 179). His new accomplishment here was successfully bringing research and imagination to bear on chronicling the epidemic in naturalistically clinical detail, as in the descriptions of the emergence of the rats and the death agonies of the human victims. He is an incisive social psychologist in his portrayal of a trapped community, a portrayal that reveals universal truths about any group of humans in crisis: the panic-stricken, uncomprehending confusion; the emergence of the best and worst in people; the compensating virtue of plagues in pulling men momentarily out of their

173

habit-bound inertia and self-absorption, raising them to a heightened intensity of living and sense of brotherhood with fellow victims; the inevitable reversion to habitual oblivion that sets in as soon as the crisis has past (reminiscent of Dostoevsky's reprieved man in *The Idiot* who quickly forgets his vow to remain conscious of being alive every minute).[1]

It is his most fully, conventionally developed novel. Rambert and Grand are his two best rounded minor characters; Rambert especially, who among Camus's fictional personalities is probably closest to the author's own temperament, is an appealing, completely credible portrait of the sensualist torn between egoistic fulfillment and social responsibility. Rambert's inclination toward egoism at the same time functions thematically to counterbalance Tarrou's aspiration toward saintly self-sacrifice and his concern over our innate egocentricity, an internal conflict that Camus returns to in *The Fall*.

Rambert the journalist, Tarrou the diarist, Grand the would-be novelist and statistician of the plague, and Rieux the retrospective chronicler compositely symbolize Camus's preoccupation with the social responsibilities of the literary artist. He develops the theme most extensively through Rieux, whose anonymity and objective tone in his chronicle reflect the obligation of the writer to efface his individuality at least part of the time to act as spokesman for the community of muted victims. Camus implicitly suggests several analogies between the occupations of physician and artist. The "true healer" is committed to easing human suffering without hopes of definitively overcoming it (there is no certainty that the plague's cessation is due to the efforts of the medical squads; it may have simply run its natural course). Likewise, the writer, according to "The Artist and His Time," "must simultaneously serve suffering and beauty," without any illusions of ultimate success. The doctor bears witness to the value of every life and takes the side of the victim rather than the plague; similarly, "Every act of creation, by its mere existence, denies the world of master and slave" (*Rebel*, p. 274). Thus the doctor and, tacitly, the artist provide an answer to Tarrou's dilemma of how to avoid siding with the executioners in today's murderous society. This answer takes on wider significance when we remember that Camus habitually

---

1. For a thorough full-length analysis of *The Plague*, see D. R. Haggis's monograph, *Albert Camus: "La Peste"* (London: Edward Arnold, 1962; Great Neck, N.Y.: Barron's Educational Series, 1962).

speaks of the artist not only literally but as a figure for a creative, humane attitude in any realm of life.

In his medical role Rieux also shares some of the artist's personal tribulations. During and after the war Camus became increasingly apprehensive over the dangers of social duties preempting the artist's private happiness, consuming all his time, emotion, and creative resources; in fighting dehumanizing political forces the artist further subjects himself to a degree of dehumanization. From the onset of the epidemic Rieux is increasingly forced to channel his personal emotions, particularly his love and concern for his wife, into abstract concern with the plague. When Rambert reproaches him for cold-heartedly undervaluing personal happiness, which impels Rambert to try to flee the quarantined city, Rieux reflects:

> To fight abstraction you must have something of it in your own make-up. But how could Rambert be expected to grasp that? Abstraction for him was all that stood in the way of his happiness. Indeed, Rieux had to admit the journalist was right, in one sense. But he knew, too, that abstraction sometimes proves itself stronger than happiness; and then, if only then, it has to be taken into account. [Pp. 83-84]

After Rambert reluctantly decides to defer his personal happiness and stay in Oran because "it may be shameful to be happy by oneself," he asks Rieux, "Have *you* made a definite choice and turned down happiness?" Rieux replies, "I simply don't know," and "A man can't cure and know at the same time. So let's cure as quickly as we can. That's the more urgent job" (pp. 188-89). The implicit analogy with the artist here is that he must be both activist and detached analyst but cannot be both simultaneously. Only after the plague is over will Rieux have time to "know," to analyze and justify his motives in the process of writing the chronicle. In the meantime he sacrifices his happiness out of instinctive compassion, the same reason that Camus gives in "The Artist and His Time" for being unable as a writer to ignore human suffering: "Not through virtue, as you see, but through a sort of almost organic intolerance, which you feel or do not feel" (*Myth,* p. 150).

To sum up *The Plague*'s strong points, it is on first reading as gripping and moving as anything in world literature. Only on subsequent, closer rereadings do its limitations become troublesome. Stylistically it lacks the enduring fascination of *The Stranger*'s verbal complexities and *The Fall*'s epigrammatic incisiveness, so that while Stuart Gilbert's translation is more faithful than *The Stranger,* it so happens that word-for-word accuracy is not as important here. The various symbolic levels and Rieux's doctor-artist dual role are rather static techniques of structural ambiguity compared to the dynamic interaction between Parts One and Two of *The Stranger* or the innumerable possible interpretations of individual passages and of that novel as a whole. It should be remembered, however, that by the time of *The Plague* Camus has become committed to a more straightforward literature, having developed an antipathy toward the abuses of linguistic ambiguity that he expresses through Tarrou: "All our troubles spring from our failure to use plain, clean-cut language" (*Plague,* p. 230).

The philosophical dialogues between Rieux, Tarrou, Paneloux, and Rambert, although substantial thematically, tend to make stilted, bombastic fiction. Perhaps they would not sound so portentous without the embarrassingly awkward stage directions that Camus inserts in an unsuccessful attempt to break them up and ground them in a realistic context: "Tarrou's gray eyes met the doctor's gaze serenely," "Rieux's face darkened," "The reply came promptly," "The answer came through the darkness in the same cool, confident tone." Tarrou's virtually uninterrupted monologue is more effective, and the discussions might have worked better presented as unbroken dramatic dialogue.

After the first reading, without the suspense and emotional involvement in the characters' fates, Rieux, Tarrou, Cottard, and Paneloux do not retain enough individual complexity or appeal to become much more than the abstract voices of philosophical positions, as Lukács has correctly though exaggeratedly observed. Camus does not succeed in establishing a credible existence for them prior to or outside of the plague; Rieux's relationships with his wife and mother are not adequately developed, and we learn nothing of Tarrou's personal life after he left home at eighteen, other than vague references to revolutionary activities. Meursault and Clamence are both more highly individualized, as are the main characters in the novels of Dostoevsky and Malraux, the two closest models for *The Plague.* In *The Brothers Karamazov* Dostoevsky develops the characters of all four brothers and even Father Zossima, who plays a similar role to Father Paneloux, with a wealth of individual traits and activities, some independent from their theoretical ideas, some anticipating them in peripheral, everyday ways. Even such a philosophical monomaniac as Kirilov in *The Possessed* is much more of a full-fleshed individual. The ideas of Dostoevsky's characters in turn motivate their subsequent actions and determine the novel's plot, as, for instance, in the father's murder, which immediately follows and is indirectly a consequence of the theories expounded in the sections on the Grand Inquisitor and Father Zossima's exhortations. The central characters of *The Plague* represent comparatively passive responses to the plague, which initiates the action and ideas.

Malraux's characters accrue individuality from acting in a specific historical setting and against fleshly, human adversaries. Camus has set himself a nearly impossible task in having to develop full novelistic characterizations within a virtual historical vacuum and severely restricted segment of time, with the impersonal plague as antagonist. When Rieux laments that in fighting an abstract enemy one's own individuality tends to give way to abstraction, Camus may be giving us a hint of the artistic problem he faced in trying to personify in fictional characters the struggle against the abstractions of both the plague and its analogous twentieth-century ideological conflicts. Thus the abstractness of Rieux and Tarrou is undoubtedly intentional to some extent, since the plague requires them to sacrifice their own sense of individuality. Camus of course was aiming more to create a mythic setting and characters than conventional realistic ones. What he loses in gradually developed characterization he compensates for in maintaining an intensity of crisis-pitched action matched by few other novelists; what he sacrifices in concrete historical detail he gains in a hermetic universality immune from the fading of immediate historical memories. Still, subtlety of characterization and exposition are traits that invite rereading more than mythic significance and suspenseful emotional intensity, so here again the power of *The Plague* declines after the first reading.

Furthermore, weak points in the book's elaborate symbolic system lead to problems in structure and interaction between characters. Camus situates his fictional Oran outside of a specific historical and political context. Consequently, he can only bring in politics through Tarrou's flashback monologue, which, though one of the outstanding parts of the novel in itself, is dramatically and thematically an artificial interpolation. Although Tarrou expresses his political concerns in the metaphor of the plague, they are rather anomalous in the middle of the real plague, as is his very presence in Oran—we never get a clear idea of what has brought him there. The only level on which his presence might make sense is the symbolic one of the Nazi occupation, in which context we can see him as the foreigner or colonial Frenchman like Camus who has chosen to join the Resistance. It is similarly anomalous when Rieux, whose concerns are with the literal plague and with metaphysical judgment, reflects on issues that are cryptopolitical. For example, on pages 120–21 Rieux attributes "the evil that is in the world" to ignorance and misunderstanding rather than malice. This idea makes sense in the context of Camus's political thought and perhaps in the theme of the Resistance, but it is quite irrelevant to the situation in which Rieux actually formulates it, the work of the sanitary squads against the literal plague.

Perhaps it is quibbling to look for precise delineations or correlations between the novel's different levels of meaning. Camus evidently expects his reader to be willing to shift back and forth without discriminating sharply between the realistic plague, the symbolic Nazi occupation, and the allegorical problem of evil, or between Rieux's metaphysical and medical world and Tarrou's historical one. His expectation, I think, strains our willingness to suspend disbelief, at least after the first reading, and entails some thematic equivocations. Camus may have conceived Rieux and Tarrou as alter egos, a Dostoevskian composite with virtually interchangeable beliefs. Certainly there is little to distinguish between their ideas: they share the desire to side with the victims and a concern for the clear use of language to avert misunderstandings. In fact, Rieux's reflection on the latter point on pages 120–21 immediately follows and in effect explicates Tarrou's cryptic statement at the end of the previous section that his code of morals is "comprehension."

But what differentiates Rieux, who survives the plague, from Tarrou, who succumbs to it? The key explanation on pages 230–31 is obscure (ironically, considering that part of it is that all our troubles spring from our failure to use plain, clean-cut language). Tarrou asks, "Can one be a saint without God?" It is unclear, however, whether his idea of saintliness is to be found in total abstention from history or some form of nonpestiferous participation in it. (Camus discusses the notion of the saint without God in a notebook entry [*N2*, p. 20], but it is too vague to be of much help.) What forms of nonpestiferous participation does Tarrou conceive of? "There are pestilences and there are victims; no more than that. If, by making that statement, I, too, become a carrier of the plague-germ, at least I don't do it willfully. I try, in short, to be an innocent murderer." The last phrase suggests "the fastidious assassins" [or 'the delicate murderers'] of *The Just Assassins* and *The Rebel* and the ideal of limited culpability in those works, but Kaliayev does reluctantly kill, whereas Tarrou has "definitely refused to kill."

Tarrou continues:

> I grant we should add a third category: that of the true healers ['les vrais médecins']. But it's a fact one doesn't come across many of them, and anyhow it must be a hard vocation. [An earlier manuscript reads more pessimistically: 'But it's a fact that one doesn't come across any of them and that it must be too difficult' (*TRN*, p. 1992).] That's why I decided to take, in every predicament, the victims' side, so as to reduce the damage done. Among them I can at least try to discover how one attains to the third category: in other words, to peace.

Rieux asks "if Tarrou had an idea of the path to follow for attaining peace." "Yes," he replied. "The path of sympathy." This explains very little. Exactly how does one take the victims' side? What is a true healer? Is he the same as the saint, and if not, what is the difference? We might suppose that Rieux represents the true healer, but he says, "You know, I feel more fellowship ['solidarity'] with the defeated than with saints. Heroism and sanctity don't really appeal to me, I imagine. What interests me is being a man." Either the true healer is not the saint, then, or Rieux is not the true healer.

We have to go outside the text itself to get some hints on how to interpret this passage. In Camus's earlier manuscript, after "The path of sympathy," Tarrou adds, "It's a matter of understanding the most men possible" (*TRN*, p. 1992). And a notebook entry in December 1942 or January 1943 says: "Tarrou is the man who can understand everything—and who suffers thereby. He cannot judge anything" (*N2*, p. 52). These extratextual additions link the passage not only to the earlier one where Tarrou says his code of morals is understanding but to the ones where Rieux reflects that one cannot know and cure at the same time. Tarrou suffers from Hamlet's paralyzing fault of thinking too precisely on

th'event. The man who understands all pardons all and becomes incapacitated from action. Rieux recognizes that one must act decisively out of
instinctive compassion for men's suffering and only afterward seek full
understanding, as he does in compiling his chronicle. It may also be that
Camus conceived Tarrou's flaw in terms of immoderation, *la démesure;*
his preoccupation with saintliness is fatally obsessive. No one can be
entirely guilt-free. Rieux presumably has involuntarily contributed to
men's deaths also but does not dwell on it to the point of immobilization.
Tarrou says that he, like all men, has been infected with the plague of
judging before he came to Oran, but his fatal infection might contain
an equal dosage of the saintliness that cannot survive in an unsaintly
world.

Rieux presumably survives Tarrou because he has no ambition to be a
saint and because his occupation of doctor (true healer?) embodies a
viable way of living without judging. But this is the most equivocal point
in the book. Rieux can find peace of mind because his realm as a physician, literally and as a symbol of metaphysical revolt, is outside the
sphere of any social conflict. For that matter, the previously immobilized
Tarrou is quite able to function fighting the plague, which, conveniently,
involves no equivalent for the political conflicts of the outside world; the
authoritarianism of Othon and Paneloux and nihilism of Cottard are portrayed as personal quirks, not institutionalized menaces. We can extrapolate
from *The Rebel* that Camus might have wanted Rieux to represent his
final position there, that of the political activist who recognizes that killing
is sometimes necessary, with scrupulous limitations, but that he was not
able to symbolize this position in Rieux's occupation or activism against
the impersonal plague.

Even the struggle against Nazism that Rieux's role in the plague symbolizes was less complex than the political issues that concern Tarrou, as
Sartre recognized when he revised his earlier enthusiastic response to the
novel in light of the controversy over *The Rebel:*

> You [Camus] were fortunate in that the common fight against the
> Germans symbolized, in your eyes and ours, the union of all men
> against inhuman fatalities. By choosing injustice, the German, of his
> own accord, allied himself with the blind forces of nature, and in
> *La Peste* you were able to have his role played by microbes, without

anyone getting the joke [literally, '. . . without anyone perceiving the mystification'].[2]

Or, as Sartre could have put it in English, Camus disguised the Germans as germs. Many critics have pointed out that the impersonal symbol of the plague also begs the questions of the necessity of killing in World War II, the ethical dilemmas involved in Resistance activities—such as Nazi reprisals against civilians or prisoners—and the human factors on the side of the Germans.

Moreover, on the naturalistic level *The Plague* conveys little consciousness of social class in Oran. We do not see enough of the difference in the effects a plague—or a military occupation—would have on the rich and the poor. As Sartre reminded Camus, "The absurdity of our condition is not the same in Passy as in Billancourt"[3] (an affluent residential neighborhood and a poor industrial suburb of Paris). Camus's class perspective here, as in most of his fiction, is limited mainly to that of the petite bourgeoisie in spite of his own lower-working-class origin, a curiosity that might be partly attributable to the fact that the French proletarian in Algeria stood in much the same relationship to the Arab population as the bourgeois to the proletarian in noncolonial countries.

The relationship between French colonials and Arabs in Oran is itself largely ignored in *The Plague,* which results in a glaring weakness in the book's literary construction. This lapse is especially striking because before the plague Rambert has been sent to Oran by his Paris newspaper to write about living and sanitary conditions among the Arabs, and in their first meeting Rieux refuses to provide information unless Rambert is free to publish a total condemnation of the situation. But once the plague has begun, Rambert's story is forgotten, as is the effect of the epidemic on the whole Arab population of Oran, which virtually disappears for the rest of the novel. Camus apparently could not imagine a means of integrating Rieux's concern for the Arabs with his subsequent concern for the victims of the plague and the symbolic occupation. Tarrou the political activist is no more interested than Rieux in the Arab problem. The symbolic machinery of the novel is simply too cumbersomely abstract and evasive to cope with so specific a social issue. Camus's only recourse is

2. *Situations*, pp. 72–73.
3. Ibid., p. 73.

what Conor Cruise O'Brien aptly terms "this artistic final solution of the problem of the Arabs of Oran."[4]

The only conceivable equivalent in real-life political activity for Rieux's role against the plague would be, as Francis Jeanson suggested unkindly, the Red Cross. Camus sagely replied to Jeanson that the Red Cross is an estimable organization, which is quite true but still leaves the problem of its ideological limitation, that it has the power only to mitigate war or political conflict, not to prevent or end it. Perhaps Tarrou's death at the very end of the plague epidemic is necessary because he could no longer function in any other social circumstances, while Rieux is able to survive and function afterward only because his work was disengaged from social conflict to begin with.

Whichever way we interpret the book's symbolism, then, it is equivocal. If Camus intends Rieux to embody a specific alternative to Tarrou, he has begged the question, since Rieux's medical/metaphysical answers are inapplicable to Tarrou's historical dilemma. If, on the other hand, he means us to accept Rieux, Tarrou, and the other positive characters simply as a composite of various, nonspecific aspects of revolt and to acknowledge, as he suggested in a 1955 letter to Roland Barthes, that *"The Plague* can apply to any resistance against any tyranny" (*LCE,* p. 340), then the whole novel becomes abstract to the point of being inapplicable to any kind of real historical conflict. Perhaps the most consistent interpretation of the book is as an elaborate parable of Camus's ideal of the artist's social role, but that ideal has the same ideological limitations as the Red Cross and is further subject to all the previously summarized leftist criticisms of his aesthetic. No matter how we read it, *The Plague* fails to substantiate Camus's epigraph from Defoe: "It is as reasonable to represent one kind of imprisonment by another, as it is to represent anything that really exists by that which exists not."

In sum, *The Plague* is an immensely absorbing and moving novel on first reading and one that readers may well return to for emotional support in times of plaguelike disaster but not one that they are likely to pick up again periodically for the satisfactions of masterly novelistic technique or ideological cogency.

4. *Albert Camus of Europe and Africa,* p. 56.

10

The Labyrinth of *The Fall*

A different critical perspective from that applicable to *The Stranger* and *The Plague* needs to be brought to bear on evaluating *The Fall*. To begin with, it contains fewer conventional novelistic elements. There is really only one character and not much of a plot; the technique derives almost exclusively from the resourceful use of first-person narrative point of view. The structure reflects Clamence's calculated entrapment of his listener/reader. By juggling the sequence of the past events he is recounting and by dropping hints of what is to come, he builds up suspense throughout the first half of the book for the successive, climactic revelations in the second half, of the story of the girl on the bridge, his possession of the stolen painting of "The Just Judges," and the identity of his confidant. He weaves a spider's web around the latter with successively more intimate forms of address: "Monsieur," "Cher compatriote," "Cher ami," "Mon cher." The encircling movement of the narrative imitates the concentric canals of Amsterdam, the spiral of Dante's hell, the Minotaur's labyrinth, in much the same kind of mingling of theme with expository technique and geographical setting that Conrad achieves in Marlow's account of his devious moral journey up the Congo to the heart of darkness. (Camus suggested another Conradian affinity in an interview, describing Clamence as "a less brilliant Lord Jim.") [1]

Camus's narrative design provides another dimension of literary ambiguity in the final identification of Clamence's "client" as a fellow Parisian lawyer. Perhaps his visitor is a hallucination, and Clamence is talking to himself. Or perhaps Clamence is not really a lawyer but alters his whole story to match that of each different client he waylays, so that

1. *New York Times Book Review*, 24 Feb. 1957, p. 36.

each of us readers too is being lured to confess our personal variant on "what happened to you one night on the quays of the Seine and how you managed never to risk your life" (*Fall*, p. 147). Certainly Clamence's strategy succeeds in making most readers see themselves in his mirror, perhaps not immediately after the first reading, but sooner or later. The quality of *The Fall* that makes it a unique masterpiece is its power slowly to get under the reader's skin and permanently haunt his conscience.

Its internal dynamics are sufficient to make *The Fall* a rewarding reading experience by itself. But to perceive all its facets it is necessary, much more than with *The Stranger* or *The Plague,* to be aware of extrinsic factors such as Camus's other works, its literary allusions and generic tradition, the events and spirit of the historical period it reflects, and its sources in the author's personal life.

As indicated throughout Part One of this study, *The Fall* marks a culmination of nearly all of Camus's main themes: metaphysical and human judgment, dandyish egoism vs. altruism, monologue vs. dialogue, Europe vs. the Mediterranean and tropics, communist and Christian authoritarianism, an antireligious, secularized Christian ethic, and conflicting loyalties and fears between maternal and paternal forces. The fullest appreciation will result from recognizing its climactic significance in the overall pattern.

Although it is his least conventional novel in plot and characterization, it is all in all his most literary fictional work. In its genre it owes much to the tradition of spiritual autobiography and confessional literature: Saint Augustine, Rousseau's *Confessions,* Musset's *Confessions of a Child of the Century,* Baudelaire's *Flowers of Evil*—fictionalized and given the twist of an untrustworthy narrator by Dostoevsky in *Notes from Underground,* Conrad in the Marlow narratives, and Gide in *The Immoralist.* *The Stranger* and *The Plague* are both calculated to give at least an illusion of nonliterary style and viewpoint, with few allusions or self-consciously polished interjections by the narrator. In contrast, Clamence's discourse is loaded with allusions to the Old and New Testaments, Dante, Janus, Du Guesclin, van Eyck, d'Artagnan, Wagner's *Lohengrin* and *Tristan und Isolde.* His language is studiously refined and elegant—"Ah, I see you smile at that use of the subjunctive. I confess my weakness for that mood and for fine speech in general" (p. 5)—studded with aphorisms destined for quotation anthologies:

A single sentence will suffice for modern man: he fornicated and read the papers. [P. 7]

A newly dead man and the show begins at last. They need tragedy, don't you know; it's their little transcendence, their *apéritif*. [P. 34]

I have no more friends; I have nothing but accomplices. [P. 73]

Adolescents lose their metaphysical unrest with their first mistress. [P. 106]

Bourgeois marriage has put our country into slippers and will soon lead it to the gates of death. [P. 106]

Too many people now climb onto the cross merely to be seen from a greater distance. [P. 114]

This extensive use of aphorisms is a trait of Latin and neoclassical epigrammatic style, and the prominent theme in them of egocentric *amour propre* especially evokes Pascal, La Fontaine, and La Rochefoucauld—e.g., the latter's "In the adversity of our best friends we always find something that is not entirely displeasing to us," or "The most disinterested friendship is only a deal in which our own self-love always intends to gain something." Camus makes a similarly classical use of anecdotes on the same theme; Clamence recounts a variant on Pascal's stories of men distracted from their grief over the death of a wife or son by a boar hunt or game of billiards:

> "You'll pay for this!" a daughter said to her father who had prevented her from marrying a too well groomed suitor. And she killed herself. But the father paid for nothing. He loved fly-casting. Three Sundays later he went back to the river—to forget, as he said. He was right; he forgot. [P. 75]

Clamence's revelation of his own personality through epigrams and anecdotes follows the form of another neoclassical genre, the character sketch in the manner of Ben Jonson, Molière, La Bruyère, or Pope, which embodies a prototype of some human foible or compulsive "humor." Two passages, for instance, on pages 56–68 and 98–101, are structured as set pieces on Clamence's character in relation to women, revealing his Don Juan-like self-centeredness, need to domineer, and, in passages like the following one, his magnetic attraction to feminine beauty at the expense of more serious concerns:

> It hurts me to confess it, but I'd have given ten conversations with Einstein for an initial rendezvous with a pretty chorus girl. It's true that at the tenth rendezvous I was longing for Einstein or a serious book. . . . And how often, standing on the sidewalk involved in a passionate discussion with friends, I lost the thread of the argument being developed because a devastating woman was crossing the street at that very moment. [P. 60]

These incidental interludes encapsulate a whole world of significance with the concise finality of a rhymed couplet by Molière or Pope, such as the latter's description, in *Moral Essay II,* of a lady who is similarly distractible but in the opposite direction, *from* lovemaking:

> She, while her Lover pants upon her breast,
> Can mark the figures on an Indian chest.

The literary classicist's witty perception of the universality of *l'amour propre* in the particular image merges witih the existentialist notions of inauthenticity or acting at life, bad faith, and exploitative reification of the Other (not only Clamence's women but the suffering humanity he is ready to desert at the raise of a skirt). It is in such passages that the less grandiose, more down-to-earth side of Camus's philosophical and literary sensibility finds its most felicitous, best integrated expression. At the same time, these classical characterizing techniques contribute to making Clamence Camus's most fully rounded fictional personality in terms of detailed psychological realism; his self-portrait is in fact a psychiatrically accurate, clinical study of the Don Juan neurosis.

II

The Fall, then, marks a successful change of form for Camus to an overtly traditional literary style and allusiveness. He obviously did not choose this style, however, simply to show that he could master it. In the unsavory character of Clamence, who represents the humanistically educated, cultivated European, he is calling into question the whole cultural tradition of Western civilization. Like *Heart of Darkness, The Fall* ex-

poses the bestiality underneath Europe's veneer of refinement. The society that creates the "Liebestod" also creates Buchenwald; as in *The
Rebel,* Camus goes so far as to suggest a causal link between them: The
expectation of apocalyptic climax conditioned by art leads us to crave
a "little transcendence" above the boredom of everyday life—"Something
must happen, even loveless slavery, even war or death" (*Fall,* p. 37).

At the same time, Europe's culture has served to euphemize the barba-
rism of its politics and to curb potential revolutionary consciousness. The
literary confession channels all its author's and reader's passions inward,
to the autistic exclusion of social commitment. Classical wit and irony are
the defense mechanisms developed by those on the margins of the ruling
class—the more refined aristocrats and patronized artists before the Revolution, the professional class in bourgeois society—to keep from admitting
or despairing over their political ineffectuality. To vary an aphorism that
recurs throughout eighteenth-century literature, one laughs to keep from
crying—or from taking action. Witty articulation or astute analysis of
one's own faults and those of his society easily degenerates into a substitute for doing anything to correct them. As Clamence says, "I have accepted duplicity instead of being upset about it" (p. 141)—accepted it,
and dotes on it. It is all very well for the aristocrat La Rochefoucauld to
claim, "One ought to find consolation for one's faults in having the
strength to recognize them," but recognizing the faults of the *ancien
régime* was not sufficient consolation for the revolutionary masses.

Clamence paralyzed on the bridge can be seen as an emblem of the
aristocratic or bourgeois intellectual, well intentioned but too comfortable
and narcissistic to be able really to commit himself. In politics this congenital intellectual inertia ends up bolstering reactionism by default, as
in Dostoevsky's and Chekhov's impotent liberals in prerevolutionary
Russia. *The Fall* anticipates the rise of Third World cultural consciousness in the 1960s and the repudiation by spokesmen like Frantz Fanon
and Malcolm X of the white, European and Anglo-American cultural
heritage for its alleged acquiescence to racism, imperialism, and economic
class exploitation.

If Clamence embodies the duplicitous side of the entire European cultural heritage, he is also, like Lermontov's *Hero of Our Time,* "the ag-
gregate of the vices of our whole generation." The generation for which
he speaks most distinctly is the one that reached maturity between the

end of World War II and the early 1960s, an age when relatively wide-spread affluence and leisure among the bourgeoisie in Europe and America fostered self-absorption while ubiquitous mass media contributed immeasurably to a mentality of trivial distraction and theatricality. *The Fall* tends to have its most devastating effect on readers of that generation. This may indicate a largely subjective identification, and it is hard to predict whether the book will retain its effect on future generations. Certainly it is Camus's most specifically situated fictitious work historically and as such is more subject than *The Stranger, Caligula,* or *The Plague* to the vicissitudes of changing historical perspectives.

III

Another extratextual dimension contributing to the complexity of *The Fall* is its elements of autobiography. Simone de Beauvoir claims, "In the first few pages I recognized the same Camus I had known in 1943: his gestures, his voice, his charm, an exact portrait." [2] Clamence's occupation as a lawyer for noble causes is an obvious analogue for Camus's public image as humanitarian author, an image he bridled at and is satirizing here. Clamence shares his creator's love of sports and playacting, his distracting weakness for attractive females. Sartre and Beauvoir have written that despite Camus's proletarian roots and socialist sympathies, he became quite fond of bourgeois comforts, that his protestations notwithstanding, he relished celebrity, night life, stylish women. Clamence's self-consciously refined language is a self-mocking commentary on Francis Jeanson's criticism of the stylistic elegance of *The Rebel* and his implication that Camus's literary tone was decreasingly that of the *engagé* and increasingly that of the aspirant to prestigious bourgeois status as a man of letters. Clamence's paralysis on the bridge has been widely interpreted as an analogy for Camus's inability to take the plunge of committing himself to one side or the other in the Algerian War.

Clamence's first effort, while still in Paris, to shatter his public image as a great humanitarian (described on pp. 91–96) fails when his misanthropic and self-chastising outbursts are taken by his public as signs of humility, only further enhancing his prestige. Camus is commenting here on the extraordinary capacity of twentieth-century society to disarm

2. *Force of Circumstance,* p. 349.

its critics and nonconformists, not by suppressing them but by elevating them to public esteem and prosperity. Camus's career as a writer, both before and after *The Fall,* is a classic example of this paradox. When Baudelaire publishes *Flowers of Evil* in 1857, reviling his "hypocritical reader—my fellow—my brother," he is prosecuted and persecuted. A hundred years later Camus similarly vilifies his reader and himself in *The Fall* and is rewarded with the Nobel Prize—the ultimate confirmation of the fruitfulness of judge-penitency.

The autobiographical element most pertinent toward fully understanding *The Fall* is the conflict between Camus and Sartre that culminated in their quarrel over *The Rebel* in 1952. In an interview with Dominique Aury, Camus said of Clamence:

> My character is a build-up. There are touches from different sources. From the existentialists comes the mania for self-accusation, so that they can accuse others more easily. That has always seemed to me to be an extra dirty little trick; it's what shocks me the most in these gentlemen's activities. This passion for accusation always ends by a defense of the servitude which is the direct issue of existentialism.[3]

If the guilt-ridden judge-penitent after the fall is a caricature of Sartre's political philosophy, the self-righteous, prelapsarian Clamence bears a striking resemblance to Sartre's portrait of Camus in his 1952 "Reply to Albert Camus." (Sartre later suggestively described *The Fall* as "perhaps the most beautiful and the least understood" of Camus's books.)[4]

According to Sartre, each individual is obliged, if he wishes to maintain good faith, to commit himself totally to the course of political action he judges to be necessary to combat the gross injustices of his historical age; as Dostoevsky put it, we are each responsible to every man for every man. This commitment is dictated not only by conscience but by long-run pragmatic considerations: we will sooner or later be confronted by the wrath of those whose persecution we have ignored. Developing the theme of objective reactionism from Marx and the contemporary French philosopher Maurice Merleau-Ponty, Sartre argues that historical retribution often does not recognize fine lines or good intentions alone; we

3. *New York Times Book Review,* 24 Feb. 1957, p. 36.
4. "Albert Camus," in *Situations,* p. 79. This essay is also translated as "Tribute to Albert Camus" in *Camus: A Collection of Critical Essays,* ed. Brée, pp. 173–75.

may be identified with our exploiting class or race whether or not we do so in our own minds. Thus the relatively guiltless bourgeois, colonial, or white man may expect someday to be condemned along with the guilty in the revolution of the proletariat, colonized, or colored—in which case all he can do is try to detach himself enough to recognize the justice, or at least the inevitability, of his condemnation.

Up to a certain point, Sartre's ethic resembles Camus's position in the introduction to *The Rebel* that once we affirm the value of our own life we become committed by empathy to uphold others' lives as well. The main point of difference is that for Sartre this commitment to others or to history must be total, while for Camus, in his wariness of any absolute value, such a commitment makes superhuman demands and must be moderated and energized by some degree of self-fulfilling appreciation of life. Camus understood the notion of objective reactionism, as he indicated in "The Artist and His Time" of 1953: "Artists of the past could at least keep silent in the face of tyranny. The tyrannies of today are improved; they no longer admit of silence or neutrality. One has to take a stand, be either for or against. Well, in that case, I am against" (*Myth,* p. 147). But in *The Rebel* he vehemently repudiated what he alleged to be the use of this notion by Marxist intellectuals to blackmail individuals into total self-abnegation and uncritical support for communist governments or revolutionary movements out of fear of being regarded as accomplices of bourgeois reactionism. The end product of Sartrean total preoccupation with historical responsibility is symbolized in Clamence, ridden with bad conscience because he is incapable of going to the length of sleeping on the floor in self-denial for an imprisoned comrade or of sacrificing his life: "Who would have believed that crime consists less in making others die than in not dying oneself!" (*Fall,* p. 113).

Furthermore, Sartrean anxiety over the impingement of others' existence on our own and of our consequent responsibility for them can lapse into theatricality or "other-direction." Like the dandy, Clamence comes to get a dramatic thrill out of parading the shortcomings in his integrity toward others. One can even fall into an apocalyptic surrender to all forms of guilt in which that of the benevolent man whose self-sacrifice is less than total becomes indistinguishable from, and in fact lends support to, that of the malevolent evildoer. Feeling that he has failed to act in full good faith, a man may consciously or subconsciously welcome any form of oppression as chastisement: "The essential is to cease being free and obey, in repentance, a greater rogue than oneself. When we are all guilty, that will be democracy" (p. 136). Here Camus was perhaps thinking of the specific political example from the Cold War of the Sartrean, left-sympathizing bourgeois who may have rationalized the worst Stalinist excesses out of compensation for his own less-than-total revolutionary commitment.

Involved here on a broader scale is the perennial ethical dilemma of egoism against altruism, which had also troubled Tarrou in *The Plague,* in a passage reminiscent of Ivan Karamazov:

> Nobody is capable of really thinking about anyone, even in the worst calamity. For really to think about someone means thinking about that person every minute of the day, without letting one's thoughts be diverted by anything—by meals, by a fly that settles on one's cheek, by household duties, or by a sudden itch somewhere. But there are always flies and itches. That's why life is difficult to live. [P. 217]

Camus's personal solution to the dilemma was to strive for a reasonable balance between egoism and altruism, and the distance that separates him in his own mind from Tarrou and Clamence—and Sartre—in their *démesure* can be seen in a work like "Return to Tipasa," written almost contemporaneously with *The Fall.*

If Sartre's political position is subject to the equivocations that Camus dramatized in the post-fall Clamence, Camus's also has its potential equivocations, which Sartre exposed in "Reply to Albert Camus" (a nasty but forceful document that has the tone of the marriage-breaking-up fight in which all the grievances that have been suppressed over the years come pouring out at once). Camus's principle of refusing to collaborate with any murderous political camp can be turned into a weak-willed evasion of the necessity of taking sides and getting one's hands dirty. His ideal of maintaining a balance between social commitment and personal fulfillment can become a self-serving device for playing both ends against the middle, as with liberals who mouth leftist, humanitarian sentiments while continuing to indulge in bourgeois comfort and inertia. *La mesure* can be a euphemism for a limbo in which one smugly sets oneself above those who have perforce recognized the existential necessity of total commitment; thus Sartre accuses Camus of carrying around a portable pedestal and tells him, "you have become a victim of a dismal self-importance, which hides your inner problems, and which you, I think, would call Mediterranean moderation."[5] Sartre repeatedly phrases his charges against Camus in the imagery of judgment: "You have so deliberately put me on trial. . . . You are an advocate who says, 'These are my brothers,' because these are the words which stand the best chance of making the jury weep. . . . The Republic of Hearts and Flowers would have named you Chief prosecutor. . . . I am involved with a judge who is condemning our case on biased police evidence. . . . In order to keep a clear conscience, you need to condemn. You need a guilty party; if it isn't you, then it must be the universe. . . . Your distrust of men made you presume that every defendant was, before the fact, a guilty man."[6] What Sartre is implying is that Camus's self-image as literary defense attorney was a devious means of judging the judges. (René Girard has suggested that in *The Stranger* Camus was really setting Meursault above his judges and that *The Fall* was his confession of this equivocation.)[7] Camus very likely modeled Clamence's personality and vocabulary at least partly on Sartre's portrait of him, thereby perhaps admitting that Sartre's attack had hit home. I have suggested that Clamence incarnates elements of Camus before the fall and Sartre afterward, but the whole hopeless confusion of roles involved in Camus and Sartre accusing each other of being guilty of accusing is undoubtedly also reflected throughout *The Fall* in the merging of judge and penitent, of Clamence and his alter ego confidant.

IV

A word should be added about Justin O'Brien's translation, the most artful one of Camus's fiction or plays. O'Brien maintains a generally high level of accuracy while managing to find inventive English equivalents for Clamence's highly idiomatic style, which intermingles elegant literary French with street-corner colloquialism, although O'Brien's versions of the latter tend to be a little prudish. In his psychoanalytic study of *The Fall*, José Barchilon astutely points out several instances where O'Brien either

5. *Situations*, p. 55.
6. Ibid., pp. 54–77 passim.
7. "Camus' Stranger Retried," *PMLA* 79, no. 5 (Dec. 1964): 519–33.

catches or misses psychological shadings in the French text. Dr. Barchilon, a French-American psychiatrist, brings to his study a fine sensibility not only in psychology but in literature and the French language and culture. For instance, in the passage on pages 38–40 where Clamence hears a laugh behind him on the Pont des Arts, Barchilon notes: "Camus wrote, 'Face au Vert-Galant, je dominais l'île.' But Justin O'Brien translated: 'Facing the statue of the Vert-Galant, I dominated the island' (p. 38). The French only says that he was facing the Vert-Galant which to any Parisian means the garden at the tip of the island. But with a marvelous intuition, O'Brien sensed that the important thing here, as we shall see, is the statue of the Green Gallant dominating the Garden from the Pont Neuf, the next bridge, which actually straddles the Garden." [8] Barchilon suggests that Clamence imagines the equestrian statue of King Henri IV, a father figure to Frenchmen, laughing at him with "a good, hearty, almost friendly laugh, which re-established the proper proportions," reducing him to an impotent infant, after which he proceeds to the rue Dauphine, the street of the prince, to buy "some cigarettes I didn't need at all," for oral reassurance.

This interpretation of the laugh is somewhat weakened by Camus's clear statement that Clamence is facing the Vert-Galant and that the laugh comes from behind him and goes downstream, away from the statue; the hallucinated laugh, however, while male, must also be associated with the woman who had jumped from the Pont Royal, downstream from the Pont des Arts, two or three years previously—a mother figure, as we have seen in chapter 4. (Barchilon further points out that the Vert-Galant marks the tip of the Ile de la Cité, the mother island of Paris and the location of Notre Dame, Our Lady of Paris, which faces Henri IV across the island at its other end.) The possibility of a hidden allusion to the statue of Henri IV, the back of whose horse Clamence was facing, is highly suggestive, particularly since there is an amusing echo of it in the episode where Clamence is humiliated by a little man on a motorcycle who tells him (in an untranslatable colloquialism that O'Brien blandly renders "go straight to hell") that "on l'emmenait à pied et à cheval," which, as Barchilon explains, is a euphemism for "I shit

8. "A Study of Camus' Mythopoeic Tale *The Fall* with Some Comments about the Origin of Esthetic Feelings," *Journal of the American Psychoanalytic Association,* Apr. 1971, p. 197 n.

on you on foot and on horseback." The little man further tells Clamence that he should "aller me rhabiller"—go dress himself again or, by implication, go home and change his diapers (O'Brien translates, "go climb a tree") and offers him a "dérouillée," a "de-rusting" (O'Brien says, "dusting off"), which, Barchilon notes, is another euphemism, for "knock the shit out of him." Similarly, Barchilon points out that after Clamence fails to jump in after the drowning woman, O'Brien says he goes away "slowly" (p. 70), whereas the untranslatable French idiom is "à petits pas" —"with small steps," carrying the connotation of "baby steps."

v

The main limitation in *The Fall* is not any weakness on its own terms, within which it is difficult to find fault, but a general one in Camus's fiction that becomes most acute here. There is a paucity throughout his work of long-term, gradually developed characterization and relationships between people in more or less normal life situations. In an essay on Roger Martin du Gard (*LCE,* pp. 254–87), he expressed admiration for Martin du Gard as one of the last novelists to excel in this aspect of fiction and regretted that most contemporary writers, presumably including himself, had exclusively pursued the Dostoevskian novel of crisis rather than the Tolstoyan novel of character.

The dimension lacking in his fiction can be pointed up by comparing him to a master of characterization like Proust, the one twentieth-century French novelist who most clearly surpasses Camus in scope. Proust and Gide were the most influential writers for Camus's generation, and while much in Gide by now seems somewhat superficial and dated—partly because Camus brought many of his themes and techniques to a fuller realization—Proust in some ways still makes Camus appear almost redundant. Despite Proust's ostensibly more restricted social and metaphysical framework, his less robust temperament, and generally lower level of dramatic intensity, he subsumes most of Camus's themes—political injustice and revolt being the most glaring exceptions—and applies similar insight to analyzing several areas outside of Camus's range, preeminently long-term interpersonal relationships, especially in love, as well as social class structure, the psychology of children (who are almost completely absent from Camus's world), and the unconscious workings of the adult mind.

The difference between Proust and Camus can be illustrated by their treatment of one similar theme, our self-centered indifference to the death of others, as expressed in *The Fall* by Clamence's story of the daughter who kills herself to spite her father, who subsequently goes on a fishing trip "to forget," and does. In Proust's *Swann's Way* Swann's father is led from his wife's death chamber weeping profusely, but when he steps outside into a sunlit park he momentarily forgets himself and launches into rhapsodic praise of the joys of living. And at the end of *The Guermantes Way* Swann tells his friends the duke and duchess of Guermantes that his doctors have said he only has a short time left to live, but they affect disbelief and flippantly postpone discussing it because they are late to a dinner party. A moment later the duke discovers that his wife's shoes do not match her dress; he insists that *this* is important enough that she take the time to change them. Camus's anecdote, marvelous as it is, has only an extrinsic bearing on the novel's characterization and action, while Proust's are not only memorable in themselves but contribute substantially to the plot and character exposition of those directly involved as well as to the general patterns of personality that dominate his fictional world. The cumulative development of the relationship between Swann and the Guermantes and of other, similar relationships through three preceding volumes builds to an excruciating dramatic climax in the incident of the duchess's shoes.

Camus, of course, expressly conceived Clamence as a totally self-absorbed character incapable of any involved relationship with other people. Similarly, all the stories in *Exile and the Kingdom* deal with the failure of the central characters to relate satisfactorily to others. Ostensibly, Camus was critically portraying a symptomatic problem of his historical time, and we must continue to beware of overidentifying him personally with his fictional subjects; still, it would be ingenuous not to suspect strongly that in these characters he was also revealing his personal psychological and artistic limitations. All of his previous characters too, even the most admirable ones, were deficient in personal relationships; those who attained solidarity with others, like Rieux, Tarrou, Rambert, Grand, Diego, Kaliayev and Dora, did so impersonally, ideologically, at the expense of private bonds.

His portrayals of marriage, family life, and women are especially restricted. It appears that the residue of his protracted childhood narcissism limited his imaginative capacity to depict mature relationships between men and women. Camus was frugal in disclosing details of his private life, and his widow has discouraged intimate biographical inquiries, but his proclivity for extramarital love affairs was public knowledge. Although Simone de Beauvoir has disavowed any close resemblance between Camus and the character of Henri Perron in her novel *The Mandarins,* it has been widely conjectured that Perron's rocky marriage was modeled in some degree on Camus's. This is not to pass moral judgment on his private life, but it certainly indicates an artistic limitation that for his writing he was able to draw so little from twenty years of marriage and raising two children to teen age. It is noteworthy that he chose not to publish some of his more detailed treatments of marriage. In *A Happy Death* Mersault's marriage (based partly on Camus's own short-lived first one) is portrayed flatly and unconvincingly, as are his other relationships with women. In *The Plague,* although the story of Grand's unhappy marriage to Jeanne is told movingly, Camus's notebook sketches for their relationship are much more extensive, as are those for Rieux's marriage. His descriptions of women, even when lyrically appreciative, are usually one-dimensional and often tainted with a Mediterranean strain of male chauvinism—less so as he matured, but embarrassingly in early works like *A Happy Death:* "A man's beauty represents inner, functional truths: his face shows what he can do. And what is that compared to the magnificent uselessness of a woman's face?" (p. 23). More than Camus would have wanted to admit, Clamence's preference for ten-minute adventures with women corresponds to his creator's attention span in portraying them.

Whether or not the isolated central characters in *The Fall* and *Exile and the Kingdom* reflect the writer's own emotional blocks, these works marked an artistic impasse for Camus. Fiction about characters unable to communicate with others, especially in monologues by solipsistic antiheroes like Clamence and the Renegade, is a tour de force that can only be sustained for so long in one book and cannot be repeated indefinitely—although, to be sure, many European, English, and American writers have continued to work this vein past the point of exhaustion since *The Fall.* Camus was probably quite aware of having run into a blind alley and was trying to work out of it in his next novel-in-progress, "The First Man," written in naturalistic style and set in Cold War Europe, which apparently would have dealt with a conflict between its hero's political commitments and his marriage, a central theme in the fiction of Malraux,

Sartre, and Beauvoir. His notebook sketches show promise in their insightful, detailed account of the evolving marital relationship, although it again appears to be a deteriorating one.

Camus did have a surprising capacity for dialectical reversals, and it is quite possible that he would have mastered the traditional techniques of interpersonal characterization and naturalistic, historically situated exposition in "The First Man." Even if he had, however, the larger, impersonal dialectic of literary and political history would have been working against him. Few enduringly great conventional novels have appeared since *The Fall*. Most of the outstanding subsequent fiction writers, including the French New Novelists and Beckett, Grass, Borges, Nabokov, Heller, and Barth, have turned the form inside out in diverse ways. Even these antinovels seem like last-ditch efforts, conveying a sense of creative desperation. *The Fall* marks a significant step in a tendency since World War II in Western Europe, England, and America—a tendency that Camus was in effect exploiting at the same time he was ostensibly criticizing it—for literature to become progressively more egocentric, technically involuted, and calculated through mirror effects to serve the purpose of the self-approval (or self-disapproval, which comes to the same thing, as Clamence knows well) of a jaded middle-class reading public. The end result has been that literary forms that had long been viable— theater and poetry as well as the novel and short story—now appear to have become inbred nearly to the point of extinction.

It is hard to avoid the conclusion that what John Barth has termed "the literature of exhaustion" represents one aspect of a general atrophy of culture under capitalism that has resulted at least in part from the complete assimilation of art as a commodity into the consumer society, with its planned obsolescence and depletion of resources, and from the triumphant credo of artistic and intellectual adaptations of bourgeois individualism. As American New Leftist literary critic Louis Kampf wrote in 1967, "We must all begin to understand that a totally self-centered individualism is not necessarily a sign of heroism or nobility; it may, in fact, serve as a mask for the competitive depredations of capitalism. The narcissistic obsession of modern literature for the self, the critical cant concerning the tragic isolation of the individual—these are notions that tie our hands and keep us from the communion necessary for meaningful action." [9]

9. "The Scandal of Literary Scholarship," in *The Dissenting Academy,* ed. Theodore Roszak (New York: Vintage, 1968), pp. 56–57.

Camus undoubtedly would have agreed in principle; and he had the *will* to progress beyond the negative truth of *The Fall* toward a literature dramatically affirming social solidarity. The question is whether he would have been able to find the necessary artistic resources and ideological foundation to do so.

The artistic impasse of *The Fall* coincided with his ideological isolation and paralysis over Algeria and conservatism on the Cold War. The shifting political perspectives of the 1960s might have undermined his vantage point from the peak of the Cold War by the time he completed "The First Man," but they also might have opened new artistic vistas. Perhaps the increased intensity of world revolution and reaction, along with the challenge of a new generation of writer-revolutionaries like Frantz Fanon and Régis Debray, would have served as a creative catalyst, or perhaps he would have felt compelled like Sartre to forsake fiction altogether in order to concentrate full attention on political journalism and theory. It would have been highly instructive to see whether he would have succeeded in readjusting to the climate of the New Left that disoriented many creative writers of his generation in Europe and America. "The First Man," however, was to remain no more than a fragment, and there appears to be little prospect of its being published even in that form by his literary executors. Like so much else in his life that was unintentionally exemplary, *The Fall* seemed destined to stand not only as his own last novel but as a historical milestone toward the exhaustion of the novel as a literary genre.

The Stories: Exile and Kingdom, Solitude and Solidarity

I

In the six stories of *Exile and the Kingdom* Camus is trying out new techniques: a relatively objective third-person narration in all of them but "The Renegade," which is his only attempt at interior monologue; a light, urbane tone in the satire on upper-bohemian Paris social life in "The Artist at Work"; a feminine point of view in "The Adulterous Woman"; extensive stretches of detailed realistic narration and description with few symbolic overtones in the early parts of "The Adulterous Woman" and "The Growing Stone" and throughout "The Silent Men." He is also trying to fill some gaps in the subject matter of his previous works: sustained accounts of marital relationships in "The Adulterous Woman" and "The Artist at Work"; mundane central characters and workaday settings in "The Adulterous Woman" and "The Silent Men"; a Parisian locale in "The Artist at Work"; most strikingly, the less attractive side of the coin of Algeria's landscape and life—"The Renegade" takes place under inhumanly hot sunlight, "The Adulterous Woman," "The Silent Men," and "The Guest" in wintry cold. The stories are woven together thematically by various paradoxical mixtures of familiar antitheses: exile and kingdom, solitude and solidarity, freedom and servitude, silence and noise or speech. Each of the central characters suffers from divided loyalties, each is literally or figuratively a foreigner, isolated in the midst of society.

With a more disenchanted vision than that which had set an Algerian kingdom in antithesis to European exile, Camus now identifies Algeria too as a place of exile for Janine, the renegade priest, Daru, and Yvars. At the end of "The Silent Men" Yvars dispiritedly dreams of fleeing from

Algeria as the characters in *The Misunderstanding* and Camus in the later lyrical essays dreamed of fleeing *to* it: "If only he were young again, and Fernande too, they would have gone away, across the sea" (*EK,* p. 84). The stories were written for the most part before the Algerian War broke out in 1954, but the change in perspective undoubtedly resulted in part from the deepening crisis in the early fifties that was cutting the ground away under Camus on which rested his nostalgia for his youthful homeland as an oasis of relative innocence. But even if war had not been brewing, he probably would have been due following his accustomed procedure to counterbalance any implications from his previous works that Algeria was a pure Arcadia, implications that only careless or hostile readers would have found to begin with, notwithstanding the limitations in his portrayals of the racial situation there.

II

At the beginning of "The Adulterous Woman," Janine feels estranged as a European and threatened as a woman by the Arab natives and barren southern Algerian landscape. She clings to her banal, philistine husband now for the same reason she has married him, out of fear of loneliness, desire for bourgeois security, and the feminine need to give authenticity to her existence by identifying with a man—a prominent theme in Beauvoir and Sartre: "By so often making her aware that she existed for him he made her exist in reality. No, she was not alone" (*EK,* p. 6). But she still feels alone when with Marcel—"They made love in the dark by feel, without seeing each other" (p. 27)—and her identity with him is also a bondage: "No, she was overcoming nothing, she was not happy, she was going to die in truth, without having been liberated ['delivered']" (p. 29). ("Délivrée" carries the connotation of childbirth; on the previous two pages we have learned that her unhappiness stems in part from being childless and that she has become like a mother to Marcel.)

She first feels lured away from Marcel when, atop the fortress of the oasis town where he is doing business, she sees in the distance the tents of a nomadic tribe, "homeless, cut off from the world," yet paradoxically, "possessing nothing but serving no one, poverty-stricken but free lords of a strange kingdom" (p. 24). She senses in their life the liberation she has been longing for, and it is their memory, her instinct of spiritual solidarity with them, that draws her back to the fortress where she undergoes her liberating, adulterous union with the cold desert night.

Camus reinforces his themes here with a development of imagery similar to that in the lyrical essays. The solitary Janine's sense of communication with the desert and distant nomads is expressed in oxymorons of noise and silence, speech and dumbness: she hears the "mute call" of the desert, and the nomads' faraway camels metaphorically "formed against the gray ground the black signs of a strange handwriting, the meaning of which had to be deciphered" (p. 23). This aural and semantic imagery merges with similar mixtures of cold and heat, dryness and wetness, weight and lightness. Camus identifies the emotional and sexual barrenness of Janine's marriage with cold, aridity, and a heaviness suggesting perpetual pregnancy without delivery, while the barren desert, in contrast to the domesticated oasis, becomes associated by metaphor with water, fertility, phallic potency, as in the following (with my italics):

> She was waiting, but she didn't know for what. She was aware only of her *solitude,* and of the *penetrating cold* [literally, 'the cold that was penetrating her'], and of *a greater weight* in the region of her heart. She was in fact dreaming, almost *deaf to the sounds rising from the street along with Marcel's vocal outbursts,* more aware on the other hand of that *sound* of a *river* coming from the window-slit and caused ['*fait naître*'—'given birth'] *by the wind in the palm trees,* so close now, it seemed to her. Then the wind seemed to increase and the *gentle ripple of waters became a hissing of waves.* She imagined, beyond the walls, a *sea of erect, flexible palm trees unfurling* ['frothing'] in the storm. Nothing was like what she had expected, but those invisible *waves* refreshed her tired eyes. She was standing, *heavy,* with dangling arms, slightly stooped, as *the cold climbed her thick legs.* She was dreaming of the *erect and flexible palm trees and of the girl she had once been.* [P. 14]

All these images culminate in the climactic two paragraphs on pages 31–33, where the cold and dryness of the desert night, the "sparkling icicles" of the stars, are melted by the liberating flow of heat and fluid from within her, suggesting both sexual orgasm and childbirth: "Then, with unbearable gentleness, the water of night began to fill Janine, drowned the cold, rose gradually from the hidden core of her being and overflowed in wave after wave, rising up even to her mouth full of moans." The stylistic virtuosity of this climax is a counterpart to that of "Summer in Algiers," where the earth, hot and dry after the long summer, is personified as a woman fecundated by the cool autumn rains.

The story's last paragraph presents an ironic anticlimax to the liquid symbolism of male potency: when Janine comes back to bed, Marcel, who has earlier warned her fastidiously against drinking the local water, gets up to fortify himself with a glass of bottled mineral water.

III

Exile and the Kingdom's most striking technical feat is the style of the interior monologue in "The Renegade," much of which is unfortunately lost in translation. These are the opening lines:

> Quelle bouillie, quelle bouillie! Il faut mettre de l'ordre dans ma tête. Depuis qu'ils m'ont coupé la langue, une autre langue, je ne sais pas, marche sans arrêt dans mon crâne, quelque chose parle, ou quelqu'un qui se tait soudain et puis tout recommence ô j'entends trop de choses que je ne dis pourtant pas, quelle bouillie, et si j'ouvre la bouche, c'est comme un bruit de cailloux remués. [*TRN*, p. 1577]

> What a jumble! What a jumble! I must tidy up my mind. Since they cut out my tongue, another tongue, it seems, has been constantly wagging somewhere in my skull, something has been talking, or someone, that suddenly falls silent and then it all begins again—oh, I hear too many things I never utter, what a jumble, and if I open my mouth it's like pebbles rattling together. [*EK*, p. 34]

The tortuously elongated sentences, ungrammatically linked without punctuation or by commas, are the antithesis of *The Stranger*'s curt, disparate sentence structure. Clamence's verbose quasidialogue, verging toward the end of *The Fall* on delirium, is reduced here to a man without a tongue raving interminably to himself—the ultimate image of everything Camus has said about the perversion of language to isolate and enslave men. A litany of anguish is created by the rhythms of three-, six-, and twelve-syllable syntactic units that suggest the French alexandrine poetic line, reinforced by internal near rhymes (*mettre/tête*), as in the first two sentences above or the following: "Quelle bouillie, quelle fureur, [/] râ, râ, ivre de chaleur" (*TRN*, p. 1586). In *The Rebel* Camus had criticized the romantic and symbolist poets, especially Baudelaire, Lautréamont, and Rimbaud, for exalting apocalyptic evil in images of exotic primitivism. "The Renegade" evokes Rimbaud's alexandrine *The Drunken Boat*—whose speaker at the end of his hallucinatory journey into tropical savagery nostalgically longs for Europe—and even more overtly *A Season in Hell*: "I called to the executioners that I might gnaw their rifle-butts while dying. I called to the plagues ['fléaux'—'scourges'] to smother me in blood, in sand. Misfortune was my God." [1]

"The Renegade" is a close companion piece to *The Fall*, which Camus originally conceived as a short story in the same collection. Jean-Baptiste Clamence is a false John the Baptist, the *vox clamans in deserto;* here the narrator, literally in the desert, asks, "God doesn't speak in the desert, yet whence comes that voice . . . ?" (*EK*, p. 61). Filled with hostility since youth against his boorish parents and "the whole of lousy Europe" (p. 36), he has set out for Africa as the missionary of brute power: "I wanted to be acknowledged by the torturers themselves, to fling them on their knees and make them say: 'O Lord, here is thy victory,' to rule in short by the sheer force of words over an army of the wicked" (p. 40). But it is he who is reduced to slavery by the Taghâsan tribe, converted to their savagery, envisioning them conquering Europe, as if Camus is reminding us that the barbarity beneath Europe's facade of civilization is still more than matched by that of the primitive world. Clamence has lamented, "Oh, sun, beaches, and the islands in the path of the trade winds, youth whose memory drives one to despair!" (*Fall*, p. 144), but the renegade, torn at last by remorse, cries, "O nights of Europe, home, childhood, why must I weep in the moment of triumph?" (p. 59). Still, in the end it is the French troops who inflict the Taghâsans' own tortures on them, they whose "handful of salt fills the mouth of the garrulous slave" (p. 61).

IV

The beginning of "The Silent Men"—"It was the dead of winter" (*EK*, p. 62)—signals that this story is a sequel to "Summer in Algiers," published nearly twenty years earlier. There Camus had written, "During

1. *A Season in Hell* (New York: New Directions, 1961), p. 3.

their entire youth men find here a life in proportion to their beauty. Then, later on, the downhill slope and obscurity. They wagered on the flesh, but knowing they were to lose" (*Myth,* p. 105), and "They go to work early and in ten years exhaust the experience of a lifetime. A thirty-year-old workman has already played all the cards in his hand. He awaits the end between his wife and his children" (p. 109). Here Camus, himself now writing from the perspective of his forties, has the forty-year-old workman Yvars reflect sadly, "The deep, clear water, the hot sun, the girls, the physical life—there was no other form of happiness in this country. And that happiness disappeared with youth" (*EK,* p. 64). The rather vague references in "Summer in Algiers" to the actual working life of the poor laborers are also supplemented here in the convincingly detailed account of vitiating labor in a barrel factory, the atmosphere of which Camus re-created partly from memories of his uncle's barrel shop in his youth.

"Solidarity" here is that of trade unionism, which has broken down, causing the coopers' wildcat strike in their single shop to fail, leaving them isolated. Camus sets up the situation of a labor-management dispute in which neither side is really at fault, each a victim of circumstances. Yet wounded pride compels the workers to refuse to speak to their employer, even to express sympathy when his child falls fatally ill. The frustrating impasses built into the human condition are repeated here at the level of men finding themselves insurmountably at socioeconomic cross-purposes through no one's fault.

Roger Quilliot says about this story "The Silent Men," "If Camus wanted to prove that he, too, was capable of not going beyond the story, and, as he told me jokingly one day, of writing in the vein of 'socialist realism,' he certainly won his bet." [2] Realistic the story is—socialistic it isn't. It does meet one criterion of recent theoreticians of socialist realism like Lukács and Fischer in conveying a sense of the general conditions in Algeria's economic development that created the local problem involved here. Nevertheless, even though Camus credibly portrays the small entrepreneur Lassalle as a sympathetic character and emphasizes that the workers' cause was too weak to gain the support of their union, the Marxist would argue that their conflict is not typical of management-labor relations in general under capitalism. Surely Camus chose the atypi-

2. "An Ambiguous World," in *Camus: A Collection of Critical Essays,* ed. Brée, pp. 164–65.

cal to point up that class conflict is not always a black-and-white matter. Still, in the absence everywhere else in his fiction of more clearcut exploitation of labor, his singling out this situation leaves the mystifying impression that it *is* typical and that there is no possible solution such as systemic political reorganization changing the distribution of wealth and placing means of production under workers' control. The Marxist literary theorist might further recommend that Camus juxtapose the plight of these silent men with the leisurely life of wealthy capitalists in Algeria or France.

It would of course be difficult to integrate a socialist perspective with the more personalized elements in the story without smothering it in revolutionary tendentiousness. Yet Camus himself, as well as Marxist critics, established some such integration of art and ideology as the ideal toward which today's writer should aspire. By failing to provide an overview beyond his characters' uncomprehending perception of their experience, Camus himself is falling victim to the totalistic unselectivity that he disapprovingly attributes to socialist realism.

When Justin O'Brien was translating the next story, "L'Hôte," he wrote to Camus asking whether to use the title "The Host" or "The Guest." Camus opted for the latter but added that it was a pity the ambiguity was lost in translation. "Host" has no less than three Latin origins: in addition to the root of its sense as the eucharistic host, *hostia*—"victim" or "sacrifice," there is *hostis*—"stranger" or "enemy," and its compounded form *hospes*—"friendly stranger," either as guest or host. Is "l'hôte" Daru or the Arab, or perhaps both? Each man is at the same time friendly stranger, victim, and enemy.

Daru at first is the host, the native. "In the beginning, the solitude and the silence had been hard for him on these wastelands peopled only by stones" (*EK,* p. 97), but by the time of the story's present action, "he who lived almost like a monk in his remote schoolhouse, nonetheless satisfied with the little he had and with the rough life, had felt like a lord. . . . Daru had been born here. Everywhere else, he felt exiled" (p. 88). He is content to lie "listening to the silence" (p. 97). By the end, however, the roles have reversed, making Daru the guest, or the unwelcome foreigner, an exile in his own homeland. In the last sentence his cherished solitude has become cause for fear: "In this vast landscape he had loved so much, he was alone" (p. 109).

Daru's voluntary solitude and silence are unavoidably, fatally intruded on with the approach of the policeman Balducci and his Arab prisoner— a tacit commentary by Camus on the impossibility of escaping political involvement. As he says in "The Artist and His Time" of 1953, "As a man, I have a preference for happiness. . . . But I have been sought out, as each individual has been sought out" (*Myth,* p. 147).

The eucharistic communion Daru reaches with the Arab is ephemeral. In spite of his good intentions he is condemned by his prisoner's brothers, one more instance in Camus of tragedy resulting from failure in communication, verbal misunderstanding. Here Camus might also be dramatizing the problem of political objective reactionism that preoccupied Sartre and Merleau-Ponty. As Sartre puts it, "We will not be judged by our intentions alone. What reveals our worth as much and more than the intentional effects of our actions, are their involuntary results." [3] Daru is unable to foresee that his humane intentions will be wasted and misunderstood. Camus suggests no alternative to this tragic dilemma, but the Sartrean leftist would draw the conclusion that Daru—literally and as a symbol for the intellectual in the real historical situation of the years leading up to the Algerian War—should have sided actively, unequivocally with the Arabs before historical retribution caught up with him in his isolation and passivity.

A fatal intrusion into a man's valued solitude and silence is again the subject of "The Artist at Work," but in the diametrically opposite setting of Parisian society and the artistic life. This is the story of the paradoxical decline of an artist due to success, with its attendant public notoriety, demands on his time for social causes, distractions by disciples, hangers-on, and resentful detractors—the same theme Federico Fellini treated a few years later in his film *8½*. After reaching the extreme point of becoming completely incapacitated in his work by social demands, the painter Gilbert Jonas lurches to the opposite pole of totally isolating himself to work in a dark loft; but there he ironically finds himself able to think only about his family and friends. Having lost the equilibrium between solitude and sociability necessary to function as an artist and man, he inevitably collapses.

"The Artist at Work" is one of Camus's more straightforward pieces of fiction. Most of its meaning is evident on the surface—some perhaps

3. "Merleau-Ponty," in *Situations,* p. 175.

above the surface, in the similarities to Camus's own personality and career as a writer; the best part of the story is the bitterly humorous barbs aimed at the Parisian artistic *haut monde,* which he must have been saving up for a long time. A symbolic level suggested by the biblical epigraph about Jonah is not fully developed. The story is a partial dramatization of Camus's concern with the occupational hazards of the artist, but it is slightly disappointing as such because he does not develop several aspects of the problem that might have added more drama, some of which he projected for the story in his notebooks, such as the tendency in the artistic temperament toward self-absorbed callousness in one's personal relationships or, worse, parasitic exploitation of them for subject matter. In one projected sketch Camus's artist triumphantly finishes his masterpiece at the same moment his neglected wife dies, and in another he impassively paints her dead face.

v

"The Growing Stone" presents the most optimistic version of the book's recurrent themes, which is undoubtedly one reason Camus placed it last. It also has the most involved plot: D'Arrast, the engineer exiled for reasons we never learn from his native France, comes to Iguape, Brazil, to build a dike protecting the poor section of the town from a flooding river. There he is annoyed by the superstitious local Catholicism and by the white bureaucracy—the mayor, the chief of police who drunkenly harasses him, the inevitable judge, predictably grandiloquent and self-righteous, who insists against D'Arrast's will that the police chief be punished for his indiscretion. He feels more companionship toward the poverty-stricken black natives, but they resent his presence. He finally befriends a mulatto ship's cook with whom he attends a night of Dionysian native dancing, but as the dancing nears orgiastic pitch, the cook approaches D'Arrast: "Coldly, as if speaking to a stranger, he said: 'It's late, Captain. They are going to dance all night long, but they don't want you to stay now'" (*EK,* p. 197). Afterward D'Arrast reflects morosely: "Yonder, in Europe, there was shame and wrath. Here, exile or solitude, among these listless and convulsive madmen who danced to die" (p. 198).

The cook, recently saved from a shipwreck, has vowed in gratitude to Jesus to carry a hundred-pound stone on his head to the church in the procession at the Festival of the Good Jesus, so named for a statue of Christ placed in a grotto where another stone miraculously grows and replaces the bits chipped off by pilgrims. But, too weak willed to refrain from dancing until dawn the night before the procession, the exhausted cook hasn't the strength to reach the church with his penitential burden. D'Arrast picks up the fallen stone for his friend, carrying it on his own head but continuing with it past the church, against the cries of the townspeople, to the cook's miserable hut, where his family, previously hostile to D'Arrast, now ask him to sit down among them.

This ending is obviously laden with symbolism. D'Arrast is rejecting official social institutions—government, church, civic endeavors (the dike he is to build)—in favor of a personal bond between men. Camus may be expressing in parable form his pessimism over all social organization, partially offset by his faith in individual relationships, particularly those between well-meaning whites and colonized natives; certainly the latter relationship ends more promisingly here than in "The Guest." By carrying the rock to the cook's hut instead of to the church, the agnostic D'Arrast affirms secular love for men over sacred love for Jesus; he feels more brotherhood with the cook for his fleshly frailty of will than for his religious resolution. In Camus's familiar technique of reversing Christian symbolism, the rock D'Arrast carries away from the church suggests the rock of Peter, on which a secular church will be built, or the cross carried by a Christ in opposition to the mystical Christianity that distracts the poor natives from their human condition. In place of the supernatural growing stone in the grotto of the Good Jesus, D'Arrast's stone grows from one man's burden into a symbol of shared, earthly responsibility. Camus must also have chosen this symbol of solidarity as a counterpart to *The Myth,* where Sisyphus's rock was his solitary burden.

"The Growing Stone" is one of Camus's weaker pieces of writing. The Crucifixion symbolism of the ending, which he has used so many times previously, has become tiresomely predictable and is exposed heavyhandedly, with too abrupt a shifting of gears from the previous realistic mode. In realistic terms it is implausible, if not downright silly; the last thing a destitute native family needs is a hundred-pound rock in the middle of their living room. The story reveals no lucid political consciousness of the colonial situation; its tone, on the contrary, is patronizing toward the noble savages. D'Arrast's background in insufficiently developed. What

has his life been previously? Why has he left Europe? What is the promise he has failed to keep (pp. 186–87)? Up to the night of dancing, the
story is too long, with tedious, superfluous stretches of local color that
Camus took from the notebooks of his 1949 trip to Brazil for realistic
authenticity. (He is a rather pedestrian writer when he attempts passages
of straight realism; he is at his best when he blends realistic with symbolic or lyrical elements.) Several strands of plot and symbolism are also
incompletely developed—for instance, the dike, which seems to be forgotten halfway through the story, or D'Arrast's attraction to the "black
Diana," presumably the cook's sister or niece. She is among the family
who welcomes D'Arrast at the end, but we get no hint of where their
potentially provocative relationship might lead. Imagery of water is prominent throughout the story, but its significance is vague. There is a suggestion, as in "The Adulterous Woman," that it is associated with sexual
potency, particularly near the end, when "the sound of the waters filled
him with a tumultuous happiness. With eyes closed, he joyfully acclaimed
his own strength; he acclaimed, once again, a fresh beginning in life. At
that moment, a firecracker went off that seemed very close" (pp. 212–13).
But this theme too is inadequately developed.

"The Growing Stone" is the most obvious instance of the impression
the whole book gives that Camus had not fully mastered the short-story
form. "The Guest" is the only story that ranks with the three novels in
successful cohesion of theme, structure, expository technique, characterization, and realistic and symbolic elements. "The Renegade" is perhaps
equally well written but is emotionally unmoving, perhaps because its
narrator is the only one of Camus's central characters who is totally un-
sympathetic. "The Adulterous Woman" is too obviously written around
the tour de force ending; like "The Growing Stone," the realistic scene
setting of its first half is somewhat listless and unnecessarily long. "The
Artist at Work," on the other hand, is a moderately effective study in
satirical realism up to the ending where, as in "The Growing Stone," the
sudden shift to highly contrived symbolism disrupts the previous development and tone. "The Silent Men" is successful as far as it attempts to
go but is too short for us to become fully absorbed in its characters or
situation. It and "The Growing Stone" might have served better as points
of departure for longer fictional works; in fact, "The Silent Men" may
provide us with a hint of the direction Camus would have taken in the

work based on his youth in Algiers that he projected in the 1958 preface to *L'Envers et l'endroit*. But the subjects of these and several of the other stories are also precisely those he had had the least success dealing with in depth: realistically portrayed working-class and colonial situations, marital relationships, the feminine viewpoint. Perhaps his very choice of the short-story medium, which is a constricted one to begin with and which by the 1950s was becoming even more obsolescent than the novel, was a tacit admission of his inability to treat these subjects with the fullness they require.

12

The Drama: An Unmastered Form

I

In spite of his lifelong passion for the theater, Camus never attained full mastery as a playwright. All four of his plays make better reading than stage pieces, although each has its moments of theatrical power. *Caligula* and to a lesser degree *The Just Assassins* were successful in their original productions and revivals in France, but neither received as much acclaim as his adaptations of Faulkner's *Requiem for a Nun* and Dostoevsky's *The Possessed*. He is rarely performed in America, except for *Caligula*, which played on Broadway (staged as a Roman spectacular) with mild success in 1960 and has had several local commercial and college productions.

His drama presents special problems for the American audience because he was writing in a tradition largely foreign to America or England, at odds with the stage fare we are accustomed to. He explains in the introduction to the American edition of the plays:

> Although I have the most passionate attachment for the theater, I have the misfortune of liking only one kind of play, whether comic or tragic. After a rather long experience as director, actor, and dramatist, it seems to me that there is no true theater without language and style, nor any dramatic work which does not, like our [French] classical drama and the Greek tragedians, involve human fate in all its simplicity and grandeur. Without claiming to equal them, these are at least the models to set oneself. Psychology, ingenious plot-devices, and spicy situations, though they may amuse me as a member of the audience, leave me indifferent as an author. [*CTOP,* p. x]

Camus was preoccupied with the challenge of finding a contemporary dramatic form equivalent to Greek tragedy (see "On the Future of

Tragedy" and "Foreword to *Requiem for a Nun*" in *Lyrical and Critical Essays*), the same attempt that T. S. Eliot, Eugene O'Neill, Arthur Miller, and William Faulkner have made in English, with equally limited success. In opposition to the prevailing modern mode of realistic drama, he was striving for classical mythic action and formal, elevated language, unity of time, place, and action concentrating the drama into a brief, intense period of crisis.

Like Racine and, even more, Corneille, his is "tragedy of the intelligence" (*CTOP*, p. vi), although not in the sense of didactic, thesis drama: the play's action is motivated by its characters' intellectual convictions—about *Caligula* he says, "For the dramatist the passion for the impossible is just as valid a subject for study as avarice or adultery" (p. vi)—and its dramatic conflicts stem from "the opposition of characters who were equal in strength and reason" (p. ix), e.g., Caligula against Cherea, Martha against Maria, Diego against Victoria, Kaliayev against Stepan, Skuratov, and the grand duchess. In "On the Future of Tragedy" he distinguishes tragedy from drama and melodrama: "The forces confronting each other in tragedy are equally legitimate, equally justified. In melodramas or dramas, on the other hand, only one force is legitimate. In other words, tragedy is ambiguous and drama simple-minded. In the former, each force is at the same time both good and bad. In the latter, one is good and the other bad (which is why, in our day and age, propaganda plays are nothing but the resurrection of melodrama)" (*LCE*, p. 301). By this standard, Shakespeare's plays, with their clearly distinguished heroes and villains, are dramas rather than tragedies. It can readily be seen, then, that Camus is writing, not in the Shakespearean tradition we are attuned to, but in that of Racine and Corneille, who have never been popular in England or America, and of Greek tragedy, which we tend to regard more as a subject for literary study than as viable stagecraft.

Even when his theater is considered on its own terms, though, it has serious limitations. There is too much talk, too little action, too little modulation in pace and mood; the unrelenting state of siege on the audience's emotions is overly demanding, more so in the theater than in a private reading that can be broken up at will. The characters are too often stiff, their dialogue pompous and stilted. Dialogue is not one of the strong points of his fiction, and his restriction to it here, with only the truncated narration and description that can be put into the characters' mouths, precludes the features that most enliven his fictional language: lyricism, ambiguities in diction and viewpoint, multiple levels of significance. Another of his general weaknesses, the portrayal of lovers, is preeminent in *State of Siege* and *The Just Assassins.* Diego and Victoria, Kaliayev and Dora love one another in the manner of Corneille's men and women who implausibly love each other in the abstract for their strength of convictions. Sartre's more positively portrayed lovers too share this trait, and it is one of those curiosities of French literary culture, in which the most rebellious writers still echo their country's standard authors (and soon join their ranks), that Camus and Sartre should share this affinity with Corneille, who in his rigid conventional moralizing and authoritarianism is their diametrical opposite.

II

Caligula has with justice been widely recognized as the one play that ranks among his best works. Theatrically, it provides an acting tour de force in the title role; in 1945 Gérard Philipe scored one of his first successes creating the part, which is reminiscent of that of Nero in Racine's *Britannicus,* the play's closest dramatic predecessor. Its secondary and minor roles are also strong, with dynamic ensemble scenes lacking in the other plays, which consist mainly of two-character dialogues. It is the only play that fully achieves Camus's distinctive resonance and complex of meanings. Because it was first produced just after the war, audiences associated Caligula with Hitler, as did the newspaper critics in their lukewarm response to it in the 1960 New York production. This is not an entirely inaccurate interpretation, but it is a superficial, incomplete one that misses Caligula's more appealing side and ignores the fact that Camus wrote the play in 1938 with the intention of playing Caligula himself at his Théâtre de l'équipe in Algiers.

Caligula has the grandeur of a classical tragic hero. He is never simply a tyrant, never impelled by pragmatically self-advancing motives, mere lust for power or sadism. He is, rather, the disillusioned romantic hero of *The Rebel,* compelled to do evil out of nostalgia for an unrealizable good. "Men die; and they are not happy" (*CTOP,* p. 8). Furthermore, every human passion is ephemeral, not only happiness and love, but despair too: "Most people imagine that a man suffers because out of the blue death snatches away the woman he loves. But his real suffering is less futile; it comes from the discovery that grief, too, cannot last. Even grief is vanity" (p. 71). These realizations drive him to strip men's illusions away. Camus suggests symbolically that Caligula, like Meursault and Dostoevsky's Kirilov, feels a Christ-like, messianic mission to make men free by forcing them to know the truth of life's absurdity. We learn at the very beginning that Caligula has returned after an absence of three days. Later he says, "I shall make this age of ours a kingly gift—the gift of equality. And when all is leveled out, when the impossible has come to earth and the moon is in my hands—then, perhaps, I shall be transfigured and the world renewed; then men will die no more and at last be happy" (p. 17). And at the end comes the predictable allusion to the Crucifixion: "But how bitter it is to know all, and to have to go through to the consummation!" (p. 72).

Caligula's assertion of egoistic freedom, then, is not self-serving so much as it is exemplary. His tragic flaw lies in not recognizing that "no one can save himself all alone and that one cannot be free at the expense of others" (p. vi). Or as Camus puts it in "On the Future of Tragedy," "The chorus knows that up to a certain limit everyone is right and that the person who, from blindness or passion, oversteps this limit is heading for catastrophe if he persists in his desire to assert a right he thinks he alone possesses" (*LCE*, pp. 301–2). In other words, freedom or any other ideal can become pernicious if it destroys life or otherwise is monomaniacally pursued to the exclusion of all other values and all sense of limits, the same criticism that Camus makes of European political ideology that turns justice into an absolute value that precludes freedom. On the psychological level *Caligula* is a cogent study of a narcissistic personality unable to perceive the reality of the autonomous existence of others, a theme symbolized in the mirror from which he effaces everyone's image but his own at the end of act 1 and that he shatters at the play's end, simultaneously with his subjects' uniting to overthrow him.

The main weakness in *Caligula* as a stage piece is its pacing, as even the unastute New York critics perceived in its production there. Nihilism is a difficult subject to dramatize without monotony: when you have wiped out all human values in the play's first ten minutes, where do you go from there? Rather than having Caligula start to pass death sentences in the first act, Camus might have better modulated the tone and built up suspense by restricting Caligula's actions at first to disrupting social and legal rituals, thereby allowing for more satirical social criticism, and only later having him escalate his caprices to killing.

III

The Misunderstanding is the play that most closely approximates Greek tragedy in its concentrated, inexorable movement toward a fatal resolution that the audience already knows (if they have read *The Stranger* or any of the several variants of the story in European folklore). It is also his most Sartrean work in portraying the subjective existences of a set of individuals at cross-purposes with one another as an aspect of the absurd (it was entitled *Cross-Purposes* in its first, British translation). The expression of this theme in a metaphysical chamber drama makes it a companion piece to Sartre's *No Exit*, which was staged the same year, 1944. Camus's darkest work, its considerable theatrical power lies in the sheer, stark anguish of human beings undone by the caprices of fate. This dramatic strength, however, is also a drawback; the sustained agony is perhaps too much to expect a modern audience to sit through for three full acts—although it must be granted that the same criticism can be directed at *Oedipus Rex*. In any case, the brief plot is somewhat padded out, and the play would probably work better on stage reduced to one act.

What has Camus added in setting, theme, and characterization to the one-paragraph version of the story in *The Stranger* to give it substance as an autonomous work? The folk versions of the story are traditionally set in Bohemia or nearby Middle Europe. Camus himself, after his depressing visit to Czechoslovakia in 1936, placed that country in antithesis to Mediterranean Italy in "Death in the Soul." The play uses a similar antithesis: Martha's and the mother's motivation for murdering the guests at their inn is to gain enough money to leave dismal, landlocked Middle Europe for a sunny, seaside climate. Jan and his wife Maria have been living in such a climate, in an unnamed, beautiful land of sun and sea that we may assume is Mediterranean. Martha's jealousy of the guest's geographical good fortune becomes an extra motive for killing Jan and taking his place in the sun. "If he is rich enough, perhaps my freedom will begin with him" (*CTOP*, p. 79).

Thus Camus introduces the same theme as in *Caligula,* one's freedom at another's expense. We cannot really deduce the same moral, though, from this play's explicit content. There is not much to indicate that one cannot be free at another's expense if the other doesn't turn out to be your son or brother. The mother has had only mild qualms about killing other guests. Martha's discovery that the latest man she has killed is her brother does not faze her in the least: indeed, she feels with some justice that his previous abandonment of her and his mother vindicated the act. For her, parents and sons, brothers and sisters live at cross-purposes no less than other humans. And for her, the cruel irony with which fate thwarts us emerges only in her mother's refusal to go through with their flight after the successful murder.

Martha's dialogue with Maria in the last act is harrowingly, unconditionally nihilistic, more so than anything else in Camus, even the end of *The Stranger,* to which it is a companion piece: "But before I go to die, I must rid you of the illusion that you are right, that love isn't futile, and that what has happened was an accident. On the contrary, it's now that we are in the normal order of things, and I must convince you of it. . . . Pray your God to harden you to stone. It's the happiness He has assigned Himself, and the one true happiness. . . . You have a choice between the mindless happiness of stones and the slimy bed in which we are awaiting you" (pp. 132–33). Maria wants not to believe it, but Martha's view is confirmed at the final curtain when Maria's prayers to God are answered only by the old manservant, who turns a deaf ear on them. Camus tries to mitigate the play's fatalism retroactively in his 1957 preface by saying the tragedy could have been averted if only Jan had spoken out in time, but this begs the question of the earlier murders. Camus would undoubtedly reply that they too could have been averted if Martha and the mother had recognized all men as brothers. Still, this view is at odds with Martha's intransigent nihilism, which as the play is written overwhelms any more positive implications.

In theatrical as well as thematic terms, Martha overpowers the other three characters. The mother is curiously, inexplicably weak before her daughter's will. Maria's is the most credible, human role, but she is necessarily a peripheral, helpless victim. The play's major dramatic flaw lies in the character of Jan, which Camus does not seem to have completely thought through. We get only a vague idea of his justification for leaving home in the first place, for not returning earlier, and for not revealing his identity when he does return. Consequently, the audience is not made to feel the sympathy for him that is necessary for the tragedy to attain its full impact.

IV

In his 1957 preface Camus emphasized that *State of Siege* was in no sense an adaptation of *The Plague*; still, it is clearly a companion piece, a variation on many of the same themes. The hero Diego, a medical student, is a younger Rieux; both their names symbolically suggest Dieu, God. Like Judge Othon and Father Paneloux, here Judge Casado and the priest justify the plague, while the nihilist Nada opportunistically collaborates with it like Cottard. The parallel between Rieux's concern with the absurdity of natural death and a capricious God and Tarrou's concern with rationalized political murder is briefly reiterated in the explanation of the collaboration between The Secretary, who personifies natural death, and The Plague, who symbolizes political tyranny. She complains to him, "You have made me the handmaid of logic, rules, and regulations" (*CTOP,* p. 225). And he boasts to the townspeople, "In the old days you professed to fear God and his caprices. But your God was an anarchist who played fast and loose with logic. He thought he could be both autocratic and kindhearted at the same time—but that was obviously wishful thinking, if I may put it so. *I,* anyhow, know better. I stand for power and power alone" (p. 226).

In Diego's love for Victoria, Camus expresses the conflict between social responsibility and personal happiness that also preoccupied Rieux and Rambert. Here the conflict is more explicitly a Corneillean one between duty and love, and the play has the dramatic advantage of the loved woman being palpably present and able to speak for herself, in contrast to the absent wife of Rieux and mistress of Rambert. Diego inevitably must sacrifice his love, along with his life, to save the people of Cadiz from their state of siege by The Plague, but Victoria makes a strong case for placing love first:

VICTORIA: When it's the utmost I can do to bear the weight of my love, how can you ask me to take on my shoulders the burden of the

> sorrows of the world as well? No, that's a man's idea of duty—one of
> those futile, preposterous crusades you men engage in as a pretext
> for evading the one struggle that is truly arduous, the one victory of
> which you could be rightly proud.
> DIEGO: What else should I struggle against in this world of ours if
> not the injustice that is done us?
> VICTORIA: The anguish ['malheur'—'unhappiness'] that you have
> within yourself. Master that, and all the rest will follow. [Pp. 198–99]

Victoria's position ties in with two prominent themes in Camus's later essays: that private love is necessary to energize social commitment, and that dictatorship and bureaucracy are able to triumph because men in the twentieth century do not love life passionately enough to stand up for it.

The most important thematic difference between *The Plague* and *State of Siege* is that The Plague in the latter more directly embodies political evils and only peripherally metaphysical ones. In the article "Why Spain?" (*RRD,* pp. 75–83), Camus confirmed that in setting the play in Spain he was expressly directing it at the Franco government, although it was equally applicable to Communist dictatorships. Some of the play's best moments are provided by the bitterly satirical observations on totalitarian government, which, Camus shows us, holds sway not only through sadistic, brute force but through keeping the ruled at each others' throats, through confusing and debilitating them with bureaucratic jargon and red tape (much as in Orwell's *1984,* published the next year, 1949), and through elevating the mediocre and maladjusted to power. Unfortunately, despite the personification of The Plague as an explicitly political force, the play as a political statement is no less vague than *The Plague,* similarly reducing ideological conflicts to oversimplified, black-and-white terms.

State of Siege is his most experimental work in form and style. As he described it, "It is not a play of traditional structure but a show whose avowed ambition is to mix all the forms of dramatic expression from the lyrical monologue to collective theater, by way of dumb-show, simple dialogue, farce, and chorus" (*TRN,* p. 187). Another important source of its form was the theory of a theater of cruelty and plague formulated by Antonin Artaud in *The Theater and Its Double.* Jean-Louis Barrault, also a devotee of Artaud, shared in the play's conception with Camus, staged the 1948 production, and played Diego. (The play's failure was certainly not due to a lack of artistic talent; Arthur Honneger composed the musical score, and the cast included some of France's leading actors: Barrault's wife and coproducer Madeleine Renaud as The Secretary, Pierre Brasseur as Nada, Maria Casarès as Victoria—she also played Martha in *The Misunderstanding* and Dora in *The Just Assassins*—and Marcel Marceau in a mimed bit part.) In this kind of experiment it is nearly impossible to predict ahead of time whether the play is going to work on stage or not. In this case it emphatically did not. The various styles fail to work individually and disastrously fight against each other collectively. As Artaudian theater of cruelty, *Caligula* is far superior; nothing here matches the stunning power of scenes like Caligula's murder of Mereia. The attempt at collective theater, an extension of Camus's communal Théâtre de l'équipe, only ends up dissipating the action and keeping the central characters, Diego and Victoria, offstage too much for us to build up sufficient sympathy for them. Above all, the symbolic stage devices exude avant-garde gimmickry, and the dialogue, especially in the choruses, is the most embarrassingly blatant instance of Camus's tendency toward portentousness. Nevertheless, the play has its appealing points, mainly in the love-duty conflict and the political satire, and if he had lived to revise it, as he likely would have, by pruning out some of the cumbersome elements like the choruses and symbolic machinery he might have salvaged it.

v

The Just Assassins (Gilbert tacked on the last word to the French title, thereby gaining graphicness but losing some shadings of meaning), produced the year after *State of Siege,* provides a striking contrast in its straightforwardly realistic structure and dialogue, controlled tone, and the subtlety of its political thought. It is much the better play and one of Camus's most mature works, even though its theatrical effectiveness is limited by an excess of talk and deficiency of onstage action, the latter perhaps partly a conscious effort toward French neoclassical decorum.

In his 1966 book *Modern Tragedy,* Raymond Williams applies a Marx-

ist perspective to Camus's plays. Taking *The Misunderstanding* as para-
digmatic, Williams argues that Camus's absurdist fatalism obscures immediate social realities:

> How fatal, how terrible, that it was a son! Yet the destructive agent
> is in fact money: not simply greed (that ethical diversion, creating a
> separate class of the guilty) but the need for money, in a society gov-
> erned by it. . . . In Camus's play, the sister's need is to get away to
> the sun, where she can reach the fullness of her own life. The frus-
> tration of life by money is known as tragedy, but its detailed work-
> ings are called Fate. . . . Certainly, I think, in Camus a false con-
> sciousness has intervened, making the recognition ambiguous. It is
> not an evasion of the permanent contradictions of life to recognize
> and name a more particular and temporary contradiction. Rather, the
> naming of the latter as Fate is itself evasion.[1]

Williams's implication is not that all tragedy could be eliminated by socialism or any political program but that some socially variable determi-
nants of tragedy can in fact be isolated in life and in literature. Williams
does recognize a progression in Camus's plays and other works toward
a more historically specific sense of tragedy, culminating with *The Just
Assassins*. The only drawback he finds in this play is that Camus is more
concerned about the conscience of the individual revolutionary than with
the historical necessity of revolution. Williams's point is well taken, but
The Just Assassins nevertheless presents the most lucid political perspective in Camus's drama or fiction.

Camus is working here in the genre of literature of political crime and
punishment that from the late 1930s through the 1940s produced such
works as Malraux's *Man's Fate* (*La Condition humaine*) and *Days of
Wrath* (*Le Temps du mépris,* a novel that Camus adapted for stage production at the Théâtre de l'équipe); Koestler's novel *Darkness at Noon*
and its stage adaptation by Sidney Kingsley; Sartre's "The Wall," *Men
without Shadows* (*Morts sans sépulture*), and *Dirty Hands;* and Orwell's
1984. He draws directly from historical accounts of the Russian terrorists
of 1905, sympathetically fleshing out his stage characters without any
ironic variations from their real-life models (as with Caligula) or from

1. *Modern Tragedy*, p. 180.

his interpretation of "The Fastidious Assassins" in *The Rebel* (pp. 164–72) two years later.

The central character is the idealistic student revolutionary Ivan Kaliayev, nicknamed "The Poet"—"He says all poetry is revolutionary" (*CTOP*, p. 237)—who is on the verge of assassinating the Grand Duke Sergei but refuses to throw a bomb at his carriage because his two young children are in it. He ultimately does kill the duke, alone, then willingly is captured and hung. Kaliayev embodies an answer to Tarrou's dilemma of how to overthrow a murderous ruling class without becoming equally murderous oneself, or at least while remaining a relatively "innocent murderer." As in the closing chapters of *The Rebel*, it is a matter of the rebel of integrity making clear to the world that if he is obliged to kill he must not be motivated by inner malevolence but by the desire to allow life to thrive, that he recognizes humane limits by refusing to kill innocents along with the guilty, and that by giving his life in return he is ruling out self-serving ambitions.

Ideologically, Kaliayev's position is somewhat shaky. Several critics have pointed out that if all the benevolent revolutionaries allow themselves to die, that will leave only the malevolent ones alive to take power. Kaliayev's ethic may be viable for the middle- or upper-class intellectual who voluntarily involves himself in revolution, but one might question, as Williams does, whether it can be prescribed for the oppressed proletarian and whether it is not perhaps designed more for maintaining the individual bourgeois's good conscience than for political efficacy. Kaliayev might be viewed as the kind of politically marginal bourgeois leftist that Sartre is preoccupied with, such as Hugo in *Dirty Hands* or Matthieu in *Roads to Freedom;* Camus does in fact embody a bourgeois revolutionary's sense of inauthenticity in the younger student, Voinov, who in a passage echoing Camus's theme of dandyism, says, "Do you know, I've never really believed in the secret police! Absurd, isn't it, for a terrorist? I'll believe they exist only when I get my first kick in the belly. Not before" (p. 266).

The play's main thematic—and dramatic—strength, however, does not lie in Kaliayev's ideology but in Camus's fairness in expressing it and measuring it against opposing views. Kaliayev's is a more tough-minded position than the ones presented in *The Plague* or *The Rebel*; he never seriously questions the revolutionary efficacy of killing the grand duke, in contrast to Camus's own views on the outcome of revolutions in general and the Russian Revolution in particular. The question is raised near the end of the play by Dora that the actions of the just assassins may set a precedent that will be exploited by unjust ones: "Sometimes when I hear what Stepan says, I fear for the future. Others, perhaps, will come who'll quote our authority for killing; and will *not* pay with their lives" (p. 296), but Annenkov, in the absence of Kaliayev, rejects this view, as eventually does Dora. Several characters represent positions antithetical to Kaliayev's, but none is portrayed villainously or even unsympathetically. Stepan is a fanatic revolutionary with unhealthily malicious motivation, yet his attitude is justified by the personal oppression that Kaliayev has not suffered, and he appears as the more authentically motivated, certainly the more efficient revolutionary. The police chief Skuratov justifies himself succinctly: "One begins by wanting justice—and one ends by setting up a police force" (p. 281). In a bit of gallows-humor comic relief suggesting the ambiguity of victims and executioners, Kaliayev's fellow convict Foka turns out also to be the hangman. The grand duchess charitably offers to spare Kaliayev's life, confronts him with the gory physical results of the bombing, and reveals the irony that the duke was a kinder person than the children Kaliayev spared. With finesse surpassing any of his other works, Camus allows Kaliayev to give each of these opposing viewpoints due consideration, yet remain steadfast to his ideals.

The Just Assassins presents Camus's most somber but most convincing variant on the conflict between personal happiness and social responsibility. Dora laments to Kaliayev, "I love you with the same love as yours: a love that's half frozen, because it's rooted in justice and reared in prison cells. . . . Summer, Yanek, can you remember what that's like, a real summer's day? But—no, it's never-ending winter here. We don't belong to the world of men. We are the just ones" (pp. 272–73). She is tempted momentarily to forsake the revolution to fulfill their personal love, as Victoria tempts Diego, but she eventually recognizes what Kaliayev does: "Those who love each other today must die together if they wish to be reunited. In life they are parted—by injustice, sorrow, shame; by the evil that men do to others . . . by crimes. Living is agony, because life separates" (pp. 289–90). In an unjust society lovers cannot pursue their private happiness in good conscience but must submerge it in collective love for the victims of injustice. The epigraph from *Romeo and Juliet*—"O love! O life! not life, but love in death!"—is fulfilled in Dora's imagining herself at the final curtain dying the same death as Kaliayev on the gallows, the only just consummation for their love. Overtones of romantic necrophilia can be found in this ending, especially from the psychoanalytic perspective, but it retains nonetheless a ring of ideological authenticity.

The subject of *The Just Assassins* gained new timeliness in America during the 1960s with the resurgence of revolutionary ideology in the New Left. Its cogent perspective on the theme of violent revolution and its classical dramatic balance make it the one play by Camus that especially deserves to be staged in the United States more often than it has been.

VI

Camus remained active theatrically throughout the decade following *The Just Assassins,* directing productions of his and other authors' plays and adapting works from other media and languages for the French stage, most of which bore a close relationship to his personal preoccupations. He evidently found in the fatalistic sense of sin in Faulkner's *Requiem for a Nun,* which he adapted in 1957, a resonance with his own waning confidence in the possibilities for human innocence, as expressed in his contemporaneous works *The Fall* and *Exile and the Kingdom.* He denied, however, that his transcription of Faulkner's Christian notions of sin and redemption—which are rather idiosyncratic in any case—signaled any increased inclination on his part toward religious conversion, squelching such speculation in his foreword to the printed text: "Please note that if I translated and staged a Greek tragedy, no one would ask me if I believe in Zeus" (*LCE,* p. 315).

Although Camus played down the racial elements in *Requiem* toward the end of greater universality, to the extent of specifying that Nancy need not be played by a black actress, there may have been an unconscious resonance between Faulkner's sensibility regarding white-black relations in the South and Camus's regarding European-Arab relations in Algeria. In any case, he was apparently not cognizant of the paternalism in Faulkner's supposition that it is the function of black people to show their nobility by sacrificing their lives to cover up their white employers' juvenile misconduct.

His stage version of Dostoevsky's *The Possessed* in 1959 counterbalanced *The Just Assassins* ideologically. He may have felt more sympathy with its counterrevolutionary politics than he had a decade earlier, as his own attitude toward revolution became more conservative through the fifties. He had long admired the novel for other reasons, though, mainly its characterizations of Stavrogin and Kirilov as adventurers in metaphysical and social absurdity.

When André Malraux became French minister of culture under de Gaulle he appointed Camus director of an experimental State theater in 1959, just before Camus's death. Camus's friends Jean-Louis Barrault and Madeleine Renaud were to find their Théâtre de l'Odéon at storm center during the Paris student uprising of 1968. It would have been highly interesting to see how Camus in a similar theatrical capacity would have responded to this combustible situation and to the other political and cultural upheavals of the sixties. Although commercial theater declined drastically, experimental theater generally showed more flexibility in adjusting to the changing times than the novel or short story. The various forms of communal creation, radical street theater, and other attempts toward reviving the notion of people's theater that evolved in Europe and America resembled Camus's earlier experiments dating back to pre-World War II Algiers. It is quite possible that the atmosphere of youthful rebellion would have helped reverse his conservative political tendency and stimulated him to the full realization in experimental theater that had eluded him previously.

CONCLUSION

13

Camus and the American Reader

I

In an article called "Camus in America," written shortly after his death in 1960, Serge Doubrovsky commented:

> Camus is the great writer American literature has waited for and who never came. The generation of Faulkner, Dos Passos, and Hemingway already belongs to the past and to history. Its value is one of example and no longer of witness. It so happens that the succession is vacant. There are a hundred authors not wanting in talent, but there is no writer who attacks the problems of our time in depth. If happy peoples can be said to have no history, perhaps prosperous peoples have no literature.[1]

Doubrovsky's judgment about the vacant succession of indisputably great American writers has been confirmed in the subsequent interval of years, while Camus has remained among the authors most admired by serious American readers in spite of a decline in his political reputation in the late 1960s resulting from shifts in the New Left perspective. By way of concluding this study and summarizing Camus's achievements and limitations, I want to delineate what I believe to be his distinctive significance for American readers since World War II in the light of the general cultural history of this period here, with the proviso that this will at times entail the purely personal judgments of the author as one American reader whose outlook has been strongly influenced by Camus.

He made only one brief visit to the United States, on the occasion of *The Stranger*'s publication here in 1946, at which time he also gave charity lectures for French war victims.[2] He found New York an extreme case

1. In *Camus: A Collection of Critical Essays*, ed. Brée, p. 17.
2. Justin O'Brien tells the story that during Camus's benefit lecture at Columbia University the box-office receipts were stolen. When the theft was announced, the audience took up

227

of everything he disliked about northern cities, as he indicated in a short essay, "The Rains of New York": "The whitened skyscrapers loom in the gray mist like gigantic tombstones for a city of the dead. . . . Eight million men, the smell of steel and cement, the madness of builders, and yet the very height of solitude" (*LCE,* p. 182). The visit also confirmed existentialist stereotypes of America: "The funeral parlors where death and the dead are made up at top speed ('Die, and leave the rest to us'), . . . the subway that reminds you of Sing Sing prison, ads filled with clouds of smiles proclaiming from every wall that life is not tragic" (pp. 184–85).

He was, however, highly cognizant of his large following in America, wrote prefaces for three American editions of his works, and maintained friendships with his publishers Alfred A. and Grace Knopf, his translator Justin O'Brien, and the critic Germaine Brée, whom he knew from wartime Algeria. Mme. Brée has done more than any other critic to promote Camus's reputation in America, and whatever reservations one might have about her interpretations or political perspective, her extensive works have provided a wealth of information and insight for subsequent critics. Just after his death Brée wrote, "Last summer Camus spoke to me of his 'dialogue' with his American readers and of the inner strength he had drawn from their understanding. He had planned to come back to America when the book he was now writing was finished." [3] His last interview was written, two weeks before his death, in response to a questionnaire from the obscure American literary journal *Venture,* where it was published as part of one of the many emotional posthumous homages to Camus here.

He greatly admired nineteenth- and twentieth-century American literature, recognizing a kinship between his sensibility and the long line of American writers with a proclivity toward solitary introspection in nature and toward individualistic political nonconformity rather than collective revolutionary organization. Like Emerson, Thoreau, and Whitman, he attempted to reconcile these egocentric inclinations with a sense of social solidarity through the vocation of artist and through a tension between his different works similar to that between Thoreau's *Walden*

---

another collection, which ended up exceeding the original sum. The evening confirmed Camus's worst and best preconceptions about Americans. See O'Brien's "Albert Camus: Militant," in *Camus: A Collection of Critical Essays,* ed. Brée, pp. 20–25.
3. "Albert Camus: An Essay in Appreciation," *New York Times Book Review,* 24 Jan. 1960, p. 5.

and *Civil Disobedience* or antislavery polemics. Perhaps his proximity to nature, his ill health and social and psychological solitude in his youth approximated the endemic isolation of writers in American society. Whatever the causes, his fiction and drama are akin to the dominant American fictional tradition of the romance, which, as distinguished by Hawthorne from the novel, is concerned more with philosophical themes, metaphysical speculation, and quasiallegorical symbolism than with the realistic portrayal of social manners or biography that has characterized the British novel. (His closest affinities to English novelists are with mavericks from the latter tradition—Defoe's *Journal of the Plague Year,* Emily Brontë's *Wuthering Heights,* Conrad, D. H. Lawrence, Orwell.) He was influenced more by Melville than by any other American or English author and paid homage to him in a 1952 essay (*LCE,* pp. 288–94).

Camus's appeal here, for readers who have grasped his full scope, can perhaps be attributed most broadly to his basic healthiness—in defiance of the tuberculosis that continually threatened his life from the age of seventeen—an emotional equilibrium and intellectual wholeness that he appeared to achieve with relatively little strain, considering that virtually no one in America seems capable of achieving them at all. He professed to be at heart an ordinary man only trying to live and write with honesty, decency, and a modest share of enjoyment; the irony of our age is that this has become a feat it takes an exceptional man to perform. He demonstrated that it is possible to face up to the worst life has to offer and still maintain a calm resoluteness—the ability, as Fitzgerald put it, to see that things are hopeless and yet be determined to make them otherwise. In his writing he encompassed the most extreme, nihilistic attitudes of his time without personally going off the deep end into suicide, violence, insanity, nervous breakdowns, or drugs.

He managed to combine diverse activities that seem to be mutually exclusive here. No contemporary American, with the possible exception of Norman Mailer, has approximated the versatility of Camus's accomplishments, not only as a novelist, literary essayist and critic, playwright and theatrical director, but as a systematic metaphysical and social philosopher, influential voice in national and international politics, and first-rate newspaper reporter and editor. He was a man of letters without being professorial or effete, an athlete, a man of action and passion who never felt obliged to play the he-man or squeamishly deny being an intellectual as prominent American writers, including Mailer, endemically do. He was an author with high artistic integrity who gained relatively popular readership and respect (even more so in Europe than here), a highbrow who tried to reconcile defenses of the Western cultural tradition with proletarian political sympathies, though he was not entirely successful in this last endeavor.

Camus provided a perspective almost totally absent from contemporary America in his diagnosis of modern social ills as products of the romantic temperament and in his application of classical humanistic values as a curative. His ideal of the classical sense of proportion is lacking in American politics and culture to the point of being a fatal national flaw. Establishment politicians and news media habitually treat issues in terms of absolute right and wrong, with oversimplified polarities like "defending the free world" against "Communist aggression," "free enterprise" against "creeping socialism," and "law and order" against "criminals and subversives." The government is consequently prone to react to conflicts with self-righteous rigidity and excessive force, as in the nuclear arms race, Vietnam, ghettos, prisons, and college campuses. With the establishment setting the pace in *la démesure,* and an intellectual establishment divided between technocratic cooperation with the power structure and apathetic withdrawal from public affairs into academic insularity or privatistic enterprises, the American counterculture is driven to react in equally excessive forms of rebellion, such as beat-generation and hippie "mind-blowing" or the urban-guerilla terrorism of the late sixties.

Camus's alternative, *le juste milieu*—which should not be confused with spineless compromise or middle-of-the-road blandness—entails recognizing that the solution to human problems is not usually to be found in absolute formulas but in perceiving exact partial degrees of right and wrong and subsequently determining where to draw the line in action. In this way he could apportion reciprocal fault in the Cold War throughout his political writing and divide responsibility between society and the criminal in "Reflections on the Guillotine," or delineate prudent limitations on revolutionary violence in *Neither Victims Nor Executioners, The Just Assassins,* and *The Rebel.* He similarly applied the principles of measure and balance to resolve the antipathy between autonomous artistic creation and ideological or emotional commitment that has divided American literary theorists throughout the twentieth century.

In short, he was the kind of complete man of letters that has been in-digenous to France from Montaigne to Gide, Malraux, and Sartre, but that has not thrived in America since at least the time of Emerson and perhaps not fully even then, if we credit Van Wyck Brooks' assertion that American intellectual life has been fragmented from the beginning between highbrows and lowbrows, serious and popular writers, men of contemplation and those of action. The stultifying cultural atmosphere of the Cold War made it more difficult than ever for intellectuals here to attain this kind of integrated sensibility.

II

Camus's depth, scope, and equilibrium provide a yardstick against which to measure the atrophy and the fluctuations between deficiency and excess in American literature between the 1940s and 1960s, after the great creative age between the first and second world wars. From the 1920s through World War II the highbrow-lowbrow split appeared to be diminishing. Writers of the lost generation and rebel thirties were by no means reconciled to American society on the whole, but more serious artists than ever before were working in diverse media, dealing with themes of broad social significance, reaching a comparatively large popu-lar audience, and gaining respected public stature. The genres of fiction and drama were at their most viable stage in American history, their practitioners having successfully fused elements from naturalism such as social determinism and cosmic irony with romantic affirmation in characters who transcend fate through heroic endurance, and with poetic, multilevel symbolism and experimental expository form. Camus's forma-tive literary influences included the leading figures of this age in the United States.

He considered William Faulkner, his elder by sixteen years, the great-est modern American writer and met him briefly when Camus staged *Requiem for a Nun* in Paris in 1956.[4] As French literary figures have

4. See Camus's essays on Faulkner in *Lyrical and Critical Essays*, pp. 311–20, and his brief tribute to Faulkner in *The Harvard Advocate*, Nov. 1951, p. 21, also reprinted in part in *Faulkner: A Collection of Critical Essays*, ed. Robert Penn Warren (Englewood Cliffs, N. J.: Prentice-Hall, 1966), p. 295. Faulkner in turn paid posthumous tribute to Camus in "L'Ame qui s'interroge," *Nouvelle Revue française*, Mar. 1960, pp. 537–38, reprinted in the collection *Hommage à Albert Camus* (Paris: Gallimard, 1967), pp. 143–44.

been inclined to do, he had a rather eccentric perspective on Faulkner by American standards; he considered *Sanctuary* and *Pylon* among his masterpieces, and the popularity of the French staging of *Requiem* was disproportionate to the American reputation of this late and racially patronizing work. In their separate, overall achievements, however, Faulkner and Camus are of equally preeminent stature among twentieth-century authors in their tragic vision of individual existence and history, their technical inventiveness, and creation of a self-contained but constantly expanding literary world.

Ernest Hemingway's impassive heroes and style influenced *The Stranger,* but Camus considered the automatonlike view of human nature that he saw implicit in Hemingway and "tough" American detective novelists to have restricted validity: "That is why, although I appreciate the real value of the American novel, I would give a hundred Hemingways for one Stendhal or one Benjamin Constant" (*LCE,* p. 348). Camus's account of him is not very accurate, but it is true that Hemingway today appears to be a more shallow writer than either Faulkner or Camus. He can imagine courageous individualism and defiance of fate or of bourgeois conformity only outside of his native American setting and in exotic circumstances—bullfighting, big-game hunting, deep-sea fishing, smuggling—while much of Camus's distinctive power comes from his revelation of the possibilities of heroism in everyday society. Camus provides a bracing antidote to Hemingway adventurism in his observation, "A sub-clerk in the post office is the equal of a conqueror if consciousness is common to them" (*Myth,* p. 51).

Camus's one other translation of an American work was a 1952 text for *The Last Flower,* James Thurber's gentle 1939 cartoon parable about the power of love and natural beauty to withstand the inevitable destructive cycles of social dissension and war. The fatalistic view over the constant frustration of grandiose romantic dreams throughout Thurber's writing can be seen as a comic counterpart to Camus's notion of the absurd.

Camus's aesthetics were a carry-over from André Malraux and his counterparts in the 1930s on the American literary left. During the Cold War it became an article of faith among American critics that left-wing literature and literary theory prior to World War II were simplemindedly propagandistic and artistically insubstantial. The fact is, however, that the more independent leftist novelists like Malraux and, in America, John Dos Passos, James T. Farrell, Richard Wright, and John Steinbeck, as well as critics like Max Eastman, Edmund Wilson, Kenneth Burke, Philip Rahv, Alfred Kazin, Lionel Trilling, and others associated with *Partisan Review,* were concerned, as Camus continued to be after the war, with striking a balance between individualistic and collective themes, aesthetic quality and social significance, ideological independence and political commitment. Camus's wartime and postwar works, along with those of Malraux and Sartre, in fact show more continuity with the American 1930s than does American writing after the war, except for that of black authors like Richard Wright—who expatriated and became part of the Sartre-Camus circle in Paris—Ralph Ellison, and James Baldwin.

The decade of the 1940s saw a serious breakdown in the continuity of American literary theory and practice, both in thematic profundity and social scope. By the early forties F. Scott Fitzgerald, Sherwood Anderson, Thomas Wolfe, and Nathaniel West were dead; most of the other important writers of the twenties and thirties had passed their creative peak and were inclining toward either conservatism or silence on social and political issues. Norman Mailer's *The Naked and the Dead* in 1948 and Arthur Miller's *Death of a Salesman* in 1949 were among the last significant vestiges of 1930s left-wing symbolic naturalism.

The cultural atrophy following the war reintensified the highbrow-lowbrow split. The triumph of technocracy, with its fragmentation of intellect and narrow specialization, was reflected literarily in a division of labor between "creative" writers and social or literary critics, most of the latter going into the academic world, with its further departmentalization. The Cold War aggravated anti-intellectualism in a rightward-moving mass public incited by McCarthyism to associate "eggheads" with communism. In France, where anti-intellectualism had never been as widespread as in America, the Cold War did not cause a similar breakdown in mutual respect between the populace and the intellectuals. There was a split between Communist party intellectuals and anticommunist leftists like Camus, but not between the latter and the working class. It is hard to imagine any influential highbrow American writer in 1953 addressing an affirmation of the common interests of intellectuals and workers to a labor council, as Camus did in "Bread and Freedom," or taking part in conferences with printers' unions seeking means to free the press from servitude to business interests and bourgeois propaganda.

One of the few remaining literary links with the thirties was the group of ex-radical intellectuals around *Partisan Review, Commentary,* and the English *Encounter,* journals that published several of Camus's articles and interviews on the artist and his time. Like him, these writers continued to combine literary and political concerns, although in a somewhat more compartmentalized manner; nor were they, for the most part, outstanding as practicing artists. Their liberal anticommunist politics were similar to his, but most of them differed from him in resigning themselves to the breach between intellectuals and the working class, highbrow and lowbrow culture, and in their increasing acceptance of a staid, upper-middle-class identity and participation in or acquiescence to the simplistic celebrations of America and capitalism prevalent in that period.

Beyond the circle of the *Partisan Review* intellectuals, Camus's theories on the literary artist and his historical time were quite alien to the prevailing literary aestheticists in postwar America, most of whom were academic critics—although their pronouncements were not audibly contradicted by practicing artists, who themselves had little of note to say on the subject. These New-Critically trained scholars were rigorous in explicating the internal complexities of literary texts, but many made no consistent effort to relate this aesthetic method to an existential or historical philosophy. (Murray Krieger in *The Tragic Vision* and R. W. B. Lewis in *The Picaresque Saint* did develop an existentialist perspective; they managed, however, not only to depoliticize Camus but to derive a message of political quietism from such authors as Malraux and Silone.)[5] Some of them, partly under the influence of T. S. Eliot, advanced a neo-Christian vision of the innate depravity of man and society that sanctioned stoic resignation to the political status quo (under which, incidentally, academics were benefiting from unprecedented prosperity). Others such as Krieger, in a skeptical reaction against the more simpleminded Marxist cultural criticism of the 1930s and in tandem with 1950s end-of-ideology theory in the social sciences, theorized that literature reflects the true complexity of human nature and historical situation and drew the

5. Krieger, *The Tragic Vision* (New York: Holt, Rinehart and Winston, 1960); Lewis, *The Picaresque Saint* (Philadelphia and New York: J. B. Lippincott, 1959).

conclusion that the literary sensibility precludes partisan political involvement, with its inevitable oversimplifications and false hopes. The
practical consequence in all these cases was a general abdication of critics
and scholars from speaking out on the pressing social issues of the time.

The revolt among college students in the mid-sixties brought in its
wake new demands for social relevance in literature and literary scholarship, but formalism or "contextualism" continued to have its defenders,
as in a 1969 article on "Autonomy and Relevance in Literature" by
Lawrence W. Hyman:

> What we find in almost all of the great literary works as they are
> interpreted by contextualist critics is not so much a moral direction
> as a sense of the limitations of any moral doctrine when confronted
> with the intractable complexity of human life. . . . As a result, when
> a modern critic examines the poem or the novel, he usually finds
> ambiguity and irony, ambivalence and paradox. To do otherwise,
> to insist as some critics still do, that a great work must furnish us
> with a noble idea, or an unambiguous morality, usually implies that
> we must sacrifice the poem to our beliefs.[6]

Camus, too, believed that literature reflects the intractable complexity of
human life but did not therefore reject it as a guide to moral and historical
commitment. In his view the highest art embodies multiplicity and complexity, but counterpoised with equal parts of unity and simplicity. The
artist's rage for order should impel him to seek a just order in his society; as Emerson said, "Justice is the rhyme of things." In the same way
that the rebellious artist "obstinately confronts a world condemned to
death and the impenetrable obscurity of the human condition with his
demand for life and absolute clarity," so he should confront the ambiguity
of political issues. The uncertain efficacy of historical involvement does
not excuse the man of letters from fully committing himself to action
according to his best literary lights. The opacity and mendacity of contemporary history will only be compounded if politics is left the exclusive
province of obfuscating and mendacious professional politicians. Noam
Chomsky echoed Camus here in 1967 (although he was alluding more
directly to Dwight Macdonald's essays following World War II on the
responsibility of intellectuals, which were closely akin to Camus) when

6. In *College English* 30, no. 8 (May 1969) : 624.

he condemned the failure of American Cold War intellectuals to speak out against the policies that led to the Vietnam War: "It is the responsibility of intellectuals to speak the truth and to expose lies."[7]

III

For all the differences between Camus's critical theory and that of postwar American aestheticians influenced by Eliot and the New Criticism, they did at least have in common a tragic vision of life. This vision became decreasingly evident in American creative literature following the war. (In one of the curious fragmentations characterizing this period, the most prominent critics were still promoting the older generation of writers including Eliot, Yeats, Pound, Stevens, Joyce, and Faulkner, while largely ignoring the younger American creative writers, who in any case were mostly working independent of any theoretical school. In contrast to most past periods, there were virtually no first-rate writers who were at once creative artists and theorists in the manner of Camus.) Thus Camus's fiction and drama between *The Stranger* in 1942 and *The Fall* in 1956 portrayed dimensions of existence that seemed to have largely disappeared from American life and literature: the devastation of habitual routine and illusions by the capriciousness of fate or the premonition of death; the sensuous exaltation of man's harmony with nature; revolt against religious and bourgeois self-righteousness; the personal dilemmas posed by the necessity of political commitment, of killing and self-sacrifice in revolution or war; the solidarity among victims of the plagues of nature and society.

Most novelists, poets, playwrights, and film makers of the postwar silent generation abandoned any comprehensive social analysis or criticism, turning inward toward depictions of neurotically self-absorbed middle-class heroes or naturalistic psychological studies of the marginal subcultures of the South, Jewishness, academia, bohemia, suburbia, or deviant sexuality. In contrast to the revolts of Cherea and Scipio in *Caligula* and Rieux in *The Plague* against metaphysical absurdity and social nihilism, and of Tarrou in *The Plague* and Kaliayev in *The Just Assassins* against political murder, the outer limits of rebellion in American Cold War culture were juvenile delinquency, dropping out of school or the corporation, having a nervous breakdown, or taking drugs—as in J. D. Salinger,

7. "The Responsibility of Intellectuals," in *The Dissenting Academy,* ed. Roszak, p. 256.

the beats, Mailer, Ken Kesey, Tennessee Williams, Jack Gelber, and (on a somewhat higher intellectual level) Saul Bellow, or the film characters played by Marlon Brando in *The Wild One* and James Dean in *Rebel without a Cause* and *East of Eden,* the latter adapted from a 1952 Steinbeck novel which itself exemplified that author's typical, egocentric postwar turn.

These writers, along with method actors, action painters, and improvisational film makers and jazz musicians, sought frenetically but aimlessly to transcend the passionlessness of the Eisenhower years with a forced hyperemotionality, like Camus's dandy acting at apocalyptic emotions in default of being able to feel any normal ones. Young followers of this "dandies' rebellion" ("rebellion" might even be a misnomer for what was more of a spasmodic reflex) chafed against grey-flannel banality but frequently ended up via narcotics or insanity in the equally banal oblivion of intellectual, and sometimes literal, suicide. In opposition to academic formalist aesthetics and in purported response to the metaphysical and moral chaos of the modern world, many of these artists lunged into utter formlessness, in disregard of Camus's intermediate notion that aesthetic form should combat the chaos of reality rather than abet it, that "even if the novel describes only nostalgia, despair, frustration, it still creates form and salvation."

The sexual attitudes expressed in much postwar American literature and some of its influential immediate predecessors similarly indicate the romantic excess that Camus diagnosed in *The Rebel.* Again, one gets the sense of excess as a desperate overreaction to deficiency in the endless parade of swaggering hypermasculinity, Reichian orgasm-ism, sado-masochism, necrophilia, and nymphetomania, intermingled with hysterical misogyny, impotence, and deviously concealed or frenetically flaunted homosexuality, that Leslie Fiedler has documented in *Love and Death in the American Novel* and *Waiting for the End.* In the kind of ironic reversal Camus describes by which a personality trait pushed to an extreme merges with its opposite, the super-maleness of the fictitious heroes of writers like Mailer, Tennessee Williams, William Inge, Edward Albee, Jack Kerouac, and Ken Kesey, or like Hemingway and Henry Miller in the previous generation, often masked their creators' insecure virility and in some cases homosexuality, on almost the same self-caricaturing level as Hollywood he-man actors.

Camus, with his fatherless, female-dominated childhood, was not without his own sexual insecurities. He frequently appeared to verge on the fear of women and association of sex and death that Fiedler regards as almost exclusively American, and his portrayals of females tend to be male chauvinistic and superficial. But he evidently managed to keep his neurotic tendencies in check and to achieve a relatively well-adjusted sex life personally. In his writing he kept his misogynistic inclinations on a discreetly subliminal level for the most part and neutralized them with lyrical appreciations of women that—sexist as they may appear from today's women's liberationist viewpoint—convey a refreshing normalcy by comparison with all the bizarre varieties of antifeminism that have monopolized American writing in recent decades.

Norman Mailer in many ways epitomized all the egocentric excesses of silent generation rebellion. He brought to mind Camus's description of the romantic hero who is "compelled to do evil by his nostalgia for an unrealizable good." In his 1957 essay "The White Negro: Superficial Reflections on the Hipster," Mailer explicitly opposed his irrationalistic, necrophilic existentialism to the life-intensifying rationalism of Sartre and Camus, advocating gratuitously flirting with death and sexual or criminal violence as forms of revolt against the banal oppressiveness of American society and the collective violence of the atomic age. We are reminded again of Camus's dandy, "incapable of love, or capable only of an impossible love," for whom "only the cry of anguish can bring us to life" and for whom consequently "the apocalypse becomes an absolute value in which everything is confounded—love and death" (*Rebel,* p. 49). One is probably not compelled to extol apocalyptic orgasms, as Mailer did, if one's ordinary orgasms are satisfactory.

With all of Mailer's excesses, it should be acknowledged that "The White Negro" was the most articulate manifesto of the beat and early hippie movement, the single literary work here of the fifties most worthy to stand against Camus and Sartre in stylistic forcefulness and comprehensive existential and social analysis. He was one of the few widely read American writers to apply a piercing, radical perspective to capitalist society during the Cold War, albeit a self-centered perspective without any viable programmatic alternatives; the alleged value of his forms of revolt was not revolutionary but individualistically therapeutic. Like Caligula, however, Mailer failed to take account of the victims of therapeutic individual violence or to define limits that would keep it from turning into as great an evil as collective violence.

IV

The Fall, published in France in 1956 and translated here in 1957, had
quite a different, though perhaps even stronger, significance for America
than his earlier works. Whereas he had previously dealt with subjects
that had disappeared from American life and literature after the war,
here he created a critical portrait of an antihero, Jean-Baptiste Clamence,
with whom American readers of the fifties could closely identify. Clamence's narcissism and the theatrical irreality of his existence were the definitive maladies of the postwar middle class in Western Europe and even
more in America. During this period unprecedented leisure and the in-
stant indulgence of material desires—even if paid for on the installment
plan—permitted total preoccupation with oneself, while suburban insulation shielded out the sight of war, poverty, disease, economic and racial
exploitation. Just after World War II Camus had written that we are
"unable to really *imagine* other people's death" and that "we kill and are
killed by proxy" (*NVNE,* pp. 3–4). This was to become even more night-
marishly true with the distant wars of Algeria and Indochina. More than
at any other time in history the bourgeoisie experienced these wars and
all of reality at second hand through the show-business cosmeticized
images of television, movies, and the mass press. Whether conservatives
or liberals, they smugly believed they could pass judgment from their
living-room box seats on a world they never really made contact with.
Clamence perfectly expresses this aura of irreality that pervaded the
middle-class consciousness: "I have never been really able to believe that
human affairs were serious matters" (p. 86), and, "Fundamentally, nothing mattered. War, suicide, love, poverty got my attention, of course,
when circumstances forced me, but a courteous, superficial attention. . . .
How shall I express it? Everything slid off—yes, just rolled off me"
(p. 49).

This theme, similar to Sartre's existential inauthenticity, can be interpreted psychoanalytically in light of the death of both authors' fathers
in their infancy, a circumstance that tends to retard the development of
the child's superego, the normal formation of his identity in opposition to
paternal authority, and his capacity to establish object relations. Perhaps
the resonance of Camus's theme in America is attributable to our being
a predominantly middle-class country whose existence preceded its essence,

a people without a superego, born like Gatsby out of our Platonic conception of ourself, insecure in our personal identities, simultaneously other-directed and narcissistic. Like the dandy in *The Rebel* who acts at life in default of being able to live it, we have always tended, and have been increasingly conditioned, to depend desperately on an audience of Others to exist, while at the same time depersonalizing them toward our own egocentric purposes: "I have no more friends," Clamence avows, "only accomplices." These traits of weak ego formation and insecure identity, leading toward schizoid tendencies in the individual, were in postwar America incessantly exploited and magnified by mercenary advertising and popular entertainment to the point of national schizophrenia.

In the 1960s the focus of Clamence's mirror accusing its spectator of smug self-righteousness might have been turned in the United States from the middle class in general toward liberal intellectuals, who during the conflictless fifties had become fixed in the comfortable pose of telescopic humanitarianism. It had been easy to approve of the civil-rights struggle in the South, to be against war and big business in the abstract. But when it came to joining forces actively with militant blacks in the North or student radicals attacking the complicity of universities and other cultural institutions with the military-industrial complex, when it came to the prospect of losing a job or going to prison in protest of the Vietnam War, most of us found ourselves like Clamence on the bridge, suddenly paralyzed by the realization that it's a long jump and the water is cold.

The Fall set the style for a rash of confessional literature through the 1960s by American writers of the pre-New Left generation—the overripe fruit of the whole Cold War culture, which after fifteen years of social disengagement seemed to have left almost nothing to write but soul-baring stripteases. These narcissistic exercises included Mailer's *Advertisements for Myself,* Arthur Miller's *After the Fall* (which might have been more aptly titled "After *The Fall,*" so derivative was its device of a guilt-ridden lawyer-narrator), Saul Bellow's *Herzog,* Norman Podhoretz's *Making It,* John Barth's *Lost in the Funhouse,* and Philip Roth's *Portnoy's Complaint* (still another author-disguised-as-lawyer narration).

The Fall did not directly inspire all these works, but it was one typical artistic portrayal of the sense of irreality that characterized this time, along with other American and foreign works popular here that dealt with autistically detached heroes or themes, including Vladimir Nabo-kov's *Lolita* and *Pale Fire,* Samuel Beckett's plays and novels, the fiction of Jorge Luis Borges and drama of Eugene Ionesco and Harold Pinter, early French New Wave films such as Jean-Luc Godard's *Breathless,* Francois Truffaut's *Shoot the Piano Player* and *Jules and Jim,* Claude Chabrol's *The Cousins,* and Serge Bourguignon's *Sundays and Cybele,* as well as many of the films of Ingmar Bergman and Michelangelo Antonioni (most definitively *Blow-Up*), Federico Fellini's *8½,* and Arthur Penn's *Bonnie and Clyde. The Fall* was distinguished, however, by its author's condemnatory attitude toward his hero and its coldly critical analysis of his time, whereas most of these fictional, dramatic, and cinematic works simply mirrored the theatricality of the age with-out trying to explain it. The major exception was *Portnoy's Complaint,* the definitive analysis of the American fifties though ten years late—the reduction to absurdity, a devastating comic purgation of silent generation narcissism.

With the reawakening of American social consciousness in the 1960s by militant blacks and other minorities, white student radicals, the anti-war movement and women's liberationists, the mirror of artistic narcis-sism was also at least cracked, if not shattered. The healthy bond that Camus advocated between the writer and the community of those in revolt, the balance between aesthetic egoism and political commitment, began to be restored with Joseph Heller's *Catch-22,* Stanley Kubrick's film *Dr. Strangelove,* Barbara Garson's *Macbird,* the American produc-tion of Peter Weiss's *Marat/Sade,* protest music in the folk and rock idioms, guerilla theater, and the mode of journalistic literature that began to appear more immediate and authentic than fiction in this period of social turmoil, including works like Paul Goodman's *Growing Up Absurd,* Michael Harrington's *The Other America,* James Baldwin's *The Fire Next Time, The Autobiography of Malcolm X,* Truman Capote's *In Cold Blood,* and Mailer's *Armies of the Night* and later reportage.

Mailer's writing improved in concreteness and ideological cogency in the late sixties as he turned from the apocalyptic individualism that had led to a literary dead end in *An American Dream* and from bizarre per-sonal antics toward more positive, communal political activism (al-though he still retained a strong residue of egocentricity; *Armies of the Night* might have been called "How I Won the Revolution"). His case was again exemplary, this time of the way that New Left social consciousness gave rebellion and writing about it a specific form, focus, and goal, in contrast to the solipsism and blind, boundless thrashing out of 1950s-style revolt, which, as Camus said of romantic revolt, is "really only useful for adventures of the imagination" (*Rebel,* p. 46) or which, as Alfred Kazin similarly characterized silent generation writing, "imagines anything because it has contact with nothing, but which, in the imagination of loneliness, cannot give us the color, the tactile feel of anything." [8] The enduring artistic quality of many of the committed works since the sixties is, of course, still problematical. On the other hand, the egocentric attitude has become an artistic dry well producing little of certain lasting value since the time of Camus's death, and as he emphasized, commitment itself neither guarantees nor precludes artistic quality; different artists will meet the challenge of combining the two with varying degrees of success.

v

In his political writing Camus presented the example of a world-famous literary artist who, while anticommunistic, remained an active advocate of democratic socialism and nonviolent militancy throughout the Cold War and as such was a more outspoken critic of capitalism than most American artists of the period, with the exception again of Mailer. That American artists were largely inaudible as political critics was, of course, not entirely their own fault; during the Cold War Americans were much more inclined to honor socialist and even procommunist artists like Sartre, Brecht, and Picasso at a distance than at home. American society to begin with has rarely granted writers the political position or influence they frequently attain in France or England, and during the McCarthy period prominent literary radicals were either blacklisted altogether or forced to mute or disguise their leftist sympathies, in

8. "Psychoanalysis and Literary Culture Today," *Partisan Review* 26, no. 1 (Winter 1959) : 48; reprinted in Kazin, *Contemporaries* (Boston: Atlantic–Little, Brown, 1962), p. 366. Kazin added, "As Albert Camus confessed in his recent Nobel Prize speech, even someone brought up in the pagan and sunlit world of North Africa finds himself unable to describe the sensuous joy of life as he once did. As man increasingly loses his connection with the world, the great world, the only world, he finds himself playing the moralist and the revolutionary as part of the same imposture—the purpose of which is to perform *some* action, to see oneself performing any role."

the manner of Arthur Miller's *The Crucible.* Furthermore, Camus's primarily literary prestige carried over here into a respect for his politics (again, a somewhat distant respect, since little of his political journalism was widely available here until the appearance of *Resistance, Rebellion, and Death* in 1960, and this was a relatively conservative sampler) greater than that accorded to comparable American-based political critics without popular reputations as creative writers, such as C. Wright Mills, Erich Fromm, Herbert Marcuse, and Paul Goodman, who received scant attention from the mass media and public before the 1960s.

In light of the recent tendency for some leftist critics of Camus's conservatism in the Algerian War and his increasing support of the West in the 1950s to dismiss his entire political stance as counterrevolutionary, it is perhaps desirable to reiterate the radical elements that persisted through his later career. In *Neither Victims nor Executioners,* his 1946 pacifist manifesto, he insisted that the fault in the Cold War lay as much in American reactionary aggression as in communist revolutionary aggression and stated bluntly, "Little is to be expected from present-day governments, since these live and act according to a murderous code" (p. 15); pending the establishment of an effective world parliament, "all we can do now is to resist international dictatorship; to resist on a world scale; and to resist by means which are not in contradiction with the end we seek" (p. 12). This essay's radicalism may account for its never having been collected in book form here and remaining somewhat of an underground document. It was first translated by Dwight Macdonald for his pacifist journal *Politics* in 1948, then reprinted in the civil-rights and antiwar movement magazine *Liberation* in 1960 with a preface by Waldo Frank and in pamphlet form by the World without War Council through the sixties, prefaced in the 1968 edition by Robert Pickus recruiting Camus posthumously against the Weatherman-style violent antiwar resistance at the end of the decade.

He denounced American and French support of the Franco government in Spain more vocally than did most American liberals, resigning from UNESCO in 1952 over its admission of Spain. He purposely set *State of Siege* in Spain to suggest an identification of the dictator The Plague with Franco.

Although he rejected those aspects of Marxism that he considered prophetic, messianic, totalitarian, and conducive to unrestrained revolutionary violence, he still showed strong affinities to Marx (although he became increasingly reluctant to identify them as such during the Cold War) in his dialectical mode of thinking and critical analysis of capitalist society. In *The Rebel* he emphasized the continuing alienation of labor even in prosperous industrial societies and under the managerialism then being extolled by James Burnham and other American liberals. In common with Marxist aestheticists, he maintained that the communal nature of even the most egocentric art should dialectically lure the aesthete into social commitment and that the ideal unity of form and content in art serves as a paradigm for the unalienated, classless society. Even a work from his more conservative period of the late fifties, "Reflections on the Guillotine," still looks as radical as ever in its tracing of the roots of crime to the example for criminal violence set by the bourgeois State and to capitalist economic priorities which perpetuate poverty while condoning profiteering from alcoholism and other crime-breeding vices. Elsewhere during the same late period he similarly pierces through bourgeois moralistic cant: "There is no reason for being surprised that such a society chose as its religion a moral code of formal principles and that it inscribes the words 'liberty' and 'equality' on its prisons as well as on its temples of finance" (*RRD*, p. 194). In condemning the communists who have aped bourgeois society in dehumanization and verbal obfuscation, Camus was faithful to the Marx who said that to be radical is to go to the root, and the root is man.

The more rebellious members of the American silent generation recognized a salutary way out of the cynical apathy of that period in Camus's affirmation that, no matter how bleak the prospects are for revolution, the individual always at least has the power actively to resist the status quo. This ethic of resistance, joined to his advocacy of militant nonviolence, made him one of the mentors of the American New Left—along with Martin Luther King, Gandhi, Tolstoy, and Thoreau—in its phase of nonviolent activism for civil rights and peace in the late fifties and early sixties and later resistance against the Vietnam War. At the height of the drive for Negro rights in the South, Robert Parris Moses, a leader of the Student Nonviolent Coordinating Committee, spoke of Camus in an interview:

When I was in jail this last time I read through *The Rebel* and *The Plague* again. The main essence of what he says is what I feel real close to—closest to. . . . It's the importance to struggle, importance to recognize in the struggle certain humanitarian values, and to recognize that you have to struggle for people, in that sense, and at the same time, if it's possible, you try to eke out some corner of love or some glimpse of happiness within. And that's what I think more than anything else conquers the bitterness, let's say.[9]

Similarly, the hedonistic foundation of Camus's politics—a benevolent anarchism and recognition that "one must keep intact in oneself a freshness, a cool wellspring of joy" to sustain political commitment—made his writing well attuned to the hippie movement of the mid-sixties, the more affirmative successor to the beats, with its short-lived faith in "flower power" and "doing your own thing."

In 1968, Catholic priests Daniel and Philip Berrigan, along with seven other nonviolent resistants against the Vietnam War, were arrested for burning draft-board files in Catonsville, Maryland. In Daniel Berrigan's play based on the courtroom proccedings, *The Trial of the Catonsville Nine,* Camus's "The Unbeliever and Christians" is cited among the defendants' justifying authorities: " 'The world expects that Christians will speak out loud and clear, so that never a doubt, never the slightest doubt, could arise in the heart of the simplest man. . . . The world expects that Christians will get away from abstractions and confront the blood stained face which history has taken on today.' "[10]

Camus's influence here extended to the governmental level of Senator Robert F. Kennedy, whose biographer Jack Newfield reports:

> The most concrete expression of Kennedy's existential quality was his involvement with the writing of Albert Camus. He discovered Camus when he was thirty-eight, in the months of solitude and grief after his brother's death. By 1968 he had read, and reread, all of Camus's essays, dramas, and novels. But he more than just read Camus. He memorized him, meditated about him, quoted him, and was changed by him.
>
> He read *Resistance, Rebellion, and Death* several times. His worn copy had a sentence or paragraph underlined on almost every page. He told me the essay in that volume, "Reflections on the Guillotine,"

9. Robert Penn Warren, *Who Speaks for the Negro?* (New York: Random House, 1965), p. 95.
10. *The Trial of the Catonsville Nine* (New York: Bantam, 1971), p. 51.

convinced him to change his mind and oppose capital punishment.

He quoted Camus on the Johnny Carson Show, in stump speeches and hamlets in Nebraska, in his televised debate with Eugene McCarthy. By the end of his campaign in California, his supporters waved signs at airports that read "Kennedy and Camus in '68." [11]

As late as 1968, Lionel Abel in the *New York Times* listed Camus as one of "Seven Heroes of the New Left," along with Chomsky, Goodman, Marcuse, Fanon, Régis Debray, and Che Guevara.[12] Unfortunately for Camus's reputation on the American left, however, the viability of his political position was waning here by the mid-sixties. His pessimism about collective revolutionary movements, which he always qualified with the imperative for the conscientious individual to continue nonetheless steadfastly to oppose the status quo, had been too easily assimilable to end-of-ideology quietism and turned into an excuse to give up on persevering to formulate a comprehensive radical analysis and program. As black leaders here were gunned down or imprisoned one after another and as the American establishment, cooptively evasive at best, repressive at worst, appeared determined to put down racial revolt and antiwar and campus protest, loving, nonviolent resistance began to appear as a policy that was meaningful only as a personal elective for middle-class and student volunteers. It sounded like dilettantism for those who had the privilege of pulling out of the game when it got too rough to be prescribing nonviolence to the victims of oppression by an implacably violent power structure.

That resort to violence by the oppressed is not so much a freely chosen act as a desperate reflex by those who have no alternative had, of course, been one of Sartre's main points in his critique of *The Rebel* and his 1961 preface to Fanon's *The Wretched of the Earth*. Fanon's book itself, with its justification of violence by colonial revolutionaries, was a seminal work for later New Left ideologists, including militant American blacks who saw themselves as a colonized people, and the startling contrast between its perspective on the Algerian War and Camus's Algerian chronicles epitomizes the shift in the sixties.

As the rhetoric and tactics of some factions in the New Left became more violent in the late sixties, it became fashionable among liberals to

11. *Robert Kennedy: A Memoir* (New York: E. P. Dutton, 1969), pp. 58–59.
12. *New York Times Magazine,* 5 May 1968, pp. 30–31.

charge that it too had become guilty of excess, an opinion with which Camus doubtlessly would have concurred. But perhaps it is unreasonable to expect a protest movement to have a perfect sense of proportion when the society it was born out of has none at all. In any case, the New Left had a long way to go before it could match the excesses built into America's official institutions. Still, by the early 1970s there were indications that practical counterproductivity and frenzied misdirections of violence by some American radicals might eventually swing leftist opinion here back toward Camus.

New Left sympathy here also shifted from Camus toward Sartre in the sixties on the issues of anticommunism and the Cold War. Although Camus, more than most American anticommunist intellectuals, continued through the fifties to acknowledge the reciprocity of fault and the human elements on both sides, the events of that decade—foremost among them what he considered to be the communist-aligned uprisings against the French in Indochina and Algeria—caused him to regard communism as a far greater menace than capitalism and to become gradually more apologetic for the West in the international conflict. His position finally came to be almost indistinguishable from American liberal Cold Warriors, although he remained more critical than they of the domestic inequities of capitalism. (It should also be remembered that being a French anticommunist in the 1950s entailed purely vocal opposition to the Communist party of France, which was one of the largest in the country and had free access to communications and educational media, in contrast to America where in the case of many intellectuals it meant acquiescing to or actively participating in hysterical repression of a relatively minute C. P. as well as other, unrelated socialist groups and individuals.) In 1957 he sounded a note familiar here when he proclaimed that "the era of ideologies is over" (*RRD*, p. 185). He did not, however, mean like Daniel Bell that the conflict between classes or between capitalist and socialist economic theories had resolved itself and that only technological problems remained to be solved—a view that he vehemently disagreed with—but only that any ideology pursued fanatically can lead to inhuman excesses and that none is worth nuclear warfare or unlimited revolutionary bloodshed.

As Camus was moving to the right in the fifties, Sartre was moving to the left. He did not join the Communist party or cease criticizing it, but he did refuse to denounce world communism unilaterally and categorically. His position, which looked extremely tenuous from here in the fifties, began to appear more defensible in the sixties as the world communist bloc was splitting up and the focus of the Cold War was moving to Third World liberation struggles where American and allied colonialist repression (for which Camus and American liberal Cold Warriors had had a blind spot) had forced nationalist revolutionary movements into communist alliances. The disfavor into which Camus had fallen among French leftists in the fifties was repeated here a decade later, first in consequence of the relative stability achieved by Algeria in its independence, against his predictions, and later with the American fiasco in Vietnam, which combined to make him appear retroactively as more of a hard-liner than he really was, since it was more evident in the sixties than in the fifties that it was possible for colonial liberation movements to maintain a large measure of independence from Moscow and Peking.

For the cause of Camus's posthumous reputation, fate played a dirty trick in timing his death at the moment when the Cold War perspective was beginning to shift. Considering the course of events in the subsequent decade—Third World revolution, Vietnam, the resurgence of the international noncommunist left that Camus and Sartre had hoped for in the mid-forties, spearheaded by students and culminating in the near revolution of 1968 in France—when many Cold War liberals of far less flexible temperament than Camus were shaken out of their acquiescence to the capitalist status quo, it seems reasonable to conjecture that if he had lived he would have moved back toward the left. On Vietnam especially he would undoubtedly have denounced the barbarity of America's intervention (granted, he would have been readier to condemn America's role there than he did France's) and would probably have come to at least a partial rapprochement with Sartre.

The experience of the American left in the 1960s indicated further weak points in Camus's general ideology. Sartre's argument that Camus was thinking wishfully to believe that one can always maintain critical detachment from both sides in violent political struggles gained credibility as the polarization of American politics brought about crisis situations such as student-police confrontations that forced those involved to forgo liberal moderation and fine balancing of faults between the opponents in face of the necessity to side either with those breaking heads or those whose heads were being broken.

Sartre and Jeanson claimed that the fallacy in Camus's principle of equal opposition to communist and capitalist world camps is that the propaganda machine of each of the major world camps is quick to pick up and blare to the world any statement from a respected public figure that is critical of the other camp while muting all qualifications or criticisms of itself. According to Sartre, blanket condemnations of communism blur the complexities of widely varying situations in different countries where communists rule or are supporting just revolutions. In some cases, then, such condemnations lend support to counterrevolutionary reaction in noncommunist countries or incite increased repressiveness in communist ones. Sartre concluded that intellectuals should more carefully guard their criticisms of communism than of capitalism because, despite greater communistic injustices in many current places and times, on a worldwide scale communism has aligned itself with more progressive forces and at least contains a potential for leading toward true socialism. Camus refused to accept Sartre's implication that one should suppress his criticisms of either side, insisting that muting one's honest opinions could never serve the cause of justice. Nevertheless, occasions such as his anticommunist sentiments being quoted on the floor of the United States Senate in 1966 by Thomas Kuchel of California in a platitudinous defense of American intervention in Vietnam must cause Camus some twinges in whatever room of that hotel in Sartre's *No Exit* he currently occupies.

Conor Cruise O'Brien's *Albert Camus of Europe and Africa* in 1970 provided the first full-scale reevaluation in English of Camus's politics from a post-Cold War, leftist perspective. Cruise O'Brien is probably Camus's closest counterpart in the English-speaking world today, both man of letters and political activist as U.N. diplomat in Africa and member of the Irish Parliament. While he acknowledges that Camus played an influential part in his intellectual formation, his own observations of colonial situations have evidently revealed to him the limitations in Camus's vision. Cruise O'Brien not only points out the numerous instances in Camus's political writing and fiction of blindness to his colonialist conditioning but notes that this peculiarity has been minimized by prominent critics here such as Germaine Brée and Emmett Parker. As late as 1965 Parker's book on Camus's political journalism, *Albert Camus: The Artist in the Arena,* completely ignored Fanon's perspective on Algeria. Similarly significant is Cruise O'Brien's observation that American critics' facile sympathy toward Camus's side in his argument with Jeanson and Sartre—most notably in Nicola Chiaromonte's influential piece translated here in *Partisan Review* and in the collection of essays on Camus edited by Brée—uniformly reflected the line of what Christopher Lasch has termed the Cultural Cold War.

Brée was on the defense by the time of her *Camus and Sartre: Crisis and Commitment* in 1972. She did present new evidence there in favor of Camus's journalistic and personal activities in Algeria but largely evaded answering Cruise O'Brien's allegations of racism in Camus's fiction. She did little to correct her own and other American critics' earlier failure to present Sartre's position fairly, and her obvious hostility toward Sartre, Beauvoir, and Fanon makes it hard to ascertain how many of the charges in the barrage she leveled against them are just. Philip Thody, another prominent promoter of Camus's reputation in America and England, was also taking a more astringent view of his politics by 1971, emphasizing that "where *The Fall* and 'The Renegade' are vulnerable to criticism is in the absence of any suggestion that the political attitudes Camus is denouncing have any origin other than the desire to rule or the longing for extremes. It is surely fair comment to say that communism is not only a means of assuaging guilt or establishing dictatorships, and that both its defects and its popularity are due to technical, political, or economic factors." [13]

Future events will undoubtedly cause us to continue revising our judgment on Camus's and Sartre's opposing positions, but one thing remains certain: that this ideological conflict between two of the most masterful minds of our time has retained and will continue to retain its urgent relevance for American politics. Meanwhile, American end-of-ideologists like Daniel Bell, who in 1960 had dismissed the Sartre-Camus debate as a manifestation of French backwardness, now appear themselves to be illustrations of discredited Cold War complacency. [14]

13. Thody, "Albert Camus," in *The Politics of Twentieth-Century Novelists,* ed. George A. Panichas (New York: Hawthorn Books, 1971), p. 203.
14. Bell, *The End of Ideology* (New York: Free Press, 1960), p. 296.

VI

Another of Sartre's and Jeanson's diagnoses of Camus's weak spots has been confirmed in America: that his writing was designed, intentionally or unintentionally, to win him comfortable bourgeois prestige as a man of letters. No matter how radical his politics are, a writer like Camus who happens to be an inventive creative artist and exemplary stylist, who composes memorable aphorisms and neat antitheses, and who eloquently applies classical measure to contemporary excesses is fated posthumously to be elevated to the literary pantheon. He will become a favored subject for safely apolitical academic studies and classroom exercises, have his pleas for moderation cited for conservative purposes in situations where his own more flexible classical sense of exactitude would dictate that outrage is in order, and have his aphorisms quoted out of the context of his complete thought in support of the most conventional causes. Thus Camus could end up being cited by the Greenwich Village Independent Democrats in their reluctant endorsement of Hubert Humphrey over Richard Nixon in the 1968 presidential election: " 'In this absurd world, the only thing one can do is make choices.' " [15] With such uses being made of him, it is not surprising that some recent American critics have reduced Camus to a dispenser of vague moral pieties. During his lifetime, the very notion of being regarded as a moralist rankled him. His reply to an interviewer's question about what compliment annoyed him most was, "Honesty, conscience, humanity—you know, all the modern mouthwashes" (*LCE,* p. 363).

While he was alive, and until about the time of the posthumous publication of *Resistance, Rebellion, and Death* in 1961, most American critical reviews of his books ranged from respectful to reverent. The decline in his reputation can be marked in the more harsh reviews of his two volumes of notebooks in 1963 and 1965 by Susan Sontag and Paul de Man in *The New York Review of Books.*[16] Paul de Man uses Camus's youthful

15. Quoted by Theodore Solotaroff in "Camus's Portable Pedestal," *The New Republic,* 21 Dec. 1968, p. 27. Reprinted as "The Young Camus" in Solotaroff, *The Red Hot Vacuum* (New York: Atheneum, 1970), pp. 276–83.
16. Sontag, "Camus' Notebooks," 26 Sept. 1963; reprinted in Sontag, *Against Interpretation* (New York: Dell, 1969), pp. 61–69. De Man, "The Mask of Albert Camus," 23 Dec. 1965, p. 10.

role as goaltender on a losing soccer team as an emblem of the waning efficacy of his beliefs in later years. By 1970 reviews and general estimates by younger critics, even when they were not primarily political, were likely to contain more censure than praise, as in Solotaroff's review of *Lyrical and Critical Essays* cited above or Leo Bersani's *Balzac to Beckett: Center to Circumference in French Fiction,* which claims, "To do justice to Camus requires an indifference to literary fashions in the light of which Camus is likely to appear quaintly archaic, as well as to the appeal of a life and a work pervaded by an apparently unattackable integrity." [17]

Some later American New Leftists who downgraded Camus's politics also tried to associate him literarily with the silent generation or the neo-Christian tragic quietism of the fifties. In 1970 Louis Kampf wrote:

> We take the concept of tragedy to represent the West's most profound understanding of man's place in the world. Yet is its counterrevolutionary acceptance of fate something we are supposed to teach as a received value? Are we really to lay today's modish subjectivism on our working-class students? The obsessive concern for the self—perhaps best exemplified by the academic popularity of Camus during the McCarthy years—internalizes all aspects of reality and immobilizes the will; it effectively disables the capacity for action.[18]

Like earlier European Marxist criticisms of Camus, Kampf's characterization can only conceivably be applied to *The Stranger, The Myth,* and *Caligula,* in isolation from his more socially committed works. Perhaps it is accurate to the extent that these works were indeed widely read here in isolation and that the metaphysical, mythic, and symbolic dimension of these and his other works was more emphasized by American critics than the social dimension; this, however, is more of a reflection on the postwar American intellectual climate than on Camus himself.

There *was* a certain apparent kinship between Meursault or Caligula and the alienated middle-class rebels without a cause in American literature. The latter, however, were too puerile even to embody the tragic profundity Kampf speaks of, lacking the existential and epistemological foundation of Meursault's and Caligula's lucid, self-determined isolation. Kampf's account, moreover, underestimates the implications for social

17. *Balzac to Beckett,* p. 247.
18. "The Trouble With Literature," *Change,* May–June 1970, p. 30.

revolt even in Camus's more egocentric works. Caligula's fatalism is opposed by Scipio's and Cherea's revolutionary action. *The Myth's* conclusion is antithetical to "the acceptance of fate"; its ethic of individual freedom and revolt against the absurdity of death and epistemological obscurity is equally applicable to revolt against political servitude, killing, and verbal mystification. *The Stranger* makes a powerful statement against capital punishment and conformity to bourgeois and Christian rituals. Camus had only to dialectically negate these "negative truths" to synthesize the philosophy of rebellious solidarity in *The Plague, The Rebel, The Just Assassins,* and his journalism.

It is true that at the time of his death Camus had not demonstrated in his fiction, drama, and aesthetic theory a strong sense of precise historical or socioeconomic situation. In his distinctive method of apportioning his total vision among different works and genres, he intentionally dealt with specific social actualities in his journalism while reserving the literary media for themes at once more universal and self-centered. His literary works, then, tended toward an ideologically vague frame of reference, toward the kind of generalization common to liberal humanism that mistakes the white, bourgeois intellectual for "man," and his restricted vantage point for the totality of the human condition or of "the modern world." One would prefer to believe that these limitations were not inevitable within Camus's system but that he could have surmounted them with growing maturity and the challenge of the changing world political perspective in the 1960s. Indeed, he likely would have succeeded in incorporating an acuter awareness of situation in his projected novel or novels drawing on autobiographical materials from his proletarian childhood in Algiers to the time of the Hungarian uprising and Algerian War.

After more than a decade, it is still difficult to talk about Camus's death without giving in to the temptation toward excessive poetic license. The unavoidable literary interpretation, that the fatal auto wreck seemed preordained as the ultimate dramatization of Camusian absurdity, tends to depersonalize the human body and mind that were crushed therein— as Camus would have been the first to point out. College students insist on mythicizing the accident into suicide, no matter how many times it is explained to them that Camus was not driving and detested speeding. And death at forty-six is by no means grossly premature compared to Keats at twenty-six, Shelley at thirty, Schubert at thirty-one, Sidney at thirty-two, Mozart at thirty-five, Byron at thirty-six, Raphael, Rimbaud, and Van Gogh at thirty-seven, Wolfe at thirty-eight, Pascal at thirty-nine, Vermeer at forty-three, Thoreau, Chekhov, and Fitzgerald at forty-four, Wilde and Orwell also at forty-six, and many other great artists, thinkers, and political leaders who have died younger. In the 1960s alone—a decade when a torrent of personal and political calamities was to reawaken the tragic sense of life in America after the quiescent postwar period—untimely death struck John and Robert Kennedy, Malcolm X, Martin Luther King, Che Guevara, Maurice Merleau-Ponty, Frantz Fanon, C. Wright Mills, Flannery O'Connor, Lorraine Hansberry, Lenny Bruce, Richard Farina, and Jack Kerouac.

Nevertheless, in spite of Camus's own early acknowledgment that a creative career usually ends not in definitive resolution but in "the death of the creator which closes his experience and the book of his genius," it remains an inconsolable outrage that a senseless accident should have cut short a life of such youthful vitality and an artistic and ideological creation of the utmost importance for our time while it was still in full evolution. For a young generation of American readers who had been sheltered from tragedy, Camus's death on 4 January 1960 was an intimation of mortality even more sobering than his works, an omen of the stormy times ahead when American life would no longer be so naïvely happy and prosperous as it appeared to Doubrovsky and the rest of us in the 1950s.

Selected Bibliography of Works on Camus

The amount of writing about Camus has reached overwhelming proportions. Robert F. Roeming catalogued 2,679 critical articles and books through 1966, and since then Camus has continued to be among the writers with most listings in the annual *PMLA* and *French VII* (*French XX* since 1969) bibliographies of scholarly studies. For purposes of selectivity I have emphasized those works of most interest to American readers, including foreign works in English translation whenever available. I have also restricted listings mainly to works from the late 1950s through 1972; for earlier works, see the bibliographical guides listed below or in books such as Brée's and Parker's.

BIBLIOGRAPHICAL STUDIES

Beebe, Maurice. "Criticism of Albert Camus: A Selected Checklist of Studies in English." *Modern Fiction Studies* 10, no. 3 (Autumn 1964) : 303–14.

Fitch, Brian T., and Hoy, Peter C. *Essai de bibliographie des études en langue française consacrées à Albert Camus. No. 1: Deuxième livraison (1937–1967)*. Paris: Minard, 1969.

Hoy, Peter C. *Camus in English*. Wymondham: Brewhouse Press, 1968. An annotated bibliography of Camus's contributions to English and American periodicals and newspapers. Includes works published in journals before book publication, often in different translations.

———. "Carnet bibliographique." In the annual volume of *Carnets Albert Camus*, 1968 to present, in *Revue des lettres modernes*.

Roeming, Robert F. *Camus: A Bibliography*. Madison: University of Wisconsin Press, 1968. Separate indexes of works on Camus by countries and, within them, by authors, journals, and chronology.

BOOKS DEVOTED ENTIRELY OR PRIMARILY TO CAMUS

Albérez, René-Marill, et al. *Albert Camus, 1913–1960*. Paris: Hachette, 1964.

Blanchot, Maurice, et al. *Hommage à Camus*. Paris: Gallimard, 1967.

Brée, Germaine. *Camus*. New Brunswick: Rutgers University Press, 1959; rev. 1961. New York: Harcourt, Brace, Harbinger Books, 1964.

———. *Albert Camus*. Columbia Essays on Modern Writers, no. 1. New York: Columbia University Press, 1964.

———. *Camus and Sartre: Crisis and Commitment*. New York: Delta, 1972.

———, ed. *Camus: A Collection of Critical Essays*. Twentieth Century Views. Englewood Cliffs, N.J.: Prentice Hall, 1962.

Brisville, Jean-Claude. *Camus*. Paris: Gaillimard, 1959.

Carruth, Hayden. *After the Stranger: Imaginary Dialogues with Camus.* New York: Macmillan, 1965.

Cruickshank, John. *Albert Camus and the Literature of Revolt.* London: Oxford University Press, 1959. New York: Oxford University Press, Galaxy Books, 1961.

Cruise O'Brien, Conor. *Albert Camus of Europe and Africa.* New York: Viking, 1970.

Durand, Anne. *Le Cas Albert Camus.* Paris: Editions Fischbacher, 1961.

Freeman, E. *The Theatre of Albert Camus: A Critical Study.* London: Methuen, 1971.

Ginestier, Paul. *La Pensée de Camus.* Paris: Bordas, 1964.

Grenier, Jean. *Albert Camus: Souvenirs.* Paris: Gallimard, 1968.

Hanna, Thomas. *The Thought and Art of Albert Camus.* Chicago: H. Regnery, 1958; Gateway ed., 1969.

Jonesco, Tony. *Un Homme, Camus et le destin; ou, Autour de la mort de Camus.* Paris: Promotion et Edition, 1968.

King, Adele. *Albert Camus.* Edinburgh: Oliver and Boyd, 1964. New York: Grove Press, Evergreen Books, 1964.

Lebesque, Morvan. *Portrait of Camus.* New York: Herder and Herder, 1971; original French ed., 1963.

Luppé, Robert de. *Albert Camus.* London: Merlin, 1966; original French ed., 1952.

Maquet, Albert. *Albert Camus: The Invincible Summer.* New York: George Braziller, 1958; original French ed., 1955.

Nguyen-Van-Huy, Pierre. *La Métaphysique du bonheur chez Albert Camus.* Neuchâtel: La Baconnière, 1962.

Nicolas, André. *Albert Camus; ou, Le Vrai Prométhée.* Paris: Editions Seghers, 1966.

Onimus, Jean. *Albert Camus and Christianity.* Tuscaloosa: University of Alabama Press, 1970; original French ed., 1965.

Parker, Emmett. *Albert Camus: The Artist in the Arena.* Madison: University of Wisconsin Press, 1965; paperback, 1966.

Petersen, Carol. *Albert Camus.* New York: Frederick Ungar, 1969; original German ed., 1961.

Pollmann, Leo. *Sartre and Camus: The Literature of Existence.* New York: Frederick Ungar, 1970; original German ed., 1968.

Proix, Robert, ed. *Albert Camus and the Men of the Stone.* San Francisco: Jack W. Stauffacher / The Greenwood Press, 1971; originally published in French as *A Albert Camus, ses amis du livre,* 1962.

Quilliot, Roger. *The Sea and Prisons: A Commentary on the Life and Thought of Albert Camus.* University, Ala.: University of Alabama Press, 1970; rev. and augmented from original French ed., 1956.

Rhein, Phillip H. *Albert Camus.* New York: Twayne, 1969; Hippocrene Books, 1972.

Sarocchi, Jean. *Camus.* Paris: Presses Universitaires de Paris, 1968.

Scott, Nathan A. *Camus.* London: Bowes and Bowes, 1962. New York: Hillary House, 1962.

Simon, Henri-Pierre. *Présence de Camus.* Brussels: Renaissance du Livre, 1961.

Thody, Philip. *Albert Camus, 1913–1960.* London: Hamish Hamilton, 1961. New York: Macmillan, 1962. Revision of *Albert Camus: A Study of His Work.* New York: Grove Press, 1959.

Willhoite, Fred. *Beyond Nihilism: Albert Camus' Contribution to Political Thought.* Baton Rouge: Louisiana State University Press, 1968.

BOOKS ON SINGLE WORKS OF CAMUS

Barrier, M.-G. *L'Art du récit dans "L'Etranger" d'Albert Camus.* Paris: A. G. Nizet, 1962.
Castex, Pierre-Georges. *Albert Camus et "L'Etranger."* Paris: Librairie José Corti, 1965.
Champigny, Robert. *A Pagan Hero: An Interpretation of Meursault in Camus' "The Stranger."* Philadelphia: University of Pennsylvania Press, 1969; original French ed., 1959.
Fitch, Brian T. *Narrateur et narration dans "L'Etranger" d'Albert Camus.* Paris: Archives des lettres modernes, 1960; rev. 1968.
Haggis, D. R. *Albert Camus: "La Peste."* London: Edward Arnold, 1962. Great Neck, N.Y.: Barron's Educational Series, 1962.
Merton, Thomas. *Albert Camus's "The Plague": Introduction and Commentary.* New York: Seabury Press, 1968.
Rhein, Phillip H. *The Urge to Live.* Chapel Hill: University of North Carolina Press, 1964. Comparison of Camus's *L'Etranger* with Kafka's *Der Prozess.*

BOOKS WITH SECTIONS ON OR SIGNIFICANT REFERENCES TO CAMUS

Alvarez, A. *The Savage God: A Study of Suicide.* New York: Random House, 1972.
Aron, Raymond. *The Opium of the Intellectuals.* New York: W. W. Norton, 1962; original French ed., 1955.
Axthelm, Peter M. *The Modern Confessional Novel.* New Haven: Yale University Press, 1967.
Barnes, Hazel. *Humanistic Existentialism: The Literature of Possibility.* Lincoln: University of Nebraska Press, 1962.
Barthes, Roland. *Writing Degree Zero.* Boston: Beacon Press, 1970; original French ed., 1953.
Beauvoir, Simone de. *Force of Circumstance.* New York: G. P. Putnam's Sons, 1965; originally published as *La Force des choses,* 1963.
———. *The Prime of Life.* New York: World Publishing, 1962; originally published as *La Force de l'être,* 1960.
Bell, Daniel. *The End of Ideology.* New York: Free Press, 1960.
Bersani, Leo. *Balzac to Beckett: Center and Circumference in French Fiction.* New York: Oxford University Press, 1970.
Blanchot, Maurice. *L'Entretien infini.* Paris: Gallimard, 1969.
Booth, Wayne C. *The Rhetoric of Fiction.* Chicago: University of Chicago Press, 1961.
Brée, Germaine, and Guiton, Margaret. *The French Novel from Gide to Camus.* New York: Harcourt, Brace and World, 1962.
Brombert, Victor. *The Intellectual Hero: Studies in the French Novel, 1880–1955.* Philadelphia: Lippincott, 1961.
Burnier, Michel. *Choice of Action: The French Existentialists on the Political Front Line.* New York: Random House, 1968. Additional chapter by Bernard Murchland: "Sartre and Camus: The Anatomy of a Quarrel."

Caute, David. *The Illusion: An Essay on Politics, Theatre, and the Novel.* New York: Harper and Row, 1971.

Cohn, Ruby. *Currents in Contemporary Drama.* Bloomington: Indiana University Press, 1969.

Cox, Harvey. *The Secular City.* New York: Macmillan, 1965.

Cruise O'Brien, Conor. *Writers and Politics.* New York: Vintage, 1967.

Engelberg, Edward. *The Unknown Distance: From Consciousness to Conscience, Goethe to Camus.* Cambridge: Harvard University Press, 1972.

Esslin, Martin. *The Theatre of the Absurd.* Garden City: Doubleday, Anchor Books, 1961; rev. 1969.

Falk, Eugene. *Types of Thematic Structure: The Nature and Function of Motifs in Gide, Camus, and Sartre.* Chicago: University of Chicago Press, 1967.

Fischer, Ernst. *The Necessity of Art: A Marxist Approach.* Baltimore: Penguin Books, 1963; original German ed., 1959.

Fowlie, Wallace. *Dionysus in Paris: A Guide to Contemporary French Theater.* New York: Meridian, 1960.

Frohock, Wilbur M. *Style and Temper: Studies in French Fiction, 1925–1961.* Cambridge: Harvard University Press, 1967.

Galloway, David D. *The Absurd Hero in American Fiction.* Austin: University of Texas Press, 1966.

Glicksberg, Charles Irving. *The Tragic Vision in Twentieth-Century Literature.* Carbondale: Southern Illinois University Press, 1963.

Guicharnaud, Jacques. *Modern French Theatre from Giraudoux to Genet.* New Haven: Yale University Press, 1967.

Hartman, Geoffrey. *Beyond Formalism: Literary Essays, 1958–1970.* New Haven: Yale University Press, 1970.

Hassan, Ihab. *The Dismemberment of Orpheus.* New York: Oxford University Press, 1971.

Hoffmann, Frederick J. *The Mortal No: Death and the Modern Imagination.* Princeton: Princeton University Press, 1964.

Hughes, H. Stuart. *The Obstructed Path: French Social Thought in the Years of Desperation, 1930–1960.* New York: Harper and Row, 1968.

Kaufmann, Walter. *Existentialism from Dostoevsky to Sartre.* New York: Meridian, 1958.

———. *Religion from Tolstoy to Camus.* New York: Harper, 1964.

Kostelanetz, Richard, ed. *On Contemporary Literature.* New York: Avon, 1964.

Krieger, Murray. *The Tragic Vision.* New York: Holt, Rinehart, and Winston, 1960.

Lewis, R. W. B. *The Picaresque Saint: Representative Figures in Contemporary Fiction.* Philadelphia: J. B. Lippincott, 1959.

Liebling, A. J. *The Press.* New York: Ballantine Books, 1964.

Lukács, Georg. *Realism in Our Time.* New York: Harper Torchbook, 1971; original German ed., 1956.

Malraux, André. *Anti-Memoirs.* New York: Holt, Rinehart, and Winston, 1968; original French ed., 1967.

Massey, Irving. *The Uncreating Word: Romanticism and the Object.* Bloomington: Indiana University Press, 1970.

Mauriac, Claude. *The New Literature.* New York: Braziller, 1959; originally published as *L'Alittérature contemporaine,* 1958.

Maurois, André. *From Proust to Camus.* Garden City: Doubleday, 1968; original French ed., 1963.

Moore, Harry T. *Twentieth Century French Literature.* Carbondale: Southern Illinois University Press, 1966.

Mueller, William R. *The Prophetic Voice in Modern Fiction.* Garden City: Doubleday, Anchor Books, 1966.

Nadeau, Maurice. *The French Novel since the War.* London: Methuen, 1967; original French ed., 1963.

Newfield, Jack. *Robert Kennedy: A Memoir.* New York: E. P. Dutton, 1969.

O'Brien, Justin. *The French Literary Horizon.* New Brunswick: Rutgers University Press, 1967.

Odajnyk, Walter. *Marxism and Existentialism.* Garden City: Doubleday, 1965.

Peyre, Henri. *French Novelists of Today.* New York: Oxford University Press, 1967.

Pierce, Roy. *Contemporary French Political Thought.* New York: Oxford University Press, 1966.

Reck, Rima Drell. *Literature and Responsibility: The French Novelist in the Twentieth Century.* Baton Rouge: Louisiana State University Press, 1969.

Robbe-Grillet, Alain. *For a New Novel.* New York: Grove Press, 1965; original French ed., 1963.

Roy, Jules. *The War in Algeria.* New York: Grove Press, 1961; original French ed., 1960.

Rysten, Felix S. A. *False Prophets in the Fiction of Camus, Dostoevsky, Melville, and Others.* Coral Gables: University of Miami Press, 1972.

Sarraute, Nathalie. *The Age of Suspicion: Essays on the Novel.* New York: George Braziller, 1963; original French ed., 1956.

Sartre, Jean-Paul. *Situations.* New York: Fawcett World Library, 1966; originally published in French as *Situations IV,* 1964.

Scott, Nathan A., Jr., ed. *The Climate of Faith in Modern Literature.* New York: Seabury Press, 1964.

——, ed. *The Unquiet Vision: Mirrors of Man in Existentialism.* New York: World Publishing, 1969.

Ullmann, Stephen. *The Image in the Modern French Novel.* Cambridge: Cambridge University Press, 1960.

Weinstein, Leo. *The Metamorphoses of Don Juan.* Stanford: Stanford University Press, 1959.

West, Paul. *The Wine of Absurdity: Essays on Literature and Consolation.* University Park: Pennsylvania State University Press, 1966.

Widmer, Kingsley. *The Literary Rebel.* Carbondale: Southern Illinois University Press, 1965.

Williams, Raymond. *Modern Tragedy.* Stanford: Stanford University Press, 1966.

Wilson, Colin. *The Age of Defeat.* London: Gollancz, 1959.

——. *The Outsider.* London: Gollancz, 1956. Boston: Houghton Mifflin, 1956.

SPECIAL NUMBERS OF JOURNALS DEVOTED TO CAMUS

Figaro, 6 Jan. 1960.
Minnesota Review, vol. 4, no. 3 (Spring 1964).
Modern Fiction Studies, vol. 10, no. 3 (Autumn 1964).

Nouvelle Revue Française, vol. 8, no. 7 (Mar. 1960).
Revue des lettres modernes, nos. 170–71 (1968). _Autour de "L'Etranger."_
————, nos. 212–16 (1969). _Langue et langage._
————, nos. 238–44 (1970). _Sur "La Chute."_
————, nos. 264–70 (1971). _Sources et influences._
Symposium, vol. 24, no. 3 (Fall 1970).
La Table ronde, no. 146 (Feb. 1960).
Venture, vol. 3, no. 4 (Spring–Summer 1960).
Yale French Studies, vol. 25 (Spring 1960).

ARTICLES IN JOURNALS AND COLLECTIONS

Abel, Lionel. "Seven Heroes of the New Left." _New York Times Magazine,_ 5 May 1968, pp. 30–31.
Aiken, Henry David. "The Revolt against Ideology." _Commentary,_ Apr. 1964, pp. 29–39.
Barchilon, José, M.D. "A Study of Camus' Mythopoeic Tale _The Fall_ with Some Comments about the Origin of Esthetic Feelings." _Journal of the American Psychoanalytic Association_ 19, no. 2 (Apr. 1971) : 193–240.
Bittner, William. "The Death of Camus." _Atlantic Monthly,_ Feb. 1961, pp. 85–88.
Brée, Germaine. "Albert Camus: An Essay in Appreciation," _New York Times Book Review,_ 24 Jan. 1960, p. 5.
Brustein, Robert. "Nihilism on Broadway." _New Republic,_ 29 Feb. 1960. Reprinted in Brustein, _Seasons of Discontent._ New York: Simon and Schuster, 1965.
Cohn, Robert Greer. "Sartre-Camus Resartus." _Yale French Studies_ 30 (Fall–Winter 1962–63) : 73–77.
Cranston, Maurice. "Albert Camus." _Encounter,_ Feb. 1967, pp. 43–55.
Driver, Tom F. "Superior Suicide." _Christian Century,_ 23 Mar. 1960, pp. 352–54.
Faulkner, William. "L'Ame qui s'interroge." _Nouvelle Revue francaise_ 8, no. 87 (March 1960): 537–38. Reprinted in Blanchot et al., _Hommage à Camus,_ pp. 143–44.
Feibleman, James K. "Camus and the Passion of Humanism." _Kenyon Review_ 25, no. 2 (Spring 1963) : 281–92.
Feurlicht, Ignace. "Camus's _L'Etranger_ Reconsidered." _PMLA_ 27, no. 5 (Dec. 1963) : 606–21.
Fiedler, Leslie A. "The Pope and the Prophet." _Commentary,_ Feb. 1956, pp. 190–95.
Fontinell, Eugene. "A Tribute to Camus: Recent Studies of His Work." _Cross Currents_ 10, no. 3 (Summer 1960) : 283–89.
Garvin, Harry R. "Camus and the American Novel." _Comparative Literature_ 8, no. 3 (Summer 1956) : 194–204.
Geha, Richard, Jr. "Albert Camus: Another Wish for Death." _Psychoanalytic Review,_ Winter 1967, pp. 106–22.
Gilman, Richard. "Two Voices of Camus." _Commonweal_ 73, no. 22 (24 Feb. 1961) : 552–53.
Girard, René. "Camus's Stranger Retried." _PMLA_ 79, no. 5 (Dec. 1964) : 519–33.
Grobe, Edwin P. "Tarrou's Confession: The Ethical Force of the Past Definite." _French Review_ 39, no. 4 (Feb. 1966) : 550–58.
Guerard, Albert J. "Fiction" (_A Happy Death_). _Esquire,_ June 1972, pp. 40–45.
Hackel, Sergei. "Raskolnikov through the Looking-Glass: Dostoevsky and Camus's _L'Etranger,_" _Contemporary Literature_ 9, no. 2 (Spring 1968) : 189–209.

Hemingway, Ernest. "Les Ecrivains nous disent." *Figaro,* 6 Jan. 1960, p. 4.

Hicks, Granville. "The Search for the Ideal Absurdity." *Saturday Review,* 3 Sept. 1966, pp. 21–22.

Hochberg, Herbert. "Albert Camus and the Ethic of Absurdity." *Ethics* 75, no. 2 (Jan. 1965) : 87–102.

Hoffman, Frederick J. "Camus and America." *Symposium* 12, nos. 1–2 (Spring–Fall 1958) : 36–42.

Hoffman, Stanley, et al. "Homage to Camus." *Massachusetts Review* 1, no. 2 (Feb. 1960) : 212–14.

Kamber, Gerald. "The Allegory of the Names in *L'Etranger.*" *Modern Language Quarterly* 22, no. 3 (Sept. 1961) : 292 : 301.

Kampf, Louis. "The Trouble with Literature." *Change,* May–June 1970, pp. 27–34.

Kaplan, Donald M. "Homosexuality and American Theatre." *Tulane Drama Review,* Spring 1965, pp. 25–55.

Kazin, Alfred. "Condemned Man." *Reporter,* 16 Feb. 1961, pp. 54–58. Reprinted in Kazin, *Contemporaries,* pp. 291–95. Boston: Atlantic–Little, Brown, 1962.

Kennedy, Ellen Conroy. "Camus at His Sources." *Kenyon Review* 31, no. 1 (1969) : 122–27.

Knopf, Blanche. "Albert Camus in the Sun." *Atlantic Monthly,* Feb. 1961, pp. 77–84.

Koppenhaver, Allen J. *"The Fall* and After: Albert Camus and Arthur Miller." *Modern Drama* 9, no. 2 (Sept, 1966) : 206–9.

Lazere, Donald. "Alas! Poor Camus; or, The Show Begins." *The Village Voice,* 14 Sept. 1961, pp. 4–6.

———. "Camus as Himself." *The Nation* 207, no. 18 (25 Nov. 1968): 569–71.

Lehan, Richard Daniel. "Camus' American Affinities." *Symposium* 13, no. 2 (Fall 1959) : 255–70.

———. "Camus and Hemingway." *Wisconsin Studies in Contemporary Literature* 1, no. 2 (Spring–Summer 1960) : 37–48.

Leites, Nathan. *"The Stranger."* In *Art and Psychoanalysis,* edited by William Phillips, pp. 247–67. New York: Meridian, 1963.

Liebling, A. J. "The Camus Notebooks." *New Yorker,* 8 Feb. 1964, pp. 128–38.

Macksey, Richard. "The Artist in the Labyrinth: Design or Dasein." *Modern Language Notes* 77, no. 3 (May 1962) : 239–56.

Madden, David. "Ambiguity in Albert Camus's *The Fall.*" *Modern Fiction Studies* 12, no. 4 (Winter 1966–67) : 46–72.

Man, Paul de. "The Mask of Albert Camus." *New York Review of Books,* 23 Dec. 1965, pp. 10–13.

McMullin, Roy. "How Relevant Is Camus Today?" *Réalités,* May 1961, pp. 66–69.

Merton, Thomas. "Camus's Journals of the Plague Years." *Sewanee Review* 75, no. 4 (Autumn 1967) : 717–30.

———. "The Other Side of Despair: Notes on Christian Existentialism." *Critic* 24, no. 2 (Oct.–Nov. 1965) : 13–23.

Merwin, W. S. "Through the Blur of Pain." *The Nation,* 16 Aug. 1958, pp. 74–75.

Molnar, Thomas. "On Camus and Capital Punishment." *Modern Age* 2, no. 3 (Summer 1958) : 298–306.

O'Brien, Justin. "Camus' *Lyrical and Critical Essays.*" *Columbia University Forum,* Spring 1969, pp. 32–33.

———, and Roudiez, Leon. "Camus." *Saturday Review,* 13 Feb. 1960, pp. 30–31.

Podhoretz, Norman. "Solitary or Solidary." *New Yorker,* 29 Mar. 1958, pp. 107–10.

Redfern, W. D. "Camus and Confusion." *Symposium* 20, no. 4 (Winter 1966) : 329–42.

Renaud, Armand. "Quelques remarques sur le style de *L'Etranger.*" *French Review* 30, no. 4 (Feb. 1957) : 290–96.

Rocks, James E. "Camus Reads Defoe: *A Journal of the Plague Year* as a Source of *The Plague.*" *Tulane Studies in English* 15 (1967) : 81–87.

Rolo, Charles J. "Albert Camus, a Good Man." *Atlantic Monthly,* May 1958, pp. 27–33.

Rossi, Louis. "Albert Camus: The Plague of Absurdity." *Kenyon Review* 20, no. 3 (Summer 1958) : 399–422.

Roudiez, Leon. "Strangers in Melville and Camus." *French Review* 31, no. 3 (Jan. 1958) : 217–26.

———. "Camus and *Moby Dick.*" *Symposium* 15, no. 1 (Spring 1961) : 30–40.

Sebba, Helen. "Stuart Gilbert's Meursault: A Strange *Stranger.*" *Contemporary Literature* 13, no. 3 (Summer 1972) : 334–40.

Seltzer, Leon F. "Camus's Absurd and the World of Melville's Confidence-Man." *PMLA* 82, no. 1 (Mar. 1967) : 14–27.

Shattuck, Roger. "Two Inside Narratives: *Billy Budd* and *The Stranger.*" *Texas Studies in Literature and Language* 4, no. 3 (Fall 1962) : 314–20.

Solotaroff, Theodore. "Camus's Portable Pedestal." *The New Republic,* 21 Dec. 1968, pp. 27–30. Reprinted as "The Young Camus" in Solotaroff, *The Red Hot Vacuum,* pp. 276–83. New York: Atheneum, 1970.

Somers, Paul P., Jr. "Camus *Si,* Sartre *No;* or, The Delightful M. Meursault." *French Review* 42, no. 5 (Apr. 1969) : 693–700.

Sonnenfeld, Albert. "Albert Camus as Dramatist: The Sources of His Failure." *Tulane Drama Review,* June 1961, pp. 106–23.

Sontag, Susan. "Camus' Notebooks." *New York Review of Books,* 26 Sept. 1963, pp. 1–3. Reprinted in Sontag, *Against Interpretation,* pp. 61–69. New York: Dell, 1969.

Spector, Robert Donald. "Albert Camus, 1913–1960: A Final Interview." *Venture,* vol. 3, no. 4 (Spring–Summer 1960).

Stamm, Julian. "Camus' *Stranger:* His Act of Violence." *American Imago* 26 (1969) : 281–90.

Starobinski, Jean. "Albert Camus and the Plague." *CIBA Symposium* 10, no. 2 (1962) : 62–70.

Thody, Philip. "Albert Camus." In *The Politics of Twentieth-Century Novelists,* edited by George A. Panichas. New York: Hawthorn Books, 1971.

Trahan, Elizabeth. "Clamence vs. Dostoevsky: An Approach to *La Chute.*" *Comparative Literature* 18, no. 4 (Fall 1966) : 337–50.

Trilling, Lionel. "*The Guest:* Commentary." In *The Experience of Literature,* edited by Lionel Trilling, pp. 370–72. New York: Holt, Rinehart, and Winston, 1967.

Updike, John. "In Praise of the Blind, Black God." *New Yorker,* 21 Oct. 1972, pp. 157–67.

Viggiani, Carl. "Camus' *L'Etranger.*" *PMLA* 71, no. 5 (Dec. 1956) : 865–87.

Wagner, C. Roland. "The Silence of *The Stranger.*" *Modern Fiction Studies* 16 (1970) : 27–40.

West, Paul. "Albert Camus and the Aesthetic Tradition." In *New World Writing,* pp. 80–91. New York: New American Library, 1958.

Index